Praise from Homeowners and Industry Professionals for
Designing Your Dream Home

"We wish that we had had a copy of this book when we built our house. Everyone who plans on building or remodeling their home should review this incredible book. It is easy to read, complete, and full of ideas that will save you time, money, and stress."

—Mark Houston, MD, and Laurie Hays, homeowners

"Building or remodeling a home can be a daunting task. This resource makes the process doable. Don't start a project without it."

—Janice and Mark Thomas, homeowners

"For the average homeowner who wants to build, Susan Lang's comprehensive book bridges the gap between the technical aspects of house infrastructure (electrical, plumbing, HVAC, etc.) and the desired end result: comfortable, convenient living. I found her extensive and thorough 'checklist' system to be especially helpful in avoiding the unpleasant surprises that come after construction is finished."

—Leora B. Allen, homeowner

"My most problematic issue as a decorator is a client's indecision. While this book may not erase indecision, it certainly empowers clients to understand where they fit into the puzzle of home-building and make preparations for navigating the process. I've never seen or even heard about a book as thorough and encompassing. In fact, I may require it for all my clients! Bravo for an insightful map to the thrilling road of building your dream house."

—Barry Williams, decorator, Williams Design, Inc.

"As owners of a historic home, our remodeling project was extensive and, quite frankly, intimidating. We were scared to death we were going to make mistakes that would not only be time-consuming but turn out to be enormously expensive, pushing us way over budget. *Designing Your Dream Home* provided the detailed support we needed to confidently move forward with our remodel. The forms in the book gave us one central reference place to capture all our concerns and ensure we hadn't overlooked anything important, truly enabling us to design the home of our dreams.

—Steve and Karen Anderson, homeowners

"With *Designing Your Dream Home,* everyone will be able to use Susan Lang's gifts and skills to help them create the home they want. This book is a must-have for every homeowner's shelf."

—Judy Pittman, realtor, Judy Pittman, Inc.

Designing Your Dream Home

every **question** to ask,
every **detail** to consider,
and **everything** you need to know
before **you build or remodel**

SUSAN LANG

THOMAS NELSON
Since 1798

NASHVILLE DALLAS MEXICO CITY RIO DE JANEIRO BEIJING

Being a native of Pass Christian, Mississippi, with family and friends
still living along the Mississippi Gulf Coast,
I dedicate this book to the victims of Hurricane Katrina.

Having lived through Hurricane Camille
and having visited the Mississippi Gulf Coast since Katrina hit,
I have experienced and seen firsthand the devastation
inflicted by these two powerful hurricanes.

It is my hope and desire that *Designing Your Dream Home*
will be an invaluable tool for those remodeling or rebuilding
their home. I am donating a copy of this book to the area libraries.

My thoughts and prayers go out to all of those still trying
to rebuild their lives and their homes. And I mourn those whose
lives were lost, including my aunt and uncle, Helen and Nip Lang.

Published in Nashville, Tennessee, by Thomas Nelson. Thomas Nelson is a registered trademark of Thomas Nelson, Inc.

Thomas Nelson, Inc. titles may be purchased in bulk for educational, business, fund-raising, or sales promotional use. For information, please e-mail SpecialMarkets@ThomasNelson.com.

This book is intended to provide general information on designing your home. Although every effort has been made to make this book as accurate as possible, the author and Thomas Nelson, Inc., assume no responsibility for errors or omissions. Neither is any liability assumed for damages resulting from the use of the information contained herein. If architectural, building, legal, or other expert assistance is required, the services of a competent professional person should be sought.

Illustrations by Jim Moore, Nashville, Tennessee.
Page design by Casey Hooper.

Library of Congress Cataloging-in-Publication Data

Lang, Susan.
 Designing your dream home : every question to ask, every detail to consider, and everything you need to know before you build or remodel / Susan Lang.
   p. cm.
 Includes bibliographical references.
 ISBN 978-1-4016-0352-6
 1. Dwellings—Design and construction. I. Title.
TH4815.L38 2008
690'.837--dc22
                                         2007045965

Printed in the United States of America
08 09 10 11 12 QW 5 4 3 2 1

Contents

Acknowledgments

First, I want to acknowledge my daughter, Suzy Foral, who believed in my book from the first moment she read a chapter and was my number one supporter. Her belief kept me going. I drew perseverance and determination from my son, Hastings Puckett. My daughter-in-law, Amanda Puckett, is the most organized person I know. From Amanda, I find affirmation in my belief that everything needs a place to be stored. My son-in-law, Ray Foral, a homebuilder (Construction Concepts of Carolina, LLC), has been a sounding board and an invaluable source of information. As I write this book, Suzy and Ray are remodeling their home and Amanda and Hastings are designing and building a home. Both couples have been invaluable resources for my book. I would also like to thank my dad, Jack Lang, and my siblings, Ann Riette, Jay Lang, and Cary Lang.

Special thanks to my many friends: Dr. Mark Houston, who immediately felt my book had merit and served as my mentor; Laurie Hays, and Leora and Gregg Allen, for their friendship and support throughout the process; my designer friends, Deborah Appleton and Karen Snyder, who willingly shared their own experiences; Melanie Hughes, a longtime friend who gave her support, and her husband, Randy Hughes, a homebuilder in Dallas who allowed me to use his job sites for research; Dana Kelly, whose e-mails of support made a difference; my chiropractor, Dr. Josh Renkens, who tended to the aches and pains that developed while I was writing this book; and Janice and Mark Thomas, Libby and Isaac Manning, and Duer Wagner III, who gave me the opportunity to provide homebuilding consulting on their homes.

Special thanks to artisan Bill Powell, Nashville; Barry Williams and Zoe Powell of Williams Design Inc., Dallas; Terry Lawler of Construction Concepts of Carolina, Greenville, South Carolina; Alex Kazerooni of Eagle Fish Technologies, Nashville; John Bell Hines, architect, of Gunn Meyerhoff Shay Architecture + Urban Development of Charleston, South Carolina; Chuck Harper of Harper Electric, Nashville; Jim Thompson of H. Hughes Properties, Inc., Dallas; Charles Poliquin of Poliquin Performance Center, North Kingstown, Rhode Island; Gary Robble, insurance specialist of the Robble Agency, Nashville; Dan Crass of Steinway Piano Gallery, Nashville; David Breed of Tasco Security Inc., Telluride, Colorado; Tim Taylor of Tim Taylor Architects, Jackson, Mississippi; Betsy Hoag and Liz Ocone of TKO Associates, Inc., Dallas; and Jerry Omstead of Village Cleaners, Nashville.

Since December 2005, this book has been my companion. I have been blessed with dozens of friends who, through e-mails, phone calls, or notes, have sent their best wishes and support: Bob Brandt, Ellen and Skipper Brown, Karen and Charles Bush, Liz Daniel, Rick Davis, Elaine DeMetz, Sue Flynn, Carolyn Goddard, Roy Guinnup, Loicka and Heyward Hodges, David Kastle, Susan Kirkman, Diane and Fletcher Lance, Mike Lawler, Anne and Richard Levy, Lee Lutrell, Joe Mansfield, Stephanie and Pat Maxwell, Deborah Montgomery, Gail and Jim Moore, Patty Neherr, Jane Newsom, Bell and Bill Newton, Coleen O'Conner, Blanca O'Leary, Deborah Owen, Raymond Pirtle, Franny and W. T. Ray, Penny Reynolds, Stacy Reynolds, Denise Rice, Ann Sams, Gary Sasser, Nigel John Scott, J. J. Sibley, Ann Smith, Jerrie Smith, Ann and Frank Sprow, Gail Stanger, Paige Stephenson, Ingrid Taylor, Mary Anna Underwood, Bob Walker, Brady Wardlaw, Bekah Weatherford, Marnie Webb, Jon Witt, and the employees in the office of Dr. Dennis Wells.

Along the way I have worked with some outstanding people in the home design and building businesses who shared their knowledge with me, most importantly, John Blankenship of Custom Cabinetmakers in Dallas. Others include Antonio Medina of Antonio Floors, Cynthia Nash of Cynthia Nash Interior Design, Nicky Oates of Custom Cabinetmakers, John Clark of John Robert Clark Interiors, Keith Applegate and Able Martinez of Champion Electric, Ken Sturrock of Ken Sturrock Wallpapers, Michael Lee of Michael Lee Interior Designs, and Rene Gamez, all of Dallas; Amy Hatfield of Greenville, South Carolina; and Bill Thomas of Nashville.

At Thomas Nelson Publishing, I would like to thank David Dunham, Pamela Clements, Damon Goude, Charlette Hale, Beth Hood, Casey Hooper, and Kristen Vasgaard, and my editors, Jennifer Greenstein and Sara J. Henry.

I would also like to thank the staff at FedEx Kinko's West End Avenue; and the staff at the Bread Company, Starbucks, and Wholefoods, who all provided a great atmosphere in which I could write and edit this book.

Finally, I would like to acknowledge my grandchildren, Peyton Puckett, Parker Puckett, and Allie Foral, all born (with one still on the way) while I was writing this book.

Introduction

It is not uncommon for homeowners to feel fearful, uncertain, and overwhelmed when they begin a homebuilding or remodeling project. The goal of this book is to ease those feelings by giving you an understanding of the process. *Designing Your Dream Home* takes a commonsense approach to helping you organize your project, avoid mistakes, and attain your desired end result: a functional and aesthetically beautiful home. I want to prevent you from saying, "I wish I had thought of that!" after your home is built.

This book is also about raising questions to discuss with your architect, interior designer, and builder. Sometimes getting the right answer involves asking the right question. That's why *Designing Your Dream Home* focuses on helping you formulate the right questions to ask. It encourages dialogue between you and your architect, interior designer, and builder. And it will arm you with critical points to discuss with your team to keep everyone on track. Using detailed and easy-to-use forms and checklists, you'll inventory and analyze each room and area to be included in your new or remodeled home. These detailed forms will help you design the home that fits your family and your lifestyle.

You'll learn how to get organized; select your architect, interior designer, and builder; prepare for meetings with your architect; and much more. You'll also learn how to avoid many common mistakes and what to look for when reviewing architectural plans. At the end of the book, you'll find a glossary of terms, abbreviations, architectural symbols, and helpful standard measurements.

As the homeowner, you play an important role in the design process. The more forethought and preparation you dedicate to this, the more satisfied you will be with the finished product. Ultimately, it is your level of satisfaction that determines whether you have the home of your dreams.

Of course, money and time are important as well. If you invest your own time and effort by completing the checklists and forms in this book, you will need fewer design and building revisions, which means saving money and time.

No matter how much planning you do, when you build a home, you have an edge if you have an insider's view of the design process. The good news is that you don't have to go to "the school of hard knocks" to obtain this knowledge, because I already have! I've spent the last 20-plus years developing plans, working with builders, and compiling notes on what works (and what doesn't) in the real world of homebuilding and remodeling.

Numerous times I have shared various lists from this book with family and friends who were either remodeling or building their dream home. One in particular was about to place an order for kitchen cabinets in her newly remodeled kitchen. When she compared the size of her plates to the size of the cabinet shelf, she realized the plates would prevent the cabinet doors from closing. Fortunately, she was able to adjust her cabinet order. She called me with heartfelt gratitude that I had raised the question about the size of her dinner plates.

This book will have fulfilled its goal when you have your own "thank goodness I read this book" moment.

1 Getting Started and Staying Organized

As you begin the laborious task of having your home designed and built or remodeled, it is imperative that you take time to get organized. Getting organized at the outset of the design process will save time and money while reducing stress and headaches.

At the end of this chapter, you'll find basic forms to keep you organized: contact information forms for team members, real estate people, and utilities; a To Do List; a Comments form; a Product Sample Manifest; a Product Sample Fact Sheet; and meeting notes forms. These forms will help you keep critical information at your fingertips, and allow you to stay on top of the communication that takes place at meetings with your team. In the following pages, I'll explain when you use these forms and where to store them.

WHAT YOU WILL NEED TO GET STARTED

I recommend using a simple system of tote bags, binders, and wheeled luggage to keep everything you need at hand. The tote bags are lightweight and the contents can be easily identified; the bags serve as a portable file cabinet. The binders are easy to use, easy to update, flexible in size, and serve as portable file folders. The wheeled luggage is an easy way to organize samples and carry them around.

TOTE BAGS
Use three to five tote bags, depending on the size of the bag. These can be inexpensive tote bags made of a soft material, the type often given away at conventions or events.

THREE-RING BINDERS
You'll want 12 three-ring binders in these sizes: 4 one-inch, 7 two-inch, and 1 three-inch. If you will not be doing due diligence (this is explained in Chapter 3) and not dealing with a

Homeowner Association, you will need two fewer of the one-inch binders. Choose binders with plastic sleeves on the front cover so you can slide in a piece of paper identifying the binder contents. You will also want to be able to slide the binder title in the spine of the binder. A plastic pouch inside the front and back cover of the binder is a convenient place to store pages temporarily that need to be inserted into the binder.

Additionally, purchase a box of heavy-duty plastic sleeves, a pack of plastic sleeves that hold business cards, and a plastic zippered pouch to hold receipts, all three-hole punched.

WHEELED LUGGAGE AND ZIPPERED PLASTIC BAGS

Use a piece of wheeled luggage with a pull-up handle to hold samples such as stone, tile, brick, carpet, hardware, and paint colors. Zippered plastic bags are a convenient place to keep samples in the wheeled luggage.

The benefit of the tote bag/binder system is that it easily keeps everything you need at your fingertips. All you have to do is grab the tote bag pertinent to the meeting you're going to or the job you're doing. You can easily have them all in the car with you at any time. As you collect information, you can slip it into the tote bag holding the pertinent binder and file it when you get home.

Or you may choose a different approach to carrying and storing the multiple items needed to keep organized. Whatever your approach, get organized!

HOW TO USE YOUR TOTE BAGS

Designate one tote bag for supplies. You'll need

- Blue painter tape
- Calculator
- Correction tape or fluid
- Paper clips

- Pens, pencils, highlighters, and erasers
- Plastic sleeves
- Post-it notes
- Retractable fifty-foot tape measure, cloth tape measure, and ruler
- Rubber bands
- Scissors
- Scotch tape
- Stapler and staples
- Three-hole punch
- Tracing paper and note-taking paper

The other tote bags will hold the three-ring binders. In the following pages you'll find recommendations for the contents of each binder. You can decide which binders you want grouped together in the same tote bag. The size of the binder and the size of the tote bag will determine how many binders will fit.

To identify easily which tote bag holds which binders, you can tie a different colored ribbon to the tote bag handles, use a luggage tag, use different colored tote bags, or come up with some other identifying mark.

HOW TO ORGANIZE YOUR BINDERS

Create cover pages and spine strips for each of the 12 binder names. Decide which binders you want in which tote bag. If identifying and coordinating with color is important to you, you can print the cover page for your binder on colored paper to match the color of the ribbon tied on the tote bag or the color of the tote bag.

The 12 binders are

Binder 1: Blank Forms (three-inch binder)
Binder 2: Hiring Your Team (one-inch binder)
Binder 3: Due Diligence (one-inch binder)
Binder 4: Design (two-inch binder)

Binder 5: Team Meetings and
   Communications (two-inch binder)
Binder 6: Existing Content/Wish List Photos and
   Tear Sheets (two-inch binder)
Binder 7: Homeowner Association (HOA) and
   Municipality (one-inch binder)
Binder 8: Financial, Legal, and Insurance
   Information (two-inch binder)
Binder 9: Shopping Forms and Checklists
   (one-inch binder)
Binder 10: Product Brochures and Specification
   Sheets (two-inch binder)
Binder 11: Final Selections (two-inch binder)
Binder 12: Builder Discussions (two-inch binder)

BINDER 1: BLANK FORMS

This binder should include blank copies of all the forms in this book related to your home. Any form that does not represent an area you will be using in your home should not be copied. This book covers 32 rooms; if your home will only have 12 of the rooms, then copy only forms for those 12 rooms. (See Appendix 1, page 348, for a complete list of forms and where you will find them in this book.)

Photocopy each form and put those blank copies in Binder 1. You will need to make multiple copies of some of the forms; these are indicated by an asterisk throughout this chapter and in the list in Appendix 1. You will need a copy of the Bathroom Checklist and Bathroom Storage Item Checklist for each bathroom, the Bedroom Checklist and the Bedroom Closet Checklist for each bedroom and bedroom closet, and the Individual Room and Closet form for every room and closet you will have in your home. Depending on how many architects, interior designers, and builders you will be interviewing, you will need multiple forms for the questionnaire.

Suggested titles for the tabs in this binder:

Architect Site Visit/Change Order Form

Architectural Plan Review Forms
Builder Discussion Forms
Comment Forms
Contact Information
Design
Due Diligence Forms
Entire-Home Selection Forms
Hiring My Team Forms
Meeting Notes Forms
Miscellaneous Storage Checklists
Noise Checklist Form
Product Sample Forms
Room Checklist Forms
Shopping Forms
To Do List

Later, once you begin completing these forms, you will transfer them to different binders, as explained in the following pages.

BINDER 2: HIRING YOUR TEAM

This binder will contain information related to hiring your architect, interior design, builder, and consultant team. This binder will contain

Architect Comparison Chart
Architect Questionnaire
Builder Comparison Chart
Builder Questionnaire
Interior Designer Comparison Chart

It will also include

○ Lists of architects, interior designers, and
   builders you are considering
○ Correspondence with potential architects,
   interior designers, and builders
○ Lists of interview questions for architects,
   interior designers, and builders, along with
   your notes on their answers. (Create your own

list of questions using the suggestions on pages 28, 31, and 34 as a guide.)
- ◖ Answers to the questions you asked when taking the potential architects and/or builders to the site. (Create your own list of questions using the suggestions on pages 28 and 34 as a guide.).
- ◖ Contract points to discuss with your attorney. (Create your own list of points, using the suggestions on pages 29, 32, and 35 as a guide.)

Suggested tabs for this binder:

Architects
Builders
Consultants
Interior Designers
Other

BINDER 3: DUE DILIGENCE

This binder will contain information related to due diligence you are performing on a piece of property you want to purchase. You'll file these filled-out forms in Binder 3:

Due Diligence Information Fact Sheet
Homeowner Association Information Fact Sheet
Municipality Information Fact Sheet
Real Estate Contact Information

This folder will also include

- ◖ All printed marketing brochures and sheets on the property and any information received from the companies involved
- ◖ Contracts
- ◖ Due diligence questions and answers (create your own list of questions using suggestions in Chapter 3).
- ◖ Notes taken when viewing property with realtors and potential architects and builders.

Suggested tabs:

Appraisal Information
Attorney Communications
Banker or Mortgage Company
Contact Information
Contracts
Due Diligence Information Fact Sheet
Due Diligence Questions and Answers
Home Inspector Information
Homeowner Association (HOA) Information
   Fact Sheet
Municipal Codes, Zoning, and Building Information
   Fact Sheet
Property Flyers or Fact Sheets
Title Company

BINDER 4: DESIGN

The information contained in this binder will communicate to your entire team your vision of your dream home and any building restrictions imposed by the Homeowner Association (HOA) or municipality. Add a plastic sleeve to hold business cards. These should be followed by all design-related forms.

Forms and checklists that will go into Binder 4, once you have filled them out:

Apartment Area Checklist
Architect Contact Information
Attic Checklist
Bar Checklist
Basement Checklist
Basic Bedroom Fact Sheet
Basic Design Fact Sheet
Bathroom Applications for Stone/Tile Checklist
Bathroom Checklist
Bathroom Storage Item Checklist
Bedroom Checklist
Bedroom Closet Checklist
Breakfast Room Checklist

Butler's Pantry Checklist

Ceilings, Doors, Floors, Lighting, Walls, and
Windows Checklist

Closets in Your Home Checklist

Common Household Item Storage Checklist

Control Room Checklist

Dining Room Checklist

Driveway Checklist

Electrical Checklist

Electrical Plan Review Checklist

Elevation Plan Review Checklist

Entry Foyer Checklist

Exercise Room Checklist

Existing Contents of the Home Checklist

Exterior and Interior Christmas Lights and
Decorations Checklist

Exterior Applications for Stone/Tile Checklist

Exterior Elements for Your Home Checklist

Exterior Front Entry Checklist

Family Room Checklist

Floor Plan Review Checklist

Garage Checklist

Garage Item Storage Checklist

Garage Vehicle Checklist

HVAC Checklist

HVAC Plan Review Checklist

Individual Room and Closet Fact Sheet

Interior Applications for Stone/Tile (Excluding
Bathrooms) Checklist

Interior Designer Contact Information

Kitchen Appliance Checklist

Kitchen Cabinet Layout Checklist

Kitchen Checklist

Kitchen Island Checklist

Kitchen Item Storage Checklist

Kitchen Pantry Checklist

Kitchen Plumbing Checklist

Laundry Room Checklist

Library Checklist

Living Room/Great Room Checklist

Mechanical Room Checklist

Media Room Checklist

Miscellaneous Information Checklist

Morning Kitchen/Counter Checklist

Mudroom Checklist

Nursery Checklist

Occupants of the Home Checklist

Office Checklist

Playroom/Game Room Checklist

Plumbing Checklist

Plumbing Plan Review Checklist

Pool House Checklist

Porch, Patio, Deck, and Balcony Checklist

Powder Room/Half Bath Checklist

Rooms in Your Home Checklist

Safe Room Checklist

Specialty Room Checklist

Stone/Tile Cuts Checklist

Things That Make Noise Checklist

Wine Room Checklist

Suggested tabs:

Architectural Plan Review Checklists

Basic Design Information Checklists

Bathrooms Information

*Ceilings, Doors, Floors, Lighting, Walls, and
Windows Checklist*

Christmas Lights and Decorations Checklist

Closet Checklists

Contact Information

Contents Checklist

Electrical, HVAC, and Plumbing

Exterior Information

Garage Information

HOA and Municipal Design Information

Kitchen Information

Noise Checklist

Room Information

Rooms in Your Home Checklist

Stone/Tile Checklists
Storage Checklist

BINDER 5: TEAM MEETINGS AND COMMUNICATIONS

This binder will contain all communications with your team:

- ◗ Discussion points for the next meeting with your team
- ◗ Timetables provided by members of your team

It will also include these filled-out forms:

Architect Meeting Notes
Builder Meeting Notes
Consultant Meeting Notes
Interior Designer Meeting Notes
Landscape Architect Meeting Notes
Subcontractor Meeting Notes

Suggested tabs:

Architect Communications
Architect Timetable
Blank Architect Site Visits
Blank Change Orders
Builder Communications
Builder Timetable
Consultant Communications
Consultant Timetable
Interior Designer Communications
Interior Designer Timetable

BINDER 6: EXISTING CONTENT/WISH LIST PHOTOS AND TEAR SHEETS

Once you have filled out the Existing Contents of the Home Checklist (page 75), file it in Binder 6. Using plastic sleeves, organize photos and tear sheets into categories and place them in this binder. One group of photos represents items you currently own that will be used in your home. These photos should include the dimensions of the item and the name of the room where you want the item placed. The other group of photos and tear sheets represents your wish list. Write on each photo, tear sheet, or the plastic sleeve you have placed it in what appeals to you about this photo or tear sheet.

Suggested tabs:

Existing Content Photos
Wish List Items Photos
Wish List Tear Sheets

BINDER 7: HOMEOWNER ASSOCIATION (HOA) AND MUNICIPALITY

This binder includes the following information you have collected:

- ◗ HOA architectural approval process
- ◗ HOA bylaws
- ◗ HOA covenants
- ◗ HOA general information
- ◗ Municipal codes
- ◗ Municipal general information
- ◗ Municipal permits
- ◗ Municipal zoning laws

Suggested tabs:

HOA Architectural Approval Process
HOA Building
HOA Bylaws
HOA Covenants
HOA General Information
HOA Permit Application
Municipal Building Permit Application
Municipal Code and Zoning Information
Municipal General Information

BINDER 8: FINANCIAL, LEGAL, AND INSURANCE INFORMATION

This binder includes

> Architect Site Visit Form
>
> Change Order Form

It also includes

- ◗ Contracts
- ◗ HOA approvals
- ◗ HOA permits
- ◗ Insurance information
- ◗ Invoices
- ◗ Municipality approvals
- ◗ Municipality permits
- ◗ Paid and unpaid invoices
- ◗ Paid receipts
- ◗ Permits
- ◗ Plastic zippered pouch for receipts
- ◗ Proposals

Suggested tabs:

> *Architect Site Visits*
>
> *Change Orders, Invoices*
>
> *HOA Approvals*
>
> *HOA Permits*
>
> *Insurance Information*
>
> *Municipality Approvals*
>
> *Municipality Permits*
>
> *Paid Invoices*
>
> *Paid Receipts*
>
> *Proposals and Contracts*
>
> *Unpaid Invoices*

BINDER 9: SHOPPING FORMS AND CHECKLISTS

This binder holds copies of all the shopping forms used when shopping for items for your home, as well as checklists to refer to when shopping. They are

Appliance Shopping Form
Bathroom Applications for Stone/Tile Checklist
Bathroom Hardware Shopping Form
Bedroom Closet Hardware Checklist
Bedroom Closet Hardware Shopping Form
Ceiling Fan Shopping Form
Door Hardware Checklist
Door Hardware Shopping Form
Electrical Item Shopping Form
Exterior and Architectural Hardware Checklist
Exterior Applications for Stone/Tile Checklist
Exterior Hardware Shopping Form
Gas Log Fireplace Shopping Form
Individual Bathroom Hardware Checklist
Interior Applications for Stone/Tile (Excluding Bathrooms) Checklist
Kitchen Hardware Checklist
Kitchen Hardware Shopping Form
Laundry Room Hardware Checklist
Laundry Room Hardware Shopping Form
Miscellaneous Rooms with Cabinet Hardware Checklist
Miscellaneous Rooms with Cabinet Hardware Shopping Form
Stone/Tile Cuts Checklist

BINDER 10: PRODUCT BROCHURES AND SPECIFICATION SHEETS

This binder holds the following pages corresponding to items in your wheeled luggage, such as paint, roofing, and stone/tile:

> Product Sample Fact Sheet
>
> Product Sample Manifest

It also will contain brochures and specification sheets you have collected while selecting items for your home. These pertain to such items as appliances, hardware, fireplaces, lighting, paint brochures, plumbing fixtures, roofing, windows, and so on. Use your three-hole punch on the brochures and use plastic sleeves for specification sheets and other information on the products to file in this binder.

Suggested tabs:

Product Sample Fact Sheet
Product Sample Manifest
Appliances
Fireplaces
Lighting
Paint
Plumbing
Roofing
Windows

BINDER 11: FINAL SELECTIONS

This binder contains the completed forms representing the final selections you have made on the various components in your home:

Entire-Home Appliance Selections
Entire-Home Built-in Selections
Entire-Home Ceiling Fan Selections
Entire-Home Computer Wiring Selections
Entire-Home Door Hardware Selections
Entire-Home Exterior Component Selections
Entire-Home Exterior Paint Color Selections
Entire-Home Fireplace Selections
Entire-Home Fixed Mirror Selections
Entire-Home Floor Selections
Entire-Home Interior Paint Color Selections
Entire-Home Plumbing Selections (Excluding Bathrooms)
Entire-Home Security Alarm and Integrated Home Automation Monitor System Selections
Entire-Home Stereo Equipment Selections

Entire-Home Stereo Speaker Selections
Entire-Home Stone/Tile Selections
Entire-Home Telephone Jack Selections
Entire-Home Television Selections
Individual Bathroom and Powder Room Plumbing Selections

BINDER 12: BUILDER DISCUSSIONS

Throughout the design process, questions will arise that you will want to discuss with your builder. You'll write those on the Builder Discussion Form (page 345) and file it in this binder.

HOW TO USE YOUR WHEELED LUGGAGE

You will collect many different types of samples representing selections you have made for your home. You can store these in the wheeled luggage. Use the Product Sample Manifest form (page 19) to list each item placed in the wheeled luggage, and the Product Sample Fact Sheet (page 20) for the pertinent information on each sample item, including the name of the room for which it is intended. As you begin filling in these sample forms, file them in Binder 10 and place a copy in the wheeled luggage with the samples.

Actual sample items might include millwork (baseboard, crown, and door trim), brick, rock, stucco, siding or other exterior wall material, flooring, paint colors, roofing, stone and tile pieces, roof material, window screens, and shades. See-through zippered plastic bags come in many sizes and are a great tool for organizing samples. Using a marker, you can write the name of the manufacturer, showroom, sales representative, lead time, and any other pertinent information on the plastic bag.

Architect Contact Information

Architectural firm _____

Address _____

_____

Office phone _____ Fax _____ E-mail _____

Contact name _____

Cell _____ E-mail _____

Contact name _____

Cell _____ E-mail _____

Contact name _____

Cell _____ E-mail _____

Contact name _____

Cell _____ E-mail _____

Contact name _____

Cell _____ E-mail _____

Emergency contact name and number _____

Interior Designer Contact Information

Interior design company _____

Address _____

_____

Office phone _____ Fax _____ E-mail _____

Contact name _____

Cell _____ E-mail _____

Contact name _____

Cell _____ E-mail _____

Contact name _____

Cell _____ E-mail _____

Emergency contact name and number _____

Builder Contact Information

Builder _____

Address _____

_____

Office phone _____ Fax _____ E-mail _____

Contact name _____

Cell _____ E-mail _____

Contact name _____

Cell _____ E-mail _____

Contact name _____

Cell _____ E-mail _____

Contact name _____

Cell _____ E-mail _____

Contact name _____

Cell _____ E-mail _____

Emergency contact name and number _____

Subcontractor Contact Information

Subcontractor company _____

Contact name _____

Address _____

_____

Office phone _____ Fax _____ E-mail _____

Subcontractor company _____

Contact name _____

Address _____

_____

Office phone _____ Fax _____ E-mail _____

Subcontractor company _____

Contact name _____

Address _____

_____

Office phone _____ Fax _____ E-mail _____

Subcontractor company _____

Contact name _____

Address _____

_____

Office phone _____ Fax _____ E-mail _____

Landscape Architect Contact Information

Landscape architect company _____

Address _____

_____

Office phone _____ Fax _____ E-mail _____

Contact name _____

Cell _____ E-mail _____

Contact name _____

Cell _____ E-mail _____

Contact name _____

Cell _____ E-mail _____

Emergency contact name and number _____

Consultant Contact Information

Consultant company_____

Contact name _____

Address _____

_____

Office phone _____ Fax _____ E-mail _____

Consultant company_____

Contact name _____

Address _____

_____

Office phone _____ Fax _____ E-mail _____

Consultant company_____

Contact name _____

Address _____

_____

Office phone _____ Fax _____ E-mail _____

Consultant company_____

Contact name _____

Address _____

_____

Office phone _____ Fax _____ E-mail _____

Utility Companies Contact Information

Your new address:

_____

_____

Electric company _____ Phone _____

Fax _____ Website _____

Gas company _____ Phone _____

Fax _____ Website _____

Phone company _____ Phone _____

Fax _____ Website _____

Cable company _____ Phone _____

Fax _____ Website _____

Internet services company _____ Phone _____

Fax _____ Website _____

Satellite television company _____ Phone _____

Fax _____ Website _____

Security company _____ Phone _____

Fax _____ Website _____

Other _____ Phone _____

Fax _____ Website _____

Real Estate Contact Information

Your realtor's name _____ Phone _____

Fax _____ E-mail _____

Address _____

Seller's name _____ Phone _____

Fax _____ E-mail _____

Address _____

Seller's realtor's name _____ Phone _____

Fax _____ E-mail _____

Address _____

Title company contact _____ Phone _____

Fax _____ E-mail _____

Address _____

Mortgage company contact _____ Phone _____

Fax _____ E-mail _____

Address _____

Other _____ Phone _____

Fax _____ E-mail _____

Address _____

Other _____ Phone _____

Fax _____ E-mail _____

Address _____

To Do List

Week of _____

1. _____

2. _____

3. _____

4. _____

5. _____

6. _____

7. _____

8. _____

9. _____

10. _____

11. _____

12. _____

13. _____

14. _____

15. _____

16. _____

17. _____

18. _____

19. _____

20. _____

Blank Comment Form

You will need numerous copies of this form, as it has multiple uses. File them in Binder 1, and move to other binders as you use them.

Comments: _____

_____

_____

_____

_____

_____

_____

_____

_____

_____

_____

_____

_____

_____

_____

_____

_____

_____

_____

_____

_____

_____

Product Sample Manifest

	Type of Sample	Model/Name	Manufacturer	Vendor	Vendor Contact
1					
2					
3					
4					
5					
6					
7					
8					
9					
10					
11					
12					
13					
14					
15					
16					
17					
18					
19					
20					

Product Sample Fact Sheet

Type of sample _____

Where in the home the sample would be used _____

Item name _____ Color _____

Manufacturer _____

Vendor/showroom _____

Vendor contact name _____ Contact information _____

Lead time _____

Special comments _____

Type of sample _____

Where in the home the sample would be used _____

Item name _____ Color _____

Manufacturer _____

Vendor/showroom _____

Vendor contact name _____ Contact information _____

Lead time _____

Special comments _____

Type of sample _____

Where in the home the sample would be used _____

Item name _____ Color _____

Manufacturer _____

Vendor/showroom _____

Vendor contact name _____ Contact information _____

Lead time _____

Special comments _____

Architect Meeting Notes

Date _____ Time _____ Location _____

Attending _____

Discussions

_____

_____

_____

_____

_____

_____

_____

Plan of action/By whom/Deadline

_____

_____

_____

_____

_____

_____

_____

_____

Next meeting date/time _____

Make copies and distribute to those attending the meeting and those who are assigned to perform the plan of action, highlighting that person's duty.

Interior Designer Meeting Notes

Date _____ Time _____ Location _____

Attending _____

Discussions

_____

_____

_____

_____

_____

_____

Plan of action/By whom/Deadline

_____

_____

_____

_____

_____

_____

_____

_____

Next meeting date/time _____

Make copies and distribute to those attending the meeting and those who are assigned to perform the plan of action, highlighting that person's duty.

Builder Meeting Notes

Date _____ Time _____ Location _____

Attending _____

Discussions

_____

_____

_____

_____

_____

_____

_____

Plan of action/By whom/Deadline

_____

_____

_____

_____

_____

_____

_____

_____

Next meeting date/time _____

Make copies and distribute to those attending the meeting and those who are assigned to perform the plan of action, highlighting that person's duty.

Subcontractor Meeting Notes

Date _____ Time _____ Location _____

Attending _____

Discussions

_____

_____

_____

_____

_____

_____

Plan of action/By whom/Deadline

_____

_____

_____

_____

_____

_____

_____

Next meeting date/time _____

Make copies and distribute to those attending the meeting and those who are assigned to perform the plan of action, highlighting that person's duty.

Landscape Architect Meeting Notes

Date _____ Time _____ Location _____

Attending _____

Discussions

_____

_____

_____

_____

_____

_____

_____

Plan of action/By whom/Deadline

_____

_____

_____

_____

_____

_____

_____

_____

Next meeting date/time _____

Make copies and distribute to those attending the meeting and those who are assigned to perform the plan of action, highlighting that person's duty.

Consultant Meeting Notes

Date _____ Time _____ Location _____

Attending _____

Discussions

_____

_____

_____

_____

_____

_____

Plan of action/By whom/Deadline

_____

_____

_____

_____

_____

_____

_____

Next meeting date/time _____

Make copies and distribute to those attending the meeting and those who are assigned to perform the plan of action, highlighting that person's duty.

2 Hiring Your Team

Your team will include an architect, an interior designer, and a builder—and you want to select ones that are right for you.

HIRING YOUR ARCHITECT

Your approach to hiring an architect will depend on if a building boom is going on in your area. If local architects have more work than they can handle, you may need to adapt this step-by-step process. Your start date could be months away. You may even be required to put down a retainer fee to get on the architect's calendar. However, if the architect is looking for work, use the following process for hiring an architect.

THE ARCHITECT HIRING PROCESS

Identify at least three firms you want to consider. Look for homes in your area that you like and find out the architect who designed those homes. Look at homes you like in magazines and note the architect's name. The benefits of using an architect in your area is having an architect who knows the municipal codes and zoning laws, understands the terrain, and has relationships with area engineers and other people involved in the process. However, you can hire a lead architect from another area and hire a local architect to assist.

Send a letter asking the architect firms you'd like to consider if they would be interested in your project. Include your timetable, the approximate size of the house, and the address of the property (if known). Explain why you are considering their firm for the project. Mention any particular homes they have designed that you like. Explain your hiring process, which includes answering the Architect Questionnaire (page 38) you are attaching and returning the answers by a set date, an interview, site visit, visits to a couple of homes they have designed, and references. File a copy of the letters and questionnaires sent in Binder 2.

Once you have received the answers to the questionnaires, file them in Binder 2. If you want to eliminate a firm due to its answers on the questionnaire, send a note saying that the firm is no longer being considered for the project and thanking it for its participation.

Set up an interview with those architects you are considering. After you have read through the questionnaire responses, you may have additional questions as a result of their answers. Use those questions plus those listed here to create your own list of interview questions. File your lists of questions, along with your notes on the answers, in Binder 2.

Interview Questions

1. How closely do your home designs meet the client's proposed budget?
2. When put to bid with builders, if your design comes in over budget, do you charge for revisions?
3. Explain how your firm works.
4. Does a model of the home come with your architecture fee? If not, how much additional would a model cost?

TIP: Some HOAs require that an architectural model of your planned home be presented to their architecture review committee.

5. What is your experience with this Homeowner Association?
6. Do you know the architect representing the architectural review committee? If so, is there any conflict between the two of you that might affect the project?
7. What will be your involvement once the house is under construction?
8. Do you charge extra for site visits during construction and if so, how much?

9. Are you currently involved in any lawsuits?
10. Have you been fined or issued reprimands from AIA?
11. How do you stay current on new products and trends?
12. Explain your approach and experiences in designing a green home.

Review the list of questions to ask your architect, and take the potential architects individually to your home site. Even if you have already hired your architect, you will still want to review this list with your architect at your home site. The potential architects may be willing to answer some of these questions and may prefer to answer the rest further along in the hiring process. Write their comments on your Architect Comparison Chart (page 42), noting which architect made which comments. This comparison chart allows you to compare the architect's answers to the questionnaire, the architect's responses during the interview, the architect's comments at the home site, and your personal opinion of each architect. File it in Binder 2.

TIP: Check Better Business Bureau reports to see if the architect you are considering has had any complaints filed. You can also ask your architect for his or her Certificate of Insurance.

Questions to Ask When Taking Your Architect to the Site

1. What is your first impression of the property?
2. Do you see any immediate concerns?
3. What is your initial thought for positioning the home on the land?
4. What city or county building codes will affect this property or home?
5. Are there any HOA covenants that will affect building on this property?

6. Are there any drainage issues to avoid when positioning the house on the lot?

7. Where do you see the driveway?

The Decision

Using your comparison chart and your intuition as a guide, decide which architect you will hire. Once this architect has accepted, inform those you are not hiring and thank them for their time. They will most likely ask why you chose the architect you chose and not them. Prepare yourself to give an appropriate answer.

THE CONTRACT

Once you have selected your architect, you will move into contract negotiations. Usually your architect will provide a contract. At that point, you will want your attorney to review it and make revisions to send back to the architect. Here are some contract points for you to discuss with your attorney.

Financial Terms

1. On what terms will the architect be paid?

2. What is the billing schedule?

3. Will there be a cap on the total amount to be paid?

4. How will you be billed?

5. Will the architect provide invoices if being paid on the percentage of construction costs?

6. If you and the architect part ways, will any of the payments be reimbursed?

7. If any additional costs incur after the contract is signed, you must agree to those costs and sign off on them. No surveys, soil tests, structural design work, or other expenses can be done without the owner or designated person signing off on such requests. The architect must produce the signed-off agreement with the invoice to be paid.

8. If site visits are an additional cost to be paid, the architect will submit signed and dated copies of the Architect Site Visit Form (page 48) provided by you.

Architect Services

1. Which architectural drawings (floor plans, electrical plans, elevations, and so on) will be provided?

2. How many copies of each plan will you receive?

3. How many revisions will be allowed?

4. Will a model of your home be provided?

5. Will a color rendering of your home be drawn?

6. What role will the architect play during construction?

7. How often will the architect visit the construction site?

8. Who will be assigned to your project and what is their experience?

Time Considerations

1. Include a timetable as part of your contract.

2. State in your contract how often the timetable needs to be updated.

3. What are the penalties if the architect does not complete the plans on time?

4. Revisions will be provided to you in a timely manner.

5. You will reply to revisions in a timely manner.

6. Iron out penalties if you or the architect cause delays to the project.

Ownership of House Plans

1. Who will own the house plans?

2. Verify that the architect cannot use your house plans for future clients or developments.

3. What if your relative or friend in another state wanted to use the plans—would that be a problem?

Revisions

1. When the architect's design of your home is put to bid, if the architect's design exceeds the budget you agreed upon at the beginning of the design process, will the revisions be free?
2. How many revisions will be allowed for the original design and if the design exceeds the budget?
3. It is extremely important to state that only you can make changes to the architectural plans, to avoid changes you are unaware of and unexpected charges. The interior designer, the builder, and any outside consultants do not have the authority to make changes to your architectural plans without your knowledge and approval.

Insurance

1. Will the architect carry liability insurance?
2. What other insurance will the architect carry?
3. Are the amounts of insurance acceptable?
4. Will the architect provide a certificate of insurance?

Contract Termination

1. If you and the architect decide to part ways, the architect will return all photos, tear sheets, notes, and fact sheets provided by you, and all architectural plans and revisions to date.
2. Who will own the architectural plans created to date?
3. List reasons that will allow either party to terminate the contract.
4. List steps to terminating the contract.

Mutual Respect

Both you and the architect agree to be on time for meetings. If either party needs to cancel a meeting, they will inform the other party as soon as possible.

ARCHITECT'S SITE VISIT FORM

If you will be charged for each site visit, give a copy of the Architect's Site Visit Form (page 48) to the architect to use each time a billable site visit occurs. Ask the architect to submit these filled-in forms with invoices. Copies of this form can also be left at the job site in the construction office or on a clipboard once the interior of the home is protected from weather. When received from the architect, file the filled-in form in Binder 8.

The architect or architect's staff should fill in the form each time they visit the site. This form includes the date, the name of the person visiting the site, the names of people the architect or architect's staff is meeting, the purpose of the visit, the outcome of the visit, the length of the visit, and the architect firm's representative's signature. This form should be submitted by the architect with monthly invoices.

HOW TO BE YOUR ARCHITECT'S BEST CLIENT

Want to get the house of your dreams? Follow these basic rules for working with your architect.

Answer questions ahead of time. Before the first design meeting, copy all the forms in Chapter 4 (pages 67–85) and fill in most answers.

Take notes at each meeting. Have numerous copies of the Architect Meeting Notes (page 21) in Binder 1. Once you have taken notes at the meetings, file the notes in Binder 5. Assign a person to each follow-up task during the meeting and a date the task is to be done. Set up the next meeting before you leave. Make copies of your notes and distribute copies to appropriate persons.

Set firm dates. At each meeting, set firm dates for any follow-ups, such as delivery of revisions. Hold your architect accountable to those dates. After receiving revisions, return them according to the revision return date that was set.

Provide photos of home furnishings. Take photos of your existing furniture, appliances, art, portraits, mirrors, sculpture, rugs, and other items that you will use in your new home. Measure and write the dimensions of each item on the photograph. Organize these and place them in Binder 6. If you want to place these items in a particular room, note that on the photograph.

Provide samples of what you like. Collect photocopies, tear sheets, and photos of the exterior and interior of homes and design elements. Organize these, noting what it is you like about them, and place them in Binder 6. These are a great resource to communicate what you need, want, and desire.

Inform your architect of any change orders. If you make any changes with your interior designer, builder, or consultants once construction begins, tell your architect promptly and in writing.

Host an open house. Once you have settled into your new home, invite the architect's staff for a tour of your home.

HIRING YOUR INTERIOR DESIGNER

The next step after hiring your architect is to hire the rest of your team. Your interior designer should be brought on board as soon as possible. Your interior designer needs to collaborate with the architect during the design process. If you already have a relationship with an interior designer, you may hire this team member first. Whatever the sequence, get your team in place.

THE INTERIOR DESIGNER HIRING PROCESS

Identify three interior designers to consider. Compile a list of questions to ask when you interview them. Take notes during the interview with the potential interior designer candidates. File your list of questions and your interview notes in Binder 2.

Nine Rules for Smooth Relationships with Team Members

By following these recommendations, you will create a smooth working relationship with your architect, interior designer, and builder. Remember that you, the homeowner, have a role to play as well as each of these team members.

1. **Always be prepared!** It is better to postpone a meeting than to attend unprepared. Being prepared and organized sets the tone for the project.
2. **Take notes.** Take your own notes at every meeting, using the specific form and filing it so you can find it easily.
3. **Don't take cell phone calls during meetings.** One of the quickest ways to delay a meeting or interrupt the flow of the meeting is by answering your cell phone. The same goes for the person you're working with.
4. **Do your tasks promptly.** Do whatever tasks you need to before the next meeting, or postpone the meeting. Reply promptly to phone calls, e-mails, and faxes to help keep the project going.
5. **Be on time.** Give advance notice if postponing a meeting or if you will be late. Constantly rescheduling the meetings does not bode well for either of you.
6. **Be decisive.** Revisions are costly and slow down the process. Put the appropriate amount of time and thought into decisions going into the project. Decisions made hastily are more likely to be changed later.
7. **Keep messages brief.** This includes both phone messages and e-mails—but ask the builder what form of communication is preferred and honor that request. These are busy people, with many people needing approvals or answers to questions contacting them.
8. **Pay your bills on time.** Never expect your architect, builder, or interior designer to meet with you when you have unpaid invoices that are past due. Pay by the due date.
9. **Be generous with praise.** When you like what is presented or a completed job, let it be known. Don't just concentrate on what you do not like.

Here are some possible interview questions.

Interview Questions

1. May I see your portfolio?
2. What is your educational background?
3. What experience have you had as an interior designer?
4. What is the most expensive and the least expensive budget you have worked within?
5. How do you derive your budget?
6. How accurate are you at coming in on budget?
7. How do you want to be compensated? (Some take a flat fee, while others take a percentage of the cost of interior furniture and accessories, or a combination of the two.)
8. Do you require a contract? If so, may I have a copy?
9. On what grounds can the contract be broken?
10. How many projects are you currently involved in?
11. How many projects are you currently being considered for?
12. What is your biggest pet peeve in working with homeowners?
13. Explain your working process.
14. Would you provide a working timetable of this project?
15. Explain the structure of your firm.
16. List any design awards, and the names and dates of any magazines in which you have been published.
17. Please provide a list of references.

Fill in the Interior Designer Comparison Chart (page 44) to use as a guide for selecting your interior designer. File this chart in Binder 2.

The Decision

Make your decision and see if the interior designer is still available and willing to work on your project. Then, tell those you are not hiring and thank them for their time. If they ask why you chose the designer you chose, give an appropriate answer.

THE CONTRACT

Once you have selected an interior designer, you will move into contract negotiations. Usually your attorney will review the contract provided by the interior designer, revise it, and send it back to the interior designer.

Some contract points to discuss with your attorney:

Financial Terms

1. On what terms will the interior designer be paid?
2. What is the billing schedule?
3. Will there be a cap on the total amount to be paid?
4. How will you be billed?
5. Does the interior designer require you to provide cash in an account or a credit card on file for use in buying items? If so, will the cash be reimbursed if the contract is terminated?
6. Will the interior designer provide invoices if being paid on a percentage of costs?
7. For what reasons can the contract be terminated?
8. What are the steps to terminate the contract?
9. What is the approval process for purchases made by the interior designer?
10. What if you find items for the home on your own, how is that handled?
11. If the interior designer purchases items from a catalog and upon their arrival you do not like the items, how will that be handled?
12. What is the hourly wage for an interior designer to sit in on meetings with the architect and builder?

Interior Designer Services

1. Will there be any drawings?

2. Will there be story boards?
3. Who will work on your project?
4. Will you and the interior designer visit showrooms together?

Time Considerations

1. Include a timetable as part of your contract.
2. State in your contract how often the timetable needs to be updated.
3. What are the penalties if the interior designer does not complete the job on time? Iron out penalties if you or the interior designer cause delays to the project.

Insurance

1. Will the interior designer carry liability insurance?
2. What other insurance will the interior designer carry?

Contract Termination

1. If you and the interior designer decide to part ways, the interior designer will return all photos, tear sheets, and house plans provided by you, as well as all notes and fact sheets.
2. Spell out reasons that will allow either party to terminate the contract.
3. Spell out the steps to terminating the contract.

Mutual Respect

Both you and the interior designer agree to be on time for meetings. If either party needs to cancel a meeting, they will inform the other party as soon as possible.

Miscellaneous

Only you can make changes to the architectural plans. The interior designer cannot make changes without your signature.

HOW TO BE YOUR INTERIOR DESIGNER'S BEST CLIENT

Besides following the basic rules for working with any of your team members, here's how to make your relationship with your interior designer both more efficient and more rewarding—and make you more likely to end up with the home you want.

Provide photos of home furnishings. Take photos of your existing furniture, appliances, art, portraits, mirrors, sculpture, rugs, and other items that you will use in your new home. Write the dimensions of each item on the photograph. Organize these and place them in Binder 6. If you want to place these items in a particular room, note that on the photograph. If you do not have time to take these photos, your interior designer may offer to do the task.

Provide samples of what you like. Collect photocopies, tear sheets, and photos of the exterior and interior of homes and design elements. Organize these, noting what it is you like about them, and place them in Binder 6. These are a great resource to communicate what you need, want, and desire.

Return samples promptly. Fabric samples, furniture catalogs, stone samples, and so forth that are loaned out to you by your interior designer need to be returned in a timely manner.

Host an open house. Once you have settled into your new home, invite the interior design staff for a tour of your home.

HIRING YOUR BUILDER

The demand for builders in your area will dictate your negotiating power in the hiring process. During a slowdown, homeowners will find that builders will jump through hoops to get the job. In a building boom, you could find yourself waiting for your phone calls to be returned.

During a building boom, builders may be unwilling to go through a hiring process. They may say, "Either hire me right now or go find someone else." You may even find you cannot start construction when you planned.

But if there is no building boom, follow the hiring process listed below.

THE BUILDER HIRING PROCESS

Identify at least three builders you want to consider. Look for homes in your area that you like and find out the builder's name. Ask your architect for recommendations.

Send a letter informing the builders you are considering them for your project. Include the basic facts such as timetable, approximate size of the home you want to build, architect's name, and if known, the address of the property. Explain why you are considering their construction company. Mention the particular homes they have built that you like. Enclose the Builder Questionnaire (page 40), and ask that it be returned by a set date. Mention that you would like an interview, a site visit, visits to a couple of homes they have built, and references.

> **TIP: Hiring a builder at the outset of the design process will allow the builder to provide input regarding the topography as well as the structural engineering specifications, possibly saving you money.**

Once you have received responses to the builder's questionnaires, begin filling in the answers on the Builder Comparison Chart (page 46), and file it in Binder 2. If you want to eliminate a builder because of answers on the questionnaire, send that company a note that it is no longer being considered for the project. Next, set up interviews with potential builders. During the interviews, take notes that can be filled in on the comparison chart. After you have read through the questionnaire responses, you

may have additional questions as a result of their answers. Use those questions plus those listed here to create a list of interview questions, and file them and the answers in Binder 2.

Interview Questions

1. How accurate are you at coming in on budget?
2. How do you keep clients within their budget?
3. Explain how you work.
4. What role will you play once the house is under construction?
5. Who will be assigned to my job and what is their experience?
6. Are you currently involved in any lawsuits?
7. How long have each of your subcontractors been working for you?
8. Will you have any subcontractors on my project that you have never previously hired?
9. Will there be a construction office on site?
10. Will my job have a job site manager?
11. Explain your approach and experiences in building a green home.
12. Explain your expectations of the builder on this project.

After the interviews, take the builders you are still considering to the site, one at a time. Have them walk the land with you. Following the site visit, add your opinion and comments about each builder to the Builders Comparison Chart and file it in Binder 2. Add any noteworthy comments made by the builders. Write their comments down as they speak, making sure you note which builder made which comment.

Questions to Ask When Taking Builders to the Site

1. What is your first impression of the property?
2. Do you see any immediate concerns?

3. What is your initial thought for positioning the home on the land?
4. What city or county building codes will affect the property or the home you wish to have built?
5. Are there any HOA covenants that will affect building on this property?
6. Are there any drainage issues to avoid when positioning the house on the lot?
7. Where do you see the driveway?

The Decision

Using your comparison chart and your intuition as a guide, decide who you will hire. Inform the builder whom you want to hire as well as those you are not hiring. Thank all of them for their time.

THE CONTRACT

After you have selected a builder, you will move into contract negotiations. As with other team members, have your attorney review the builder's contract and make revisions. Here are some contract points for you to discuss with your attorney.

Financial Terms

1. How will the builder be paid?
2. What is the billing schedule?
3. Will there be a cap on the total amount to be paid?
4. How will you be billed?
5. Will the builder provide invoices if being paid on the percentage of construction costs?
6. If you and the builder part ways, will any of the payments be returned?
7. If any costs are incurred outside the contract, you must agree to those costs before they are incurred. Make it clear that any additional costs exceeding the budget will be paid only if you have authorized these expenses before they are incurred.

8. No changes can be made by anyone except you. The Change Order Form (page 49) should be a part of the contract, noting both you and the builder must sign off.
9. The builder must produce the signed-off agreement or change order with the invoice in order to be paid.

Builder Services

1. Who will be your project manager? What is that person's experience?
2. Set a particular day of the week and time of the day for a standing meeting.
3. Will there be a trailer on the job site?
4. Will there be a phone and fax on the job site?
5. What days of the week and what hours will the contractor work?
6. What holidays will be observed?
7. Specify that no new subcontractors will be used on this project. (You do not want your job to be the testing or training ground for a new subcontractor.)
8. The builder will keep the site clean as well as the interior of the home under construction.
9. List how the builder will prevent damage to building materials, appliances, plumbing fixtures, stone, tile, glass, and so on during construction. Some examples would be placing protective coverings over all glass windows to prevent them from being scratched, covering the tub and sinks so that workers cannot pour anything into them, and not allowing the HVAC system to be operated.

Time Considerations

1. Include a timetable as part of your contract.
2. State in your contract how often the timetable needs to be updated.
3. State the penalties if the builder does not complete the job on time.

Insurance

1. How much liability insurance will the builder carry? Ask for a copy of the builder's Certificate of Insurance.
2. Will the builder provide workman's compensation?
3. Will the builder carry insurance to cover the materials used for the job?
4. Does the builder's insurance cover theft of materials? If not, who will be liable for items stolen?
5. Will the builder carry fire insurance?
6. What other insurance will the builder carry?

Contract Termination

1. If the builder and you decide to part ways, the builder will return all photos, tear sheets, notes, and fact sheets provided by you, and all architectural plans.
2. Spell out reasons that will allow either party to terminate the contract.
3. Spell out the steps to terminating the contract.

TIP: Consider asking your builder to take out a performance bond, insurance that protects you if your builder's business fails. You should check out builders you are considering with the Better Business Bureau. You can ask to see builders' financial statements, but they may decline to provide them. Also check that your builder's business license is current.

Mutual Respect

Both you and the builder agree to be on time for meetings. If either party needs to cancel a meeting, they will inform the other party as soon as possible.

CHANGE ORDER FORM

The Change Order Form (page 49) should be filled out by the builder each time a change is made to the existing architectural plans after construction begins. It is imperative that you issue strict guidelines regarding who is authorized to make changes. Even if you are the only one allowed to make changes, each time a change is made, the builder should fill out this form. The form should include the date, name of the person making the change, description of the change, and any costs associated with making the change. Copies should be made of each change order and passed out to the architect, interior designer, builder, and any consultant, and keep one in your binder. Give blank copies to your builder to use and leave blank copies at the job site on a clipboard. File completed forms in Binder 8.

HOW TO BE YOUR BUILDER'S BEST CLIENT

Besides following basic rules for dealing with your team members, you can make the job go much more smoothly by following these guidelines.

Be prepared before breaking ground. Delaying the start of a job will be less wasteful of time and money than hurrying a start and ending up making change after change.

Take notes. Take notes at every builder meeting. Have numerous copies of Builder's Meeting Notes Form (page 23) in Binder 1, and file them in Binder 5 after you've taken notes. Assign a person to each follow-up task during the meeting and a date the task is to be done. Set up the next meeting before you leave. Make copies of your notes and distribute copies to appropriate persons.

Discuss construction site visits. Discuss how often and when your builder prefers that you visit the site. Some homeowners and builders meet every week on a specified date at a specified time. Some builders like homeowners to visit the site often so that subcontractors can ask them questions. Other builders feel a homeowner's presence distracts subcontractors, delaying your job and interfering with their work schedule.

Have the builder present when you discuss change orders with subcontractors. Subcontractors are instructed that the only changes they can make come from the builder. They cannot take orders from you, the architect, or the interior designer. Change orders must be controlled by the builder.

Don't call Monday morning. Monday morning is the most hectic time for the builder, project managers, and superintendents. Unless you have a time-sensitive reason to call the builder, wait until Monday afternoon or Tuesday.

Occasionally provide lunch for the workers. This gesture goes a long way. However, plan this with the builder or superintendent. If it's an extra busy week, stopping for a group lunch could be best saved for another day. In some cases it is best if you provide the money for pizza or sandwiches and have the builder handle it. Let it be the builder's call. Your builder knows the situation best.

Remember that job sites are often parking nightmares. Ask your builder where the best place is to park when you visit the site. You do not want to block in a worker, prevent delivery of materials, or get blocked in.

Treat workers with respect. Remember that those doing the work on your house are humans. A "thank you" for doing good work is appreciated. A simple nod of acknowledgment and a hello is appreciated.

Remember the builder has another life. Be considerate of the builder's time when asking him or her to meet you at the job after hours or on weekends. Also be considerate when calling after hours.

> **TIP: Discuss with your builder the team's approach to designing built-ins and cabinets. Some builders prefer these to be designed by your architect, while others ignore the architect's plans and have the homeowner work directly with the carpenter and cabinetmaker. If your builder prefers that you work directly with the carpenter and cabinetmaker, you will not need your architect to spend time drawing those plans, which could save you money.**

Now that you have hired your team, it is a high priority for you to set boundaries and establish communication channels between the members of your team. Make it clear to each member of your team what authority each person has in making decisions and whether all decisions must go through you. Creating a team atmosphere and managing the team will go a long way in the design and construction of your home.

Architect Questionnaire

1. How many homes have you designed with construction costs of $ _____ ? _____

2. How many homes have you designed with approximately _____ square feet? _____

3. What is the most expensive construction costs for a home your have designed? $ _____

4. What is the largest home you have designed? _____ square feet.

5. Check any of these situations for which you have design experience. Note the number of homes you have designed in these situations.

On a cliff _____	Flood-prone area ____	Sandy soil area _____
Dry desert area _____	Humid wet area _____	Steep slope _____
Dry mountain area ____	Hurricane area _____	Tornado area _____
Earthquake area _____	Rocky ground _____	

6. How many homes have you designed dealing with this particular Homeowner Association? _____

7. How many homes have you designed dealing with this city or county? _____

8. What is your educational background? _____

9. What is your background and experience as a home architect? _____

_____

10. How many homes are you currently involved in designing? _____

11. How many homes are you currently bidding to design? _____

12. How long do you think this particular home will take to design? _____

13. How are you compensated? _____

What is the schedule of payments? _____

14. What type of insurance do you carry? _____
Please provide a copy of your current Certificate of Insurance

15. Are you a member of AIA? _____ Any other organizations? _____

_____

16. Please provide the names and contact information of the owners of last five homes you have designed. Also give a brief explanation of the job you did.

_____

_____

_____

_____

_____

_____

_____

_____

_____

17. Please provide proof that you are licensed to work in this state.

18. Have any of your home designs been featured in magazines? If so, list the publications and dates.

_____

19. Have you won any design awards? If so, provide a list. _____

_____

Please submit these answers on or before _____

You can mail them to _____

_____

_____

Or fax them to _____

Thank you for your time and efforts.

Builder Questionnaire

1. How many homes have you built with construction costs of $ _____ ? _____

2. How many homes have you built with approximately _____ square feet? _____

3. What is the most expensive home you have built? $ _____

4. What is the largest home you have built? _____ square feet.

5. Check any of these situations for which you have building experience. Note the number of homes you have built in these situations.

On a cliff _____	Flood-prone area _____	Sandy soil area _____
Dry desert area _____	Humid wet area _____	Steep Slope _____
Dry mountain area _____	Hurricane area _____	Tornado area _____
Earthquake area _____	Rocky ground _____	

6. How many homes have you built dealing with this particular Homeowner Association? _____

7. How many homes have you built dealing with this city or county? _____

8. What is your educational background? _____

9. What is your home construction background and experience? _____

_____

10. How many homes are you currently involved in building? _____

11. How many homes are you currently bidding to build? _____

12. How long do you think this particular home will take to build? _____

13. How are you compensated? _____

14. Please provide a copy of your current Certificate of Insurance.

15. Do you have workman's compensation? _____

16. Are you a member of any home builder associations? If so, list. _____

_____

17. Please provide the names and contact information of the owners of the last five homes you have built. Also give a brief explanation of the job you did.

_____

_____

_____

_____

_____

_____

_____

_____

_____

_____

18. Please provide proof that you are licensed to build in this state.

19. Have you received any building awards? _____

20. Have any homes you have built been featured in magazines? If so, list the publications and dates.

_____

Please submit these answers on or before _____

You can mail them to _____

_____

_____

Or fax them to _____

Thank you for your time and efforts.

Architect Comparison Chart

Architect Firm	Contact Name	Address	Phone	Fax	E-mail Address
A					
B					
C					

Answers to Questionnaire	Architect Firm A	Architect Firm B	Architect Firm C
Number of homes designed with approximately ____ square feet			
Largest square foot home designed			
Most expensive home designed			
Number of homes designed on a similar challenge as this lot			
Number of homes designed in this HOA			
Number of homes designed in this municipality			
Number of years of experience			
Number of projects currently working			
Number of projects currently being considered to design			
Compensation plan			
Type of insurance carried			
Percentage of time design comes within 5 percent of the proposed budget			
If over budget, are revisions free?			
Involved in any lawsuits			
Licensed by state			

Interview: Noteworthy comments made by architects _____

_____

_____

_____

_____

_____

_____

Site visit: Noteworthy comments made by architects _____

_____

_____

_____

_____

_____

_____

Overall impression of architects on site visit _____

_____

_____

_____

_____

Rate your personal impression

Compatibility _____

Intuitive feeling _____

Interior Designer Comparison Chart

Interior Design Firm	Contact Name	Address	Phone	Fax	E-mail Address
A					
B					
C					

Answers to Questionnaire	Designer A	Designer B	Designer C
Rate the portfolio			
Education background			
Years of experience as an interior designer			
Most expensive budget for an interior design job			
Least expensive budget for an interior design job			
Is a contract required?			
Penalties for terminating contract			
Number of current projects			
Number of projects being considered to do			
Biggest pet peeve a homeowner can do			
Rate how you perceive the process of doing business			
Timetable provided			
Organization structure of interior design firm			
Other comments			

Interview: Noteworthy comments made by interior designers _____

_____

_____

_____

_____

_____

_____

Site visit: Noteworthy comments made by interior designers _____

_____

_____

_____

_____

_____

_____

Overall impression of interior designers on site visit _____

_____

_____

_____

_____

Rate your personal impression

Compatibility _____

Intuitive feeling _____

Builder Comparison Chart

Builder Name	Contact Name	Address	Phone	Fax	E-mail Address
A					
B					
C					

Answers to Questionnaire	Builder A	Builder B	Builder C
Number of homes built with approximately ____ square feet			
Largest square foot home built			
Most expensive home built			
Number of homes built on a similar challenge as this lot			
Number of homes built in this HOA			
Number of homes built in this municipality			
Number of years of experience			
Number of projects currently working			
Number of projects currently being considered to build			
Biggest pet peeve a homeowner can do			
Compensation plan			
Type of insurance carried			
Percentage of time building costs comes within 5 percent of the proposed budget			
Involved in any lawsuits			
Licensed by state			

Interview: Noteworthy comments made by builders _____

_____

_____

_____

_____

_____

Site visit: Noteworthy comments made by builders _____

_____

_____

_____

_____

_____

Overall impression of builders on site visit _____

_____

_____

_____

_____

Rate your personal impression

Compatibility _____

Intuitive feeling _____

▶ File in Binder 8: Financial, Legal, and Insurance Information

Architect Site Visit Form

Date of visit _____

Person making the visit _____

Did you meet with anyone at the site? If so, who? _____

Purpose of the site visit

_____

_____

_____

_____

_____

Outcome of the visit

_____

_____

_____

_____

_____

_____

_____

_____

_____

Length of time of the visit _____

Signature of person visiting _____

Change Order Form

Date _____ Trade _____

Ordered by _____

Description

_____

_____

_____

_____

_____

_____

_____

_____

_____

_____

_____

1. _____ $ _____

2. _____ $ _____

3. _____ $ _____

4. _____ $ _____

5. _____ $ _____

Total cost $ _____

Homeowner signature _____ Date _____

General contractor signature _____ Date _____

3 Purchasing Land, a Home, or a Condominium

When buying land or a home, you want to make sure that you don't encounter unpleasant surprises—such as zoning laws that won't let you build the house you envision. (If you have already bought land, a home, or a condominium, you can jump ahead to Chapter 4.)

WHAT IS DUE DILIGENCE?

Due diligence is the research and analysis of a piece of property or condominium done by the prospective buyer along with his or her realtor before a final decision is made about buying. The property is usually under contract during the due diligence process, with the buyer and seller agreeing to a specified amount of time for the due diligence. The prospective buyer may ask for additional time if needed, but if the seller has another interested party that extension may not be granted. At the end of the due diligence period, the prospective buyer can go forward with the purchase or terminate the contract.

Performing due diligence when buying raw land to build a home, a tear-down to build a home, a home to remodel, or a condominium is a way to find out if you will be able to create your vision on this property. Important information to obtain during due diligence includes the Homeowner Association covenants and bylaws, and municipal codes and zoning laws that would restrict what you want to build or remodel. During due diligence, you could discover the home is on the historic registry and cannot be torn down. Other things that might be uncovered are nuisances such as a volatile neighbor, neighbor pet issues, or an odor that appears when the wind blows from a certain direction.

You can ask that the seller identify the setbacks from the property line that identify the building envelope, the area in which your house could be built. Depending on the motivation of the seller or the housing market, the seller may or may not be willing to have this done. The potential buyer may have to pay to have this done.

(If you already own the property you can hire a surveyor to identify the building envelope and setbacks based on the municipal codes and HOA. You may also measure these yourself.)

DUE DILIGENCE INFORMATION FACT SHEET

As you gather information, fill in the Due Diligence Information Fact Sheet (page 60) and file it in Binder 3. This fact sheet contains the address of the property under consideration, the seller's realtor's name, the seller's name, the most pertinent answers to the due diligence questions, a list of your concerns, and any follow-up questions.

HOMEOWNER ASSOCIATION INFORMATION FACT SHEET

Fill in the Homeowner Association Information Fact Sheet (page 61) and file it in Binder 3. This fact sheet contains the name, address, and contact information of the HOA, the board members' names and contact information, the name and contact information of the architectural review committee, any pertinent HOA information discovered, and any follow-up questions for the HOA.

MUNICIPALITY INFORMATION FACT SHEET

Fill in the Municipality Information Fact Sheet (page 62) and file it in Binder 3. This fact sheet should contain the names, addresses, and contact information of the Director of the Codes Department, the Zoning Department, the Building Permit Department, and any other departments that will be involved in granting a building permit and a Use and Occupancy Certificate. List any pertinent information you receive from these departments during your due diligence process. Also list any questions and follow-up needed from the municipality.

DUE DILIGENCE BEFORE BUYING RAW LAND OR A HOME

Compile a list of questions with your realtor to be given to the seller's realtor. An experienced realtor who knows the area will aid you in reviewing the questions and adding to the list. It is important to request that these questions be answered in writing and signed by the seller. They should become a part of the contract. Include a date you would like for the answers to be returned. File a copy of your questions and the answers obtained from the seller in Binder 3.

QUESTIONS TO ASK THE SELLER

1. Why is this property being sold?
2. Are soil test results, surveys, or architectural plans available? If so, will these be provided?
3. Are there current property line markers on the property? If not, can a survey be done and the property line marked?
4. Explain the availability of gas, electricity, water and sewer, cable television, internet services, and telephone. Are all available? Will there be any fees to bring these services to the lot?
5. Are there any utility boxes on the property or, if a new development, where will they be located?
6. Are there any unsightly utility poles on the property? If so, are there any plans for underground utilities? Do you have the option to pay to move the utility wires underground?
7. Are there any utility easements? Explain.
8. Is there any possibility of a major power line planned for the neighborhood?
9. Are there any pipelines running through the property? If so, are they properly marked on the property?

10. Explain any rights of way running through the property.
11. Are there any mineral rights that go with the property?
12. Explain any restrictive covenants.
13. Explain any deed restrictions.
14. Are there any known water sources running under or through the property, such as springs, creeks, and so on? Describe.
15. Is the property in a flood plain?
16. Does the property require flood insurance?
17. Is there a public transportation route near the property?
18. What school system serves the property?
19. What fire and police force serves the property?
20. How close is a fire station to the property?
21. Is there a fire hydrant near the property?
22. Are there any new developments planned in the area that would affect the value of this property positively or negatively? Explain.
23. Are there any proposed zoning changes we should be made aware of? Explain.
24. Are there plans for a new school or other government building that through eminent domain could affect the property?
25. Are there plans for new roads or interstate highways planned or being considered for the neighborhood? Explain.
26. If applicable, please provide a copy of the Homeowner Association bylaws and covenants.
27. How much are the HOA dues and how often are they paid?
28. If applicable, are there any homeowner assessments planned? Please provide the history of homeowner assessments for the past ten years.
29. If applicable, does the Homeowner Association have plans to raise the monthly, quarterly, or annual dues for common areas?

TIP: If you are purchasing land that has previously been used for growing fruits or vegetables, have a pesticide test done on the soil.

30. What is the process required by the Homeowner Association to receive approval to build?
31. What is required by the city or county to obtain a building permit?
committees or approval process for tear-downs?
33. How much is the property tax?
34. How much do monthly utilities (water, electric, and gas) cost?
35. Are there any odor problems? If so, explain what kinds and suggested treatments.
36. Has there been a meth lab, murder, suicide, or any other event that would affect the property value?
37. What is the crime rate in this area?
38. Have there been any incidents with neighbors such as domestic violence, abnormal behavior, or disturbances? Have the police ever been called?
39. Have there been any nuisances or incidents with neighbor's pets? Do any pit bulls or other dangerous dogs live in the neighborhood?
40. Is this piece of property affected by the noise of trains, planes, or automobiles?

SITE VISITS: ISSUES TO ADDRESS

When you meet architects and builders at a property you are considering for purchase, there are many issues to address. The list here includes examples of questions to discuss and features of the property to check. Use this list as a guide to come up with your own list of issues. (If you have already purchased property, your list can help you determine how to position your home on the property.) Bring your list to the site and be sure to take detailed notes.

Place a copy of your list and your notes in Binder

Examples of HOA Bylaws and Municipal Codes

The building fees and penalties assessed by some homeowner associations can be substantial. It will help to have a clear understanding of all fees and penalties. Some HOA bylaws have a time frame for new construction to be completed. If not completed, you will be fined each day until completion.

Many homeowner associations require payment to begin the architectural review process and have an architect on retainer giving input. Some homeowner associations assess fees for approval to build. These fees are for street wear and tear and other expenses incurred during the construction process.

The following are examples of HOA bylaws and municipal codes from various parts of the country. Some are more stringent than others. It is important to understand what bylaws and codes might affect the vision you plan for your home.

No freestanding structures. All structures on the property must be connected.

Setbacks from property lines may be substantial.

Height restrictions.

Maximum and minimum number of square feet for a house.

Maximum number of square feet for a garage.

Number of balcony square feet.

Maximum amount of heated sidewalks.

Maximum amount of paving/concrete for a driveway.

Maximum degree of mountain slope on which a home can be built.

Stringent rules regarding tear-downs and recycling materials.

Color of materials to be used on the exterior of the house.

Restrictions on materials that can be used on the exterior of the house.

Roofing materials must be approved.

Architectural design must be approved.

Maximum amount of glass windows that can be used.

Noise restrictions such as not allowing exterior speakers.

Restrictions on height of fences

Exterior lighting restrictions such as not allowing flood lights on the house.

Swimming pool cannot be seen from neighbor's homes sitting above your home.

Environmental laws that must be met.

Wildfire, wildlife, avalanche reports must be submitted.

Any tree removal or replacement must be approved, even dead trees.

No dirt work can be done for landscape or any other purpose without HOA approval.

Strict guidelines for construction worker parking.

Start and stop times and days of the week for building.

3 behind the Due Diligence Questions and Answers tab. File any information about the design of the home in Binder 4.

1. What part of the property receives the western sun? How does this affect the positioning of the house on the lot?
2. Which part of the property faces north? (Snow will pile up on that side of the house and cold air will blow from that direction.)
3. Will any windows line up with the next door neighbor's windows?
4. What will the view be from each window of the house?
5. Climb on a ladder to see the view from the second level.
6. Walk the property line and see what actually borders the land.
7. Identify the height restrictions at the property site.

TIP: Before you visit raw land or a tear-down with your architect and builder during the due diligence period, obtain the setbacks and height restrictions so that the architect can show you how those affect the property. Make sure your realtor has requested that the property line be clearly marked. Obtain a survey of the land and a survey showing all structures on the property. Take a tape measure and, if possible, a tall ladder to help you see the view from upper levels. If you have a style or shape of house in mind, your architect can help you determine if the property can accommodate that style or shape.

8. Where will the driveway enter from the street? Which side of the property would be best for the driveway and why? If you live in a frigid climate, will the location of the driveway receive direct sun to melt the snow and ice?

9. Would there be a blind spot when entering or exiting the driveway? What is the traffic pattern during rush hours? Is there room for a gated entry to the driveway?

10. Discuss any trees or shrubs you want to save.

11. Listen for traffic noise and note what side of the house would be closest to the noise.

12. Will there be parking issues in front of the property if there is a nearby school or public venue?

13. Are there any telephone or power poles on the property? Will they be an eyesore? Will they interfere with radio transmissions?

14. Are there any drainage issues to consider when positioning the house on the lot?

15. Visit the property during a heavy rain and note how the water drains. Will this affect where you position the home?

16. Is there a storm drain at the property? Note the amount of water flowing into it during a storm.

17. Are there any pipeline markers on the property? These could affect where you position your home.

TIP: If building where the HOA has an architectural review committee, have your preliminary architecture plans approved before you spend the time and money to do a complete set of plans that may end up being rejected. Sometimes HOA architectural review committees can be very demanding.

18. Are there any utility boxes on the property? Will these be an eyesore?

19. Does your cell phone work on the property?

20. Can you get cable television? If not, is the site suitable for a satellite dish?

21. Is high-speed internet available?

22. Are there any rights of way through the property that would have an adverse effect on where you position the house?

23. How is garbage pickup handled on the property?

24. What city or county building codes will affect the property or the home you wish to have built?

DUE DILIGENCE BEFORE BUYING A CONDOMINIUM

If you are considering buying an existing condominium, one under construction, or one that will soon be built, ask the following questions during the due diligence process. After reviewing this list with your realtor, compile a final list of questions

True Stories of Condominium Woes

There are many pitfalls to watch out for when you buy a condominium. For example, if a unit has had water damage accompanied by an insurance claim, a new homeowner may be denied insurance coverage. This happened in the late 1990s when mold was the lawsuit du jour. A prospective buyer waited until the day of closing to inquire about insurance and was turned down due to a water damage claim from a few years earlier. The claim was due to a faulty toilet and no mold was involved. Even so, she was denied coverage. The prospective homeowner closed on the unit without insurance with plans of contacting another company for an insurance policy.

In another situation, the police were called numerous times for domestic disturbances involving a resident with alleged mental and drug problems. This resident entered another resident's unlocked condominium on the same floor without permission and used the shower; burned food while cooking, causing residents in the building to call the front desk to ask if there was a fire; and drove off in someone else's car that the valet had brought up from the garage! Two years later, the board was still dealing with this condominium owner.

In another condominium, the service elevator vestibule, a small room outside the service elevator on each floor, was smaller than the actual service elevator. The door leading out of the service elevator vestibule required a 90-degree left turn from the service elevator. When a moving company tried to move furniture from the service elevator into the elevator vestibule, it would not fit. One long sideboard could not make the 90-degree turn. The homeowner ended up paying the movers to carry the very heavy piece up the fire stairwell ten floors.

The design for one penthouse remodeling job called for tall panels of mirror on certain walls. The homeowner had to use a helicopter to lower the sections of mirror into the penthouse because they were too large to fit in the elevator.

Another building did not provide any service elevators to its hundred-plus units, even though the marketing material stated there would be one. Service elevators are typically used for moving in and out, remodeling or any construction within the resident units, repairmen and housekeepers, taking pets in and out of the building, and delivering large purchases. With only one service elevator and several construction projects going on, jobs were delayed, not to mention residents inconvenienced.

The opening to the trash chute in one building was so small that a super-sized laundry detergent bottle or a pizza box would not fit through it. Residents had to take the elevator down to the dumpster to throw out any trash that did not fit in the chute.

The bylaws of one Homeowner Association in a high-rise would not allow any type of Christmas decorations on the balconies. The same bylaws also stated curtains or curtain lining had to be a white or cream color.

In one high-rise building that presold numerous units before breaking ground, buyers were allowed to make changes to the architectural plans. All changes would be made by the construction company hired to build the building. Once construction got underway, the buyers learned that neither they nor their interior designer would be allowed to enter the building until they closed on the unit , so they could not oversee the remodel job. When the buyers saw the final product at closing, to their dismay, they discovered many mistakes and misinterpretations of the design plans.

for the seller or developer. It is important to get the answers in writing and make those answers a part of the contract should you buy the condominium.

File the questions and pertinent answers in Binder 3. File any answers returned in writing in Binder 8.

QUESTIONS TO ASK THE SELLER BEFORE BUYING A CONDOMINIUM

1. How many parking spots come with the unit? Is there tandem parking? Is parking additional to the sales price? How is the location of the

parking spot determined? How close is it to the elevator? Ask to see the actual parking spots. Is it deeded to the condo owner? Is there property tax on the parking space? Is the spot near a column that prevents a driver from fully opening the door? Is it near a maintenance area and does the vehicle need to be moved occasionally? Is there a monthly fee for parking garage cleaning, security, and upkeep in addition to the condominium fees? Are the residents allowed to park their own vehicle or is a valet required to park all vehicles?

2. Do storage units come with the building? Are they deeded? Where is the storage unit to the residence located?

3. Is there a drain at the bottom level of the multilevel underground parking garage? (This is desirable to allow water to drain out of the garage when it is power washed.)

4. Does each condominium have its own HVAC control or does the building superintendent control the temperature?

5. If the building superintendent controls the HVAC, what are the temperature settings?

6. Is the output for air conditioning adequate for comfort?

7. Does the unit get so much western sun that the curtains need to be drawn every afternoon? Does the western sun heat up the condo? Has the sun faded furniture, rugs, or wood floors?

8. Is this unit near the trash chute? Is there noise froom trash going down the chute or from the trash chute door opening and closeng? How many trash chutes are located per floor? What is the location relative to the unit? How large is the actual opening to the trash chute? (Some are so small you cannot fit a pizza box or large detergent jug into them.)

9. Is there pickup for recycling? If so, where is it, and how often is it picked up?

10. Is this unit located near an alley? If so, is there noise from dumpsters?

11. Is this unit on a bus route? If so, is there noise from buses early in the morning or late at night?

12. Is this unit near an elevator? Are there noises from the ding of the door opening, the sound of occupants talking, or the sound of it going up and down?

13. Is this unit on a busy street? (A one-way street that approaches a stop sign will be quieter because drivers will be taking their foot off the gas pedal in preparation to stop. If the unit faces a one-way street just beyond a stop sign, cars pulling away from the stop sign will be giving the vehicle gas to pick up speed, which is noisier.)

14. Are pets allowed? Is there a limit on the number of pets per residence? What are the pet rules and regulations?

15. Do any of the neighbors have pets? If so, have these pets created any problems such as barking?

16. Is there any litigation pending with the construction company? If so, explain.

17. Is any litigation pending with the Homeowner Association? If so, explain.

18. Please provide bylaws, covenants, and any other pertinent Homeowner Association information.

19. How much are the Homeowner Association dues? Are these paid monthly, quarterly, bi-annually, or annually? How many increases have occurred in the past ten years? When is the next increase expected? (Ask to see the HOA budget.)

20. Please provide copies of the board meeting minutes for the past year.

21. Have the homeowners ever been assessed by the HOA? If so, how much was the assessment and what was the reason? Are any planned?
22. Are there any HOA rules governing curtains on the windows? Christmas decorations? Balcony objects? Stereo speakers on the balcony?
23. Have there been any termite problems or damage due to termites? If so, what was the damage and how was the problem treated?
24. Have there been any repairs for water leaks or damage due to the water leaks in this unit? Has there been an insurance claim? If so, explain.
25. Has there ever been any mold in the unit? Has there been an insurance claim regarding mold? Explain both.
26. Have there been problems with neighbors living on the same floor, above, or below? (Things that you should be concerned with may include people with alcohol issues, domestic violence problems, noisy neighbors, or any other problems that have involved police.)
27. Has the building had a structural, mechanical, electrical, plumbing, or other audit done? If so, why? Is there a report from this audit on file?
28. Please provide a copy of the certificate of occupancy or use and occupancy certificate.
29. Has the developer's master plan met all code requirements and been signed off on as compliant by the codes division?
30. How is furniture moved into the unit? Is there adequate space to load and unload furniture in the elevator vestibules? How many service elevators are there? Is a reservation required for the elevator on moving day?

    Will large furniture fit into the elevator or in the elevator vestibules? (Armoires, large art and mirrors, pianos, oversized sofas, and hunting trophies can be problematic.)

31. Describe the fire drill. Will fire ladders reach the height of the unit?
32. What is the fire escape plan?
33. Identify any load-bearing walls. (You need this information if you plan to remodel.)
34. How much is the property tax?
35. What do the HOA bylaws say about remodeling?
36. What type of security system does the building offer?
37. Does the building have security personnel on duty? Are they armed? Are they on duty 24/7?
38. Does the building require employees to sign a confidentiality agreement?

ADDITIONAL QUESTIONS FOR NEW CONDOMINIUMS

If you are purchasing a mid-rise or high-rise condominium that is either under construction or will be built in the near future, there are questions to ask specific to a new development during the due diligence process. Use the following list of questions and discuss each point with your realtor when you visit a condominium that you are interested in buying. Your realtor may have additional questions to add to the list. File pertinent information in Binder 3. Add any answers that relate to design to Binder 4. Always get any promises made by the developer in writing as part of your contract.

1. Will you be able to make buyer changes?
2. Will you be granted reasonable access during construction to oversee the buyer changes?
3. Will you be allowed to bring in your own plumber to check plumbing before drywall is installed? High-rise condos are known for having plumbing leaks. Ask to have your own plumber check the work that has been done. If you know your neighbors, especially the person above you, encourage them to have their plumbing checked, too.

4. If you are one of the first to close on the unit and the full support staff has not been hired and some of the amenities are not ready for use, will you be expected to pay the full amount of common area dues?

5. At what point does the developer begin paying the common area dues for unsold units?

6. How long will the developer be allowed to post marketing or For Sale signs on the property?

7. What are the specifications of materials that will be used in the finish-out? Make the specifications and tear sheets for these items part of the contract. These include the floors, counters, lighting fixtures, appliances, fireplace mantel, type of fireplace, type of gas logs, photo of proposed fireplace and logs, plumbing fixtures and fittings, ceiling fan photos, balcony railing, balcony flooring, closets, cabinets, and so on.

8. What comes with the property? Get it in writing. Will there be a lawn sprinkler system, sodded grass installed, water fountain, pool, hot tub, weight room and equipment, furnishings in the common areas, wine storage area, or garage storage? How many passenger elevators and service elevators will there be? What services will the staff provide and what type of security system will there be? What types of trees and shrubs will be planted and how many? Some developers verbally promise many amenities but end up not providing them—so get it in writing.

9. What are the proposed HOA monthly dues? Ask how this figure was reached. Ask for a

Check Out Condo HOA Bylaws

Condominium HOA bylaws can affect the lifestyle you envision due to restrictions on remodeling, restrictions on the use of your condominium, and restrictions on the number of occupants.

Bylaws may place restrictions on

- Number, size, or type of pets (if any are allowed)
- Number of household occupants allowed in your unit
- Use of your condominium for any type of business
- Swimming pool use
- Use of Christmas lights or decorations on balconies
- Window treatments
- All objects placed on a balcony, including the weight and the aesthetics
- Use of the party room
- Hosting parties or social events in your condo. (Some HOAs even require you to provide a security officer and valet parking if you have more than a set number of guests.)
- Hosting Tupperware, jewelry shows, clothing shows, or other type of retail parties
- Days of the week and hours of the day construction workers can work in your unit
- Leasing your unit
- Grilling on your patio or balcony

guarantee on how long the monthly dues will remain at the price quoted when the unit was purchased. Sometimes monthly fees are set too low for selling purposes and are increased within a short period of time.

Due Diligence Information Fact Sheet

Seller's name _____ Phone _____

Property address

_____

_____

Seller's realtor _____ Phone _____

Buyer's realtor _____ Phone _____

Pertinent information architect needs regarding property that was discovered during due diligence

_____

_____

_____

_____

_____

_____

_____

_____

_____

_____

_____

_____

_____

Homeowner Association Information Fact Sheet

Name of Homeowner Association _____

Phone _____ Fax _____

Mailing address

_____

_____

HOA president _____ Phone _____

HOA e-mail _____ President e-mail _____

Board members and contact numbers

_____

_____

_____

HOA fees for building approval _____

HOA architectural approval process pertinent facts

_____

_____

_____

_____

_____

HOA design criteria information

_____

_____

_____

_____

_____

_____

Municipality Information Fact Sheet

City or county name _____

Contact names, contact numbers, fax, e-mail

_____

_____

_____

_____

Address

_____

_____

Building permit fee information

_____

_____

Building permit approval process

_____

_____

_____

_____

_____

_____

Codes and zoning design criteria information

_____

_____

_____

_____

_____

_____

4 How to Be Prepared When Working with Your Architect

Once you have hired an architect, you will need to prepare for the first meeting to discuss the house you want designed. Remember, your architect cannot read your mind. Your architect will not live in your house. The more prepared you are for the first meeting, the more likely the first set of architectural plans will meet your expectations. Your architect's job is to design the house you want by listening to your needs. Your architect should first listen to your ideas and review your photos and tear sheets, and then ask questions. If you do not have ideas for a certain room, ask your architect for suggestions and then ask why he or she is making those suggestions. Your architect should make recommendations, but not intimidate or persuade you into agreeing to a house you did not have in mind.

A house evolves from meeting to meeting. If something you want does not fit into the plans, challenge your architect to find solutions. Trust your intuition. If you do not feel something is what you really wanted, reject it. If you do not understand what is being proposed, speak up.

If you have not already assembled your binders, before you begin working with your architect you will definitely want to assemble Binder 1, Binder 4, Binder 5, and Binder 6. These four binders are important in keeping you organized while working with your architect.

BINDER 1: BLANK FORMS

Make copies of all of the forms pertinent to your house (refer to Appendix 1, pages 348–351) and file them in Binder 1. Note which forms need multiple copies.

BINDER 4: DESIGN

Fill in the forms, checklists, and fact sheets as well as you can. These forms are thorough, and completing them will be an ongoing process. All of these forms, checklists, and fact sheets will be the cornerstone for your design and building process. The information you fill in will be invaluable to your architect, interior designer, builder, and you, representing every decision you make on the design of your home.

It is important to date all of these forms, checklists, and fact sheets every time you add a new item or make a change so you will know which sheet contains the most up-to-date information. When you make additions or changes, provide the newly dated sheet to the architect, interior designer, and builder, and replace your old sheet in your binder with the updated copy.

Basic Design Fact Sheet (page 67). This form will help you identify your needs, wants, and desires for your home as you prepare for your first meeting with your architect.

Occupants of the Home Checklist (page 68). For a better understanding of the design project, your architect needs to be acquainted with basic information regarding the people and animals that will call this house a home.

Rooms in Your Home Checklist (page 69). This indicates the rooms that you want in your home, including the floor level and the approximate sizes of the rooms.

Closets in Your Home Checklist (page 70). This indicates the closets that you want in your home, including the floor level and the approximate sizes of the closets.

Basic Bedroom Fact Sheet (page 71). Fill in this grid based on the number of bedrooms and the size of the beds you want in your home. See Bed Sizes and Measurements (above right) for specifics.

BED SIZES AND MEASUREMENTS

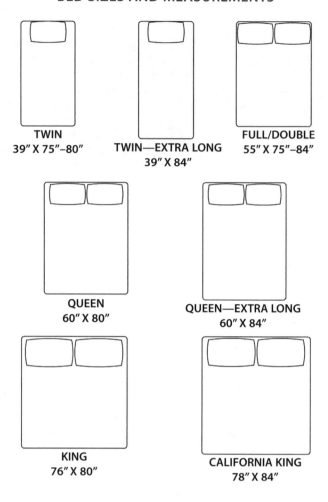

TWIN
39" X 75"–80"

TWIN—EXTRA LONG
39" X 84"

FULL/DOUBLE
55" X 75"–84"

QUEEN
60" X 80"

QUEEN—EXTRA LONG
60" X 84"

KING
76" X 80"

CALIFORNIA KING
78" X 84"

Miscellaneous Information Checklist (page 72): This represents a range of possibilities for you to consider for your home, including consultants, natural gas, pets, and game tables and video game machines.

Exterior Elements for Your Home Checklist (page 73): This checklist covers everything from the foundation, roof, walls, doors, windows, water features, and exterior living areas. Refer to Roof Shapes (page 65).

Existing Contents of the Home Checklist (page 75): This form covers all items you own that will become a part of the new home: furniture, art, portraits, mirrors, rugs, trophies, musical instruments, chandeliers, antique doors, mantels, appliances, audio visual equipment, office equipment, and patio furniture. Where applicable, describe the item, its desired location and dimensions, and note if you will be providing a photo. If any items will be located in a specific room, record that on the particular room's individual fact sheet.

Common Household Item Storage Checklist (page 79): If you expect to find a place for everything when you move into your home, you'll need to identify the items you own that need to be stored and where you want those items stored. This information will need to be discussed with your architect.

Individual Room and Closet Fact Sheet (page 81): This will become the most important and detailed checklist regarding decisions for your home.

Make a copy of this form for every room and closet you will have in your home and record every detail about each room or closet in your home. As you read through the book and fill in the multiple forms and checklists, you will find more and more information to add to this fact sheet. You will be asked questions about particular rooms that may have never even crossed your mind, and may end up listing needs, wants, and desires that you might have otherwise forgotten. You'll record information on this fact sheet about appliances, built-ins, ceiling fans, computer wiring connectors, fireplaces, fixed mirrors, the integrated home automation monitor, security alarm pads, stereo components, stereo speakers, individual speaker volume controls, telephone jacks, televisions, wall treatments, window treatments, electrical needs, storage needs, existing contents, ceilings, doors, floors, HVAC, and paint colors .

Individual room checklists (pages 128–203): At the end of Chapter 5, you'll find checklists for the following possible rooms and areas in your home. Copy any that you will have in your home. You will file the filled-out forms in Binder 4.

ROOF SHAPES

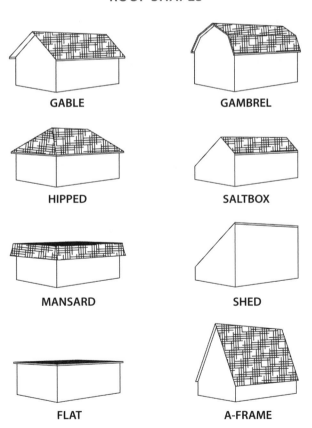

GABLE   GAMBREL

HIPPED   SALTBOX

MANSARD   SHED

FLAT   A-FRAME

Apartment Area
Attic
Bar
Basement
Bathroom
Bathroom Item Storage
Bedroom
Bedroom Closet
Breakfast Room
Butler's Pantry
Control Room
Dining Room
Driveway
Entry Foyer
Exercise Room
Exterior Front Entry

TIP: Before putting any furniture, art, rugs, or other items into storage, photograph them and write the dimensions on the back of the photo.

Family Room

Garage

Garage Item Storage

Garage Vehicle

Kitchen

Kitchen Appliance

Kitchen Cabinet Layout

Kitchen Island

Kitchen Item Storage

Kitchen Plumbing

Kitchen Pantry

Laundry Room

Library

Living Room/Great Room

Mechanical Room

Media Room

Morning Kitchen

Mudroom

Nursery

Office

Playroom/Game Room

Pool House

Porch, Patio, Deck, and Balcony

Powder Room/Half Bath

Safe Room

Specialty Room

Wine Room

BINDER 5: TEAM MEETINGS AND COMMUNICATIONS

File all communications you have with your team in Binder 5, including any pertinent information obtained at your meeting as well as the meeting notes you have taken.

BINDER 6: EXISTING CONTENT/WISH LIST PHOTOS AND TEAR SHEETS

Before meeting with your architect, organize the photos and tear sheets with dimensions noted, and place these in Binder 6. Make photocopies of any information in your binders that you give to your architect. Ask if you can access your architect's library of architectural design books. Once your architect has an idea of the style of the home you want, ask your architect to designate pages in books that represent the type of home you want designed. Spend time studying other books in your architect's library and indicate any page that represents your desires.

TIP: Your architect may assign an associate to be the point person on your job. Ask for references from home-owners who have worked with this associate, and find out if they were satisfied. If you do not feel comfortable with the associate, let your architect know immediately. You will spend a great deal of time on the phone and in person with that associate. It is imperative that you feel comfortable with the associate and confident in this person's ability.

Basic Design Fact Sheet

Homeowner _____ Date _____

Budget _____ Number of square feet _____

Break ground date _____ Move-in date _____

Circle those that apply.

One level   Two-story   Three-story   Attic   Basement

If you want a multistory home, do you prefer that the top floor be a complete floor with an attic above?
If the top floor is located within the roof, do you want dormers? Note any comments.

_____

_____

_____

_____

_____

_____

_____

_____

_____

_____

_____

_____

_____

_____

_____

_____

_____

_____

_____

_____

_____

Occupants of the Home Checklist

Name	Age	Sex	Height	Weight	Left or Right Handed	Shoe Size	Special Needs

PET OCCUPANTS

Name	Type of Pet	Age	Indoor or Outdoor	Pet Weight	Special Needs

Rooms in Your Home Checklist

Check all rooms you want designed in your home. Fill in the approximate size of the room and the floor level the room should be located. There are multiple entries for bathrooms, bedrooms, bedroom closets, offices, and porches, patios, decks, and balconies—you may want to assign a name or number to the bedrooms and bathrooms in your home. For the porch, patio, deck, and balcony entries, circle the items you want and indicate the floor level and size for each.

ROOM	FLOOR LEVEL	SIZE
☐ Apartment	_____	_____
☐ Attic	_____	_____
☐ Bar	_____	_____
☐ Basement	_____	_____
☐ Bathroom, master	_____	_____
☐ Bathroom, guest	_____	_____
☐ Bathroom 1	_____	_____
☐ Bathroom 2	_____	_____
☐ Bathroom 3	_____	_____
☐ Bathroom 4	_____	_____
☐ Bedroom, master	_____	_____
☐ Bedroom, guest	_____	_____
☐ Bedroom 1	_____	_____
☐ Bedroom 2	_____	_____
☐ Bedroom 3	_____	_____
☐ Bedroom 4	_____	_____
☐ Bedroom closet, master	_____	_____
☐ Bedroom closet, guest	_____	_____
☐ Bedroom closet 1	_____	_____
☐ Bedroom closet 2	_____	_____
☐ Bedroom closet 3	_____	_____
☐ Bedroom closet 4	_____	_____
☐ Breakfast room	_____	_____
☐ Butler's pantry	_____	_____
☐ Control room	_____	_____
☐ Dining room	_____	_____
☐ Entry foyer	_____	_____
☐ Exercise room	_____	_____
☐ Family room	_____	_____
☐ Garage	_____	_____
☐ Kitchen	_____	_____
☐ Kitchen pantry	_____	_____
☐ Laundry room	_____	_____

ROOM	FLOOR LEVEL	SIZE
☐ Library	_____	_____
☐ Living room/great room	_____	_____
☐ Mechanical room	_____	_____
☐ Media room	_____	_____
☐ Morning kitchen	_____	_____
☐ Mudroom	_____	_____
☐ Nursery	_____	_____
☐ Office	_____	_____
☐ Office	_____	_____
☐ Porch, patio, deck, and balcony	_____	_____
☐ Porch, patio, deck, and balcony	_____	_____
☐ Porch, patio, deck, and balcony	_____	_____
☐ Porch, patio, deck, and balcony	_____	_____
☐ Porch, patio, deck, and balcony	_____	_____
☐ Playroom/game room	_____	_____
☐ Pool house	_____	_____
☐ Powder room/half bath (formal)	_____	_____
☐ Powder room/half bath (second)	_____	_____
☐ Safe room	_____	_____
☐ Specialty room	_____	_____
☐ Wine room	_____	_____
☐ Other _____	_____	_____
☐ Other _____	_____	_____
☐ Other _____	_____	_____
☐ Other _____	_____	_____
☐ Other _____	_____	_____

Closets in Your Home Checklist

Check all closets you want designed in your home. Fill in the floor level you want that closet located, as well as the approximate size of the closet.

CLOSET	FLOOR LEVEL	SIZE
❑ Art supplies closet	_____	_____
❑ Baby equipment closet	_____	_____
❑ Broom closet*	_____	_____
❑ Cedar closet*	_____	_____
❑ Coat closet, main at front door	_____	_____
❑ Coat closet, secondary at front door	_____	_____
❑ Coat closet, mudroom	_____	_____
❑ Craft storage closet	_____	_____
❑ Decorations, Christmas	_____	_____
❑ Decorations, miscellaneous holiday	_____	_____
❑ Entertaining pieces closet	_____	_____
❑ File storage closet	_____	_____
❑ Fishing equipment closet	_____	_____
❑ Flower arranging closet	_____	_____
❑ Folding chair and table closet	_____	_____
❑ Gardening tool closet	_____	_____
❑ Gift storage closet	_____	_____
❑ Gift wrap closet	_____	_____
❑ Golf equipment closet	_____	_____
❑ Gun closet	_____	_____
❑ Hunting equipment closet	_____	_____
❑ Ice chest/picnic closet	_____	_____
❑ Linen/towel closet*	_____	_____
❑ Luggage closet*	_____	_____
❑ Office equipment closet	_____	_____
❑ Out-of-season clothing closet	_____	_____
❑ Pet equipment closet	_____	_____
❑ Photo album closet	_____	_____
❑ Skiing equipment closet	_____	_____
❑ Silver closet	_____	_____
❑ Sports equipment closet	_____	_____
❑ Toy closet	_____	_____
❑ Other _____	_____	_____

*If more than one, note the additional information out to the side.

Basic Bedroom Fact Sheet

	Master Bedroom	Guest Bedroom	Bedroom 1	Bedroom 2	Bedroom 3	Bedroom 4
Approximate dimensions of room						
Size of bed(s)						
Number of beds						
Number of occupants						
List occupants and indicate which side of the bed they prefer to sleep on						
Does the person sleeping in this room need to be close to the bathroom?						
Will this bedroom have a private bathroom?						
Do you want windows on the headboard wall?						

See Bedroom Checklist (page 143) and Bed Sizes and Measurements (page 64).

Miscellaneous Information Checklist

CONSULTANTS *Check any you plan to hire.*
- ❑ Closet designer
- ❑ Communications consultant
- ❑ Feng Shui consultant
- ❑ Interior designer
- ❑ Kitchen consultant
- ❑ Landscape architect
- ❑ Lighting consultant
- ❑ Owner-building representative
- ❑ Personal home building consultant
- ❑ Security consultant
- ❑ Swimming pool consultant
- ❑ Other _____

NATURAL GAS *Check any that will use natural gas.*
- ❑ Dryer
- ❑ Exterior lampposts
- ❑ Exterior lanterns
- ❑ Fire pit
- ❑ Fireplaces
- ❑ Grill
- ❑ Heating system
- ❑ Hot tub
- ❑ Ovens
- ❑ Pool
- ❑ Stove top/range top
- ❑ Water heater
- ❑ Other _____

HVAC *Check any that apply.*
- ❑ Air conditioning
- ❑ Forced air for heat
- ❑ Heat pump
- ❑ Geothermal system
- ❑ Radiant floor for heat
- ❑ Solar heat
- ❑ Other type of heat _____
- ❑ Surface or walls heated with radiant heat—if so, which ones?
- ❑ Other _____

OVERALL PLUMBING *Check any that apply.*
- ❑ Tank water heater
- ❑ Tankless water heater
- ❑ Recirculation pump on water heater
- ❑ PEX pipe
- ❑ PEX pipe and copper pipe combination
- ❑ Copper pipe
- ❑ Copper and PVC pipe combination
- ❑ Geothermal desuperheater to heat water tank
- ❑ Other _____

INTERIOR PLUMBING *Check any that apply.*
- ❑ Sink in the bar
- ❑ Sink in the laundry room
- ❑ Sink in the garage
- ❑ Sink in the morning kitchen
- ❑ Sink in the media room
- ❑ Sink(s) in the pool house
- ❑ Sink in the wine room
- ❑ Indoor water wall
- ❑ Indoor water fountain
- ❑ Aquarium
- ❑ Indoor pond
- ❑ Dog bath area
- ❑ Hot/cold water faucet in the garage
- ❑ Other _____

PETS *Check any that apply.*
- ❑ Aquarium
- ❑ Bird cage
- ❑ Dog run, doggie door, dog room
- ❑ Cat area, litter area
- ❑ Other _____

GAME TABLES AND VIDEO GAME MACHINES *Check any that you will have in your home.*
- ❑ Dartboard
- ❑ Foosball table
- ❑ Pinball machine
- ❑ Ping-Pong table
- ❑ Pool table
- ❑ Shuffleboard
- ❑ Video games
- ❑ Other _____

Exterior Elements for Your Home Checklist

Check those that apply.

TYPE OF FOUNDATION

❑ Slab

❑ Pier and beam

❑ Footers and walls

COMMON ROOF SHAPES (See Roof Shapes, page 65)

❑ A-frame

❑ Flat

❑ Gable

❑ Gambrel

❑ Hipped

❑ Mansard

❑ Saltbox

❑ Shed

❑ Other _____

COMMON ROOF MATERIAL

❑ Architectural shingle

❑ Ceramic tile

❑ Metal sheets

❑ Slate

❑ Wood shake

❑ Other _____

COMMON EXTERIOR WALL MATERIALS

❑ Adobe

❑ Brick

❑ Log

❑ Natural stone

❑ Stucco

❑ Synthetic siding

❑ Synthetic stone

❑ Wood siding

❑ Other _____

COMMON TYPES OF EXTERIOR DOORS

❑ Paneled wood doors

❑ Glass and wood

❑ Glass and metal

❑ Glass and iron

❑ Glass, wood, and iron

❑ Glass and aluminum clad to match window package

❑ Other _____

COMMON TYPES OF WINDOWS (See Types of Windows, page 210)

❑ Awning

❑ Casement

❑ Double-hung sash

❑ Fixed

❑ Pivot

❑ Sliding

❑ Other _____

COMMON ORNAMENTAL EXTERIOR MATERIALS

❑ Balustrade

❑ Chimney cap

❑ Conductor head or leader box

❑ Cupola

❑ Decorative dormers

❑ Finials and spires

❑ Louver and soffit vents

❑ Pinnacles

❑ Roof panels

❑ Tower

❑ Weather vane

❑ Other _____

WATER-RELATED ITEMS

❑ Endless pool

❑ Fountain

❑ Hot tub

❑ Lap pool

❑ Pool house

❑ Steamer

❑ Swimming pool

❑ Waterfall

❑ Other _____

ITEMS OUTSIDE THE HOME

❑ Basketball goal

❑ Fire pit(s)

❑ Greenhouse

❑ Outdoor fireplace

❑ Outdoor grill(s)

❑ Outdoor television

❑ Putting green

❑ Skinning rack/cooler

❑ Smokehouse

❑ Smoke pit

❑ Tackle room

❑ Tennis court

❑ Other _____

MISCELLANEOUS

❑ Air purification system

❑ Awning

❑ Chimneys

❑ Dormers

❑ Dumbwaiter

❑ Elevator

❑ Fanlight

❑ Generator

❑ Geothermal system

❑ Humidifier system

❑ Integrated home automation system

❑ Laundry chute

❑ Porte cochere

❑ Sauna

❑ Tank water heater

❑ Tankless water heater

❑ Transom

❑ Water purification system

❑ Water softener system

❑ Other _____

EXTERIOR LIVING AREAS

Check any of the following you want for your home, and fill in the location. For example, you might want a balcony off the master bedroom or a porch off the master bedroom.

❑ Balcony _____

❑ Deck _____

❑ Gazebo _____

❑ Patio _____

❑ Porch _____

❑ Veranda _____

❑ Other _____

Will any porches be screened? If so, do you want a motorized retractable screen or a fixed screen? List.

_____

_____

Are there any items that need to be placed in the backyard before the house is built (trees, boulders, hot tub, etc.)? If so, list.

_____

_____

Existing Contents of the Home Checklist

FURNITURE

Type of furniture _____ Dimensions _____

Desired location _____ Photo: Yes or No

Type of furniture _____ Dimensions _____

Desired location _____ Photo: Yes or No

Type of furniture _____ Dimensions _____

Desired location _____ Photo: Yes or No

Type of furniture _____ Dimensions _____

Desired location _____ Photo: Yes or No

Type of furniture _____ Dimensions _____

Desired location _____ Photo: Yes or No

Type of furniture _____ Dimensions _____

Desired location _____ Photo: Yes or No

❑ Check if more furniture is listed on an attached page.

ART, SCULPTURE, MIRRORS, PORTRAITS, RUGS

Note any special lighting or display needs

Item _____ Dimensions _____

Desired location _____ Photo: Yes or No

Special needs _____

Item _____ Dimensions _____

Desired location _____ Photo: Yes or No

Special needs _____

Item _____ Dimensions _____

Desired location _____ Photo: Yes or No

Special needs _____

❑ Check if more art, sculpture, mirrors, or portraits are listed on an attached page.

ANIMAL TROPHIES, OTHER TROPHIES

Item _____ Dimensions _____

Desired location _____ Photo: Yes or No

Item _____ Dimensions _____

Desired location _____ Photo: Yes or No

Item _____ Dimensions _____

Desired location _____ Photo: Yes or No

Item _____ Dimensions _____

Desired location _____ Photo: Yes or No

❑ Check if more animal trophies or other trophies are listed on an attached page.

MUSICAL INSTRUMENTS, PIANO, ORGAN, HARP, OR OTHER

Item _____ Dimensions _____

Desired location _____ Photo: Yes or No

Special needs _____

Item _____ Dimensions _____

Desired location _____ Photo: Yes or No

Special needs _____

❑ Check if more musical instruments are listed on an attached page.

CHANDELIERS, WALL SCONCES, LIGHT FIXTURES

Item _____ Dimensions _____

Desired location _____ Photo: Yes or No

Item _____ Dimensions _____

Desired location _____ Photo: Yes or No

Item _____ Dimensions _____

Desired location _____ Photo: Yes or No

❑ Check if more light fixtures are listed on an attached page.

ANTIQUE DOORS, MANTELS, STAINED GLASS

Item _____ Dimensions _____

Desired location _____ Photo: Yes or No

Item _____ Dimensions _____

Desired location _____ Photo: Yes or No

❑ Check if more door, mantels, or other items are listed on an attached page.

APPLIANCES

Item _____ Dimensions _____

Desired location _____ Photo: Yes or No

Item _____ Dimensions _____

Desired location _____ Photo: Yes or No

Item _____ Dimensions _____

Desired location _____ Photo: Yes or No

Item _____ Dimensions _____

Desired location _____ Photo: Yes or No

Item _____ Dimensions _____

Desired location _____ Photo: Yes or No

❑ Check if more appliances are listed on an attached page.

AUDIOVISUAL EQUIPMENT

Item _____ Dimensions _____

Desired location _____ Photo: Yes or No

Item _____ Dimensions _____

Desired location _____ Photo: Yes or No

Item _____ Dimensions _____

Desired location _____ Photo: Yes or No

Item _____ Dimensions _____

Desired location _____ Photo: Yes or No

❑ Check if more audiovisual equipment is listed on an attached page.

OFFICE EQUIPMENT

Item _____ Dimensions _____

Desired location _____ Photo: Yes or No

Item _____ Dimensions _____

Desired location _____ Photo: Yes or No

Item _____ Dimensions _____

Desired location _____ Photo: Yes or No

Item _____ Dimensions _____

Desired location _____ Photo: Yes or No

❑ Check if more office equipment is listed on an attached page.

PATIO FURNITURE

Item _____ Dimensions _____

Desired location _____ Photo: Yes or No

Item _____ Dimensions _____

Desired location _____ Photo: Yes or No

Item _____ Dimensions _____

Desired location _____ Photo: Yes or No

Item _____ Dimensions _____

Desired location _____ Photo: Yes or No

❑ Check if more patio furniture is listed on an attached page.

Common Household Item Storage Checklist

For each item listed that you own, indicate the room where you will store it. If you plan to store the item in a specific location within that room, indicate the location in the right column (examples: inside a sideboard, in a drawer in the entertainment center, on a self in the closet).

ITEM	ROOM(S) WHERE ITEM WILL BE STORED	LOCATION IN ROOM
Baby equipment	_____	_____
Baskets	_____	_____
Board games	_____	_____
Books, children	_____	_____
Books, nonfiction	_____	_____
Books, novels	_____	_____
Broom, mop, bucket, vacuum	_____	_____
Camera equipment	_____	_____
Candles, votives	_____	_____
Christmas decorations, exterior	_____	_____
Christmas tree, artificial	_____	_____
Christmas tree decorations	_____	_____
Christmas wreaths, garlands, decorations	_____	_____
Cleaning products	_____	_____
Cleaning rags	_____	_____
DVDs, videos, cassettes, albums	_____	_____
Entertaining decorative items	_____	_____
Entertaining serving pieces	_____	_____
Files, filing cabinets	_____	_____
Firewood, inside and outside	_____	_____
Fishing equipment	_____	_____
Gifts on hand	_____	_____
Gift-wrapping paper, supplies	_____	_____
Golf equipment	_____	_____

ITEM	ROOM(S) WHERE ITEM WILL BE STORED	LOCATION IN ROOM
Household tools		
Hunting equipment		
Ice chests		
Keepsakes		
Luggage		
Linens (quilts, blankets, sheets, comforter)		
Linens (towels)		
Magazines		
Office equipment (printer, fax)		
Off-season clothing		
Telephone books		
Pet equipment (kennel, leashes)		
Pet food		
Photos in frames (hanging)		
Photos in frames (tabletop)		
Photo albums		
Silver flatware		
Silver serving pieces		
Skiing equipment		
Sports equipment		
Stationery, notepads, correspondence items		
Toddler equipment		
Toys		
Other _____		
Other _____		
Other _____		

Individual Room and Closet Fact Sheet

Homeowner _____ Date _____

ROOM OR CLOSET _____ Approximate size _____

Will this room or closet have any of the following? List any comments.

YES   NO

❏   ❏   Appliances—if so, list them.

_____

_____

❏   ❏   Built-ins—if so, what kind? See Entire-Home Built-in Selections (page 309) for options.

_____

_____

❏   ❏   Ceiling fan

_____

_____

❏   ❏   Computer wiring connector

_____

_____

❏   ❏   Existing contents to be used in this room—if so, list the items.

_____

_____

_____

_____

❏   ❏   Fireplace—if so, approximate size? _____ Gas or wood burning? _____ Remote starter? _____

Floor or raised hearth? _____ If so, approximate height and width of raised hearth? _____

❏   ❏   Fixed mirror—if so, on the walls, ceiling, or doors? Explain.

_____

❏   ❏   Integrated Home Automation Monitor—if so, approximate location.

_____

_____

ROOM OR CLOSET _____

❏ ❏ Security alarm pad—if so, approximate location.

_____

_____

❏ ❏ Stereo components—if yes, which ones?

_____

_____

❏ ❏ Stereo speakers

_____

_____

❏ ❏ Individual speaker volume control

_____

_____

❏ ❏ Telephone jack—if so, how many? _____

Do you want a combination telephone jack and cable connector? _____

❏ ❏ Television—if so, how many in this room? _____ Cable or dish? _____

Circle how the television will be displayed.

Drop-down screen   Pop up out of furniture   In an armoire   In a bookcase   Other _____

❏ ❏ Wallpaper or fabric walls—if so, on walls and ceiling? Cloth or paper? Explain.

_____

_____

❏ ❏ Window treatment—if so, curtain, shades, shutters, other?

_____

_____

❏ ❏ Motorized window treatment—if so, curtains, shades, or other?

_____

_____

ROOM OR CLOSET _____

Ceiling comments for this room.

_____

_____

Door comments for this room.

_____

_____

Floor comments for this room.

_____

_____

Lighting comments for this room.

_____

_____

Wall comments for this room.

_____

_____

Window comments for this room.

_____

_____

Hardware

List specific hardware items that will be used in this room.

_____

_____

_____

Stone/Tile

List specific applications for stone or tile in this room and the name of the stone or tile to be used.

_____

_____

_____

ROOM OR CLOSET _____

Electrical Needs

Outlets

List specific items that will need an outlet in this room

_____

_____

_____

List any outlets that need to be connected to a light switch. Note location of light switch and location
of outlet connected to that light switch.

_____

_____

_____

_____

_____

Floor Outlets

List specific area of the floor and what will be plugged into that outlet._____

Does the floor outlet needs one receptacle or two? _____

Once plugged into the outlet, does the plug need to be flush with the floor?

_____

_____

Light Switches

Three-way, four-way, five-way light switches:

List the location of each switch and what item it will be turning on.

_____

_____

_____

_____

_____

_____

ROOM OR CLOSET _____

Light Switches (continued)

Motion sensor, jamb, or other special type of light switch:

Note what you want to turn on or off. _____

_____

_____

Lighting

Circle the type of lighting to be used in this room.

Chandelier   Sconce   Recessed can lights   Ceiling light   Light on fan   Art light   Other_____

List any items such as art, portraits, sculptures, or trophies that require specialty lighting, and describe the lighting needs.

_____

_____

Storage

Referring to the Common Household Item Storage Checklist (page 79), list items that will be stored in this room.

_____

_____

Paint*

Wall paint color, brand, type of paint _____

Ceiling paint color, brand, type of paint _____

Trim paint color, brand, type of paint _____

Comments _____

_____

_____

_____

_____

_____

*The paint information can be filled in later in the process.

5 The Rooms in Your House

Many homeowners beginning the house building process have vague ideas about the home they want designed. This chapter is devoted to helping you solidify your thoughts. You will find a list of 32 possible rooms plus the driveway, exterior front entry, and garage. With each is a list of common mistakes related to that room or area of the home, and at the end of the chapter you'll find checklists for each of these areas.

Begin filling in the checklists as soon as you have made the decision to build or remodel. In fact, you can begin filling in these checklists years before you even make such a decision. Once you are ready to discuss the home you want to build with your architect, revisit these checklists and update them.

By filling in the checklist for each room, you will gain more clarity in what you want designed. Some of the information on the checklist may evoke an immediate answer, while other information may require more thought and time. Filling in these checklists is an ongoing process. Circle unanswered questions in pencil to remind yourself that they still need to be answered. The checklists will be most helpful when you meet with your architect.

As you decide which rooms you want in your home, begin filling in the checklist for that room. Also make a copy of the Individual Room and Closet Fact Sheet (page 81) for each room and fill in the room name. File the room checklists and the Individual Room and Closet Fact Sheet in Binder 4.

APARTMENT AREA

An apartment area in a home has many uses: rental income, caretaker quarters, elderly relatives' housing, boomerang kid housing, or guest quarters. With so many potential uses, an architect can take many approaches when designing this room or rooms.

FORMS TO USE

Apartment Area Checklist (page 128)

Individual Room and Closet Fact Sheet (page 81)

HOW TO AVOID COMMON APARTMENT AREA MISTAKES

1. If the apartment is connected to your home, tell your architect if you want to be able to lock the apartment off from the main house.

2. Tell your architect and security consultant if you want a security system in the apartment and if you want it to operate separately from your house.

3. Discuss caretaker or tenant parking options with your architect.

4. Tell your architect if you want the apartment to be metered separately for utilities.

5. Discuss with your architect and lighting expert your concern that the exterior lighting on the apartment might affect the occupants of your home.

6. Make sure the driveway to the apartment is not near bedrooms of the main house.

7. Read your HOA bylaws and covenants and ask your city or county code department about property rental restrictions.

ATTIC

It is important for you to discuss your vision for your attic space with your architect early in the design process. The amount of space available for an attic is determined by the size of your home, the shape of your home, the shape of the ceiling, and the shape of the roof. In some designs, you will have one large attic, in others, several small attic spaces. If you have many heirlooms to store in your attic and need a substantial amount of attic space, tell your architect this before beginning to design your home.

FORMS TO USE

Attic Checklist (page 129)

Individual Room and Closet Fact Sheet (page 81)—if you need an area in your attic high enough to stand in, note that on this sheet.

HOW TO AVOID COMMON ATTIC MISTAKES

1. The joists in your attic should run parallel to any hallway or area where you plan to install a fold-down stairway.

2. Identify on the floor plans where your attic stairway will be located. If located in a hallway, make sure the hallway is wide enough to handle the fold-down stairway. Also make sure the fold-down stairway is centered in that hallway. This can be affected by the location of the joists. A fold-down stairway that is off to one side of the hallway will look odd and when carrying items up the stairs, you will likely bump your walls, causing marks.

3. If you will be placing large or heavy boxes, tubs, or other items in your attic, or the person who will be climbing the fold-down stairway is heavy, consider a wide and heavy-duty fold-down stairway. Ask your architect for options.

4. If your fold-down stairway will be in your garage, ask your architect and builder if it can be placed so that you can use it without moving a vehicle.

5. Use a three-way light switch with your fold-down stairway. Place one switch at floor level and the other in the attic. With only one light switch in the attic at the top of the stairway, invariably you will climb down and realize you forgot to turn off the light.

6. Have adequate lighting to illuminate all areas.

7. If you will use your attic often and will need a large area for storage, have the entire attic floor covered with flooring. Do not leave uncovered areas where a person can accidentally step through the ceiling of the floor below.

8. Tell your architect and your builder that you

expect all wiring and duct work located in the attic to be neat and orderly. You do not want it installed haphazardly, creating an obstacle course.

9. If the HVAC system will be located in your attic, provide adequate space around the HVAC for servicing.

10. Have your architect specify rolled insulation. It is more expensive than blown insulation, but does a better job, and over time you will recoup the expense by savings in heating and air conditioning bills.

11. If in the future the attic could be finished out for living space, discuss with your architect and builder what preliminary work should be done during construction.

12. If you have plastic storage bins, plastic tubs, or boxes to place in your attic, make sure any shelves you have built in the attic will accommodate those storage components.

13. Once your home is built, make sure all vents are clear of insulation, especially if you are using blown insulation.

14. If you live in a hot or humid climate, consider a motorized vent system or discuss other options with your architect. There should also be vents in the soffits and at the ridge of the roof to create air flow. You will want screens on all vents to prevent squirrels and other animals from entering your attic.

BAR

Some people want a bar hidden behind louvered or closet doors; others want it to resemble a commercial bar. Some want their bar in the main living area of the home; others want it in the game room on the basement level. Share your vision for your bar with your architect.

FORMS TO USE

Bar Checklist (page 130)
Individual Room and Closet Fact Sheet (page 81)

HOW TO AVOID COMMON BAR MISTAKES

1. Have a trash can built into the cabinets. It should be generous in size, especially if you and your friends are beer drinkers. Under-Cabinet Trash Storage (page 90) shows two styles. Design A provides a taller trash can by incorporating a false drawer into the pull-out cabinet front. Design B provides a true working drawer with a shorter trash can that is located only behind the false cabinet door.

2. Give your architect and builder the length and diameter of your liquor and wine bottles for the cabinetmaker. Not all bottles are equal in size.

3. Make sure your electrical plan has outlets near the bar counter, located to accommodate using a blender, coffeemaker, and other small appliances.

4. When selecting your bar sink, if you want to be able to stand glasses upright in the bottom of the sink, avoid vessel-type sinks, which do not have a flat bottom.

5. If the back of the bar wall is an outside wall, instead of giving up a window for upper storage cabinets, store your bar glasses in a drawer, as shown in the illustration on page 90.

6. If your bar and wine room are on different levels or at opposite ends of the house, plan for wine storage in your bar area. You can see several wine storage options on page 91. Design A has an open area in the upper half of the cabinet in which to store numerous wine bottles. Design B has the same configuration as design A, but with cabinet doors. Design C offers a horizontal shelf for wine bottle storage in the above-counter cabinet. In design D, wine bottles are stored vertically in the above-counter cabinet. And design E offers both above- and below-counter wine storage, including pull-out drawers. (In place of the drawers, you could install a wine chiller.)

7. If you are a cigar aficionado, plan for a custom location for a humidor in your bar area. Give your architect the dimensions of your humidor.

8. Choose a layout that does not allow sunlight

to shine on liquor or wine bottles, because it can damage the contents.

9. If needed, allow additional interior height in the bar drawers so the drawer will not jam due to bar utensils.

10. Identify any wine openers, wine decanters, or other items that will require a special location or installation. Discuss these with your architect, builder, and cabinetmaker before the cabinets are designed and made.

11. Make sure the HVAC vents will not blow directly on any person sitting at the bar.

12. Use stone, tile, or other material instead of glass for exposed bar shelves to cut down on visible dust collection and maintenance.

13. Use self-closing drawer runners on bar drawers.

14. The direction any appliance door opens should be the most convenient for ease of use.

15. Make sure light switches are aesthetically placed and are not an eyesore.

BASEMENT

Through the years, the word "basement" has taken on many different meanings. It is important that you and your architect discuss the meaning of the word and agree on how you will use your basement. If the basement is another level of the house with bedrooms, playroom/game room, and so forth, skip filling out the Basement Checklist and fill out the checklist for the actual rooms in your basement level. If you will use your basement for storage or to finish out in the future, fill out the Basement Checklist.

UNDER-CABINET TRASH STORAGE

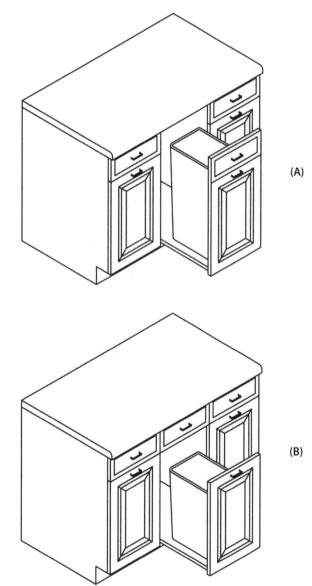

(A)

(B)

BAR GLASSES STORED IN DRAWER

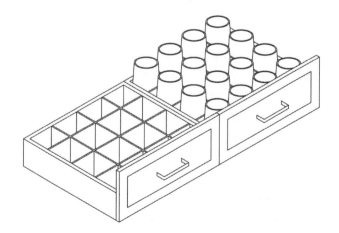

WINE STORAGE OPTIONS

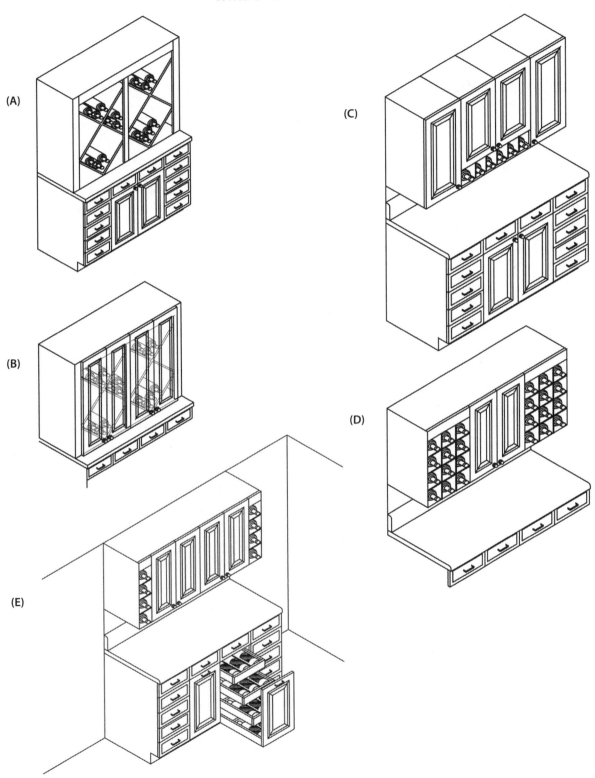

FORMS TO FILL OUT

Basement Checklist (page 133), if your basement
   is unfinished or is a storage area
Individual Room and Closet Fact Sheet (page 81)

HOW TO AVOID COMMON
BASEMENT MISTAKES

1. Be diligent in understanding the drainage
design around your basement. A poor design may
result in water leaking into your basement, which
may not show up for several years. This can create a
host of issues, structural as well as mold.

2. Discuss with your architect and builder what
measures can be taken to ensure proper waterproofing around the basement walls.

3. Discuss with your architect and your builder
the height measurements for the stairway header
leading to the basement. Often these are too low.

4. Discuss with your architect any plans to finish
out your basement in the future and what preliminary electrical, plumbing, or other work should be
done during construction.

5. Know your city and county fire inspection
codes for basements. Often a use and occupancy
certificate is denied due to basements not meeting
code requirements regarding fire escapes.

BATHROOMS

The bathroom is one of the most used rooms in a
home. Most homeowners have a definite idea about
what they want in their bathroom. Because of the
enormous range of options, mistakes can be made
when designing your bathroom.

At the beginning of the design process, give a
name to each bathroom in your home. This name
can be the name of the person who will use the
bathroom, such as Bill's bathroom, or a generic
name such as guest bedroom bathroom. Be consistent in whatever name you choose, and use that

name when referring to that bathroom throughout
the design and building of your home.

FORMS TO USE

Bathroom Checklist (page 134)
Bathroom Storage Item Checklist (page 140)
Individual Room and Closet Fact Sheet (page 81)

HOW TO AVOID COMMON BATHROOM
MISTAKES

1. Identify which vanity drawer will hold which
items. Measure the tallest and widest items to make
sure your inside drawer dimensions will accommodate them.

2. Have drawers built into your vanity. It is much
easier to reach into a drawer than to stoop down to
look for items on shelves behind lower cabinet doors.

3. Make sure the knee-hole dimensions for
your seated makeup counter are tall enough for you
to sit in your chair or stool without scraping your
knees.

4. Study your floor plans to see where you can
place a scale or decorative trash can—some bathroom floor plans have no open wall for these items.
Trash cans may also be built into a vanity. See
Under-Cabinet Trash Storage on page 90.

5. If you need additional storage space and have
a generous amount of counter space, counter cabinets above the vanity can provide more storage
space, as shown in the illustration on page 93 (left).
If your counter is extra long, you can also add
counter cabinets between the two sinks.

6. For additional storage space, add drawers
underneath the cabinet doors located below the
sink. (See illustration, page 93, right.) The taller the
counter height, the taller the drawers can be.

7. Think outside the box and have a custom-
made medicine cabinet built, which can be taller
and deeper in size.

8. Discuss with your architect and cabinetmaker

options to put locks on medicine cabinets. This is a safety factor for children, grandchildren, and visitors you may not want looking through your medicine cabinets.

9. If you prefer an uncluttered bathroom counter, consider storing your toothbrush, electric razor, and products in a medicine cabinet with an outlet inside, and your hair dryer in a drawer with an outlet located inside the drawer.

10. The standard depth of a bathroom counter is 24 inches. When selecting your sink and faucet, make sure the depth of the sink, front to back, will allow ample room for cleaning between the faucet and the backsplash, as shown in Faucet/Backsplash Relationship (page 94). If using a self-rimming sink, you will want ample space between the back outside edge of the rim and the backsplash to be able to clean.

11. If the distance between the faucet handles and the faucet is too narrow, cleaning between them will be more difficult.

12. When purchasing a bathroom faucet, make sure you can comfortably reach your hand under the flow of water to rinse off shaving cream or rinse off your face.

13. Avoid black and stainless steel sinks, which show water and soap spots and require constant wiping to look clean.

14. Though attractive, pedestal sinks in a bathroom may not be practical unless you have shelves or a counter nearby to hold the products you use.

15. A one-piece faucet with attached controls requires only one cut into the countertop, which creates less clutter and fewer knobs to clean around.

16. Measure your shampoo and conditioner bottles and any other items used in the shower and make

CABINETS ABOVE VANITY COUNTER

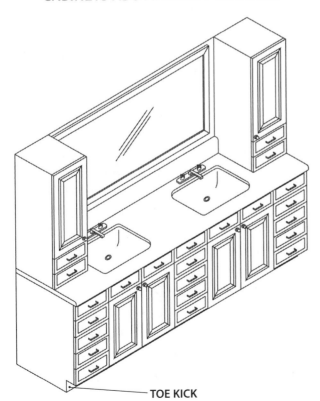

TOE KICK

DRAWERS UNDERNEATH CABINET DOORS

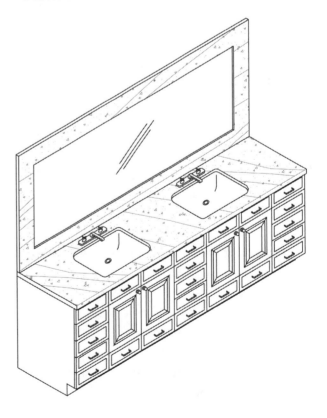

FAUCET/BACKSPLASH RELATIONSHIP

TOO TIGHT TO CLEAN

AMPLE ROOM TO CLEAN

NICHE FOR CANDLES

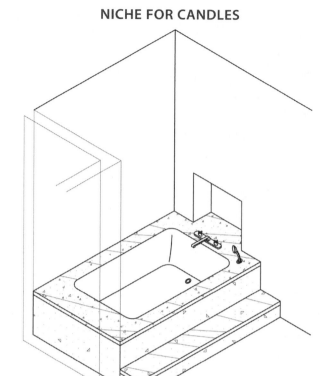

sure the finished height and width of the shower shelf is ample.

17. Avoid glass walls in the shower, unless you have daily housekeeping help. Otherwise, cleaning water spots from shower glass will become your daily chore!

18. Specify the location and height for a hand-held shower to be mounted and the location of the on/off controls. Consider if you want to use it as a showerhead or when you bathe or shave your legs while sitting on the bench.

19. Be sure the floors, bench, wall shelves, door curb in the shower are sloped properly to avoid creating a constant puddle of water.

20. Your soap dish in the shower should be mounted away from the spray of the shower water so your soap will not get mushy.

21. If your shower is large enough, discuss with your architect whether you need two steam heads.

22. The walls and ceiling of your steam shower should be covered in a waterproof material such as stone or a waterproof paint to prevent mildewing.

23. If you use a washcloth when taking a shower, plan for a hook to hang the washcloth to dry.

24. Municipal codes restrict the size of plumbing pipes. Before purchasing elaborate shower systems, make sure you will have enough water pressure to operate them.

25. Locate the towel warmer within reaching distance of the shower and tub.

26. The controls to your bathtub should be easy to reach when standing outside the bathtub as well as when sitting in the bathtub. The faucet and faucet handles should be positioned at one of the ends or corners of the tub. The faucet, if separate from the

handles, can also be positioned on the inside side of the tub. Avoid having these on of the outside side of the bathtub as they will interfere with entering or exiting the tub.

27. If your bathtub adjoins a closet wall, water closet wall, a storage room, or closet below, access to the jetted motor may be obtained through this wall or ceiling. If not, you will need access along the side apron of the tub.

28. If you want the ambiance of a fireplace, but it will not fit your budget or the size of the room, consider adding a niche in the wall around the bathtub deck to place multiple candles. See Niche for Candles (page 94).

29. Tell your architect what type of bathtub mount you want, and have it specified in the plans. When the bathtub deck is made of stone or tile, the most common styles are self-rimming or drop-in mounts and under-mounts. See Bathtub Mount Options (this page).

30. If you have a cabinet above the back of the toilet, make sure the cabinet is not so deep that it hits your back when you sit on the toilet.

31. Consider a built-in ledge behind the toilet tank, which supplies a place to put candles, flowers, or potpourri. It also allows for added depth for cabinets mounted on the wall above the toilet, as shown on page 96.

32. Taller toilet seats are more comfortable, as are padded seats.

33. Self-closing toilet seats are a nice option to prevent the toilet seat from slamming shut.

34. A shower with a dry area, an enclosure outside the shower, gives you more privacy as well as a place to stay warm when drying off. See the illustration on page 97.

35. Show the framer the location of a recessed magazine rack or recessed toilet paper holder so he can avoid putting a stud in that location.

36. A wall-mounted phone near a toilet should

BATHTUB MOUNT OPTIONS

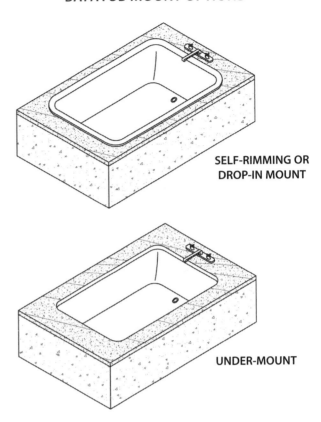

SELF-RIMMING OR
DROP-IN MOUNT

UNDER-MOUNT

be mounted in line with the back of the toilet seat. If mounted too far forward, it will be knocked off the hook when the person turns to flush the toilet.

37. If you plan to use a lighted wall-mounted magnifying mirror, this needs to be called out on the architectural plans so that there is electrical power and wall space to mount the mirror.

38. Think about how many bathroom outlets you use. Hair dryers sometimes have a bulky plug and will cover two receptacles when plugged in. Other items that require outlets may include an electric toothbrush, night-light, electric razor, curling iron, hair straightening iron, electric rollers, clock radio, CD player, MP3 player, foot bath, paraffin wax heater, and cell phone charger.

39. A towel bar mounted on a side wall might interfere with an outlet mounted nearby. Once your

LEDGE BEHIND TOILET

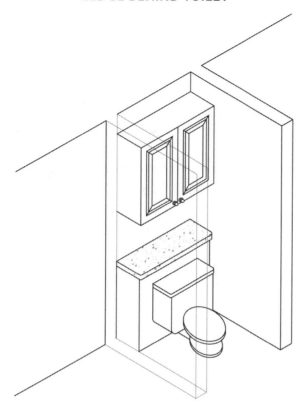

home is framed in, and before the electrical system is roughed in, check out this relationship in all bathrooms.

40. Avoid using too many round bulb lights around the vanity mirror, as they will emit excessive heat.

41. If possible, always have an outlet on each side of the sink. This accommodates both a right-handed and left-handed person.

42. Be aware that shell stone or a porous material in the bathroom will be stained forever if a bottle of makeup, lotion, or nail polish spills.

43. Work with the stone installer to determine where the cuts in stone will be made. The illustration on page 239 (top) shows options for centering shower and tub fixtures on tiles, and what to avoid. Bathtub Stone Cut Options (page 239) shows three ways you can choose to have stone cut around a tub.

44. Using polished stone or tile pieces on your bathroom floor that are larger than six inches creates a dangerous surface for slipping. In a shower, pieces no larger than four-inches square are safest. A tumbled finish or a honed finish is less slippery, and wider grout will give added traction.

45. Discuss with your architect, builder, and designer the kind of windows and window treatments that will be used in the bathroom. You may want a motorized opener, which will create special requirements, including a power source.

46. Consider if others can see in the bathroom window from outside: you don't want to plan window treatments to cover half of your bathroom window only to discover that the neighbors can see inside from their second level.

47. Make sure the opening mechanism for the curtains, blinds, or shutters on the windows around your tub is easy to reach and you don't have to climb into the tub to operate it.

48. If you are considering a skylight in your bathroom, think about privacy. Can someone climb onto the roof and look in?

49. Calculate the direction the sun will shine through your bathroom skylight. You do not want the sun on your perfume tray or other products on your counter.

50. Make sure any appliance, mini-refrigerator, ice maker, or wine cooler that may be stored behind a cabinet door has proper ventilation according to the appliance specifications. You don't want to have to leave the door open to let heat from the motor escape.

51. Review the master bath floor plan and note the proximity of any appliance with a running motor to the bedrooms. Do not let someone tell you the motor will not be heard when the cabinet door is closed—the vents in the cabinet door that are nec-

SHOWER WITH A DRY AREA

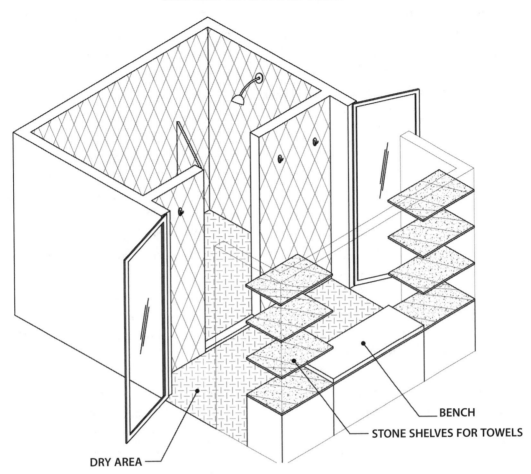

BENCH

STONE SHELVES FOR TOWELS

DRY AREA

essary for heat to escape will also allow noise to escape. This means that closing the cabinet door will not stop the noise.

52. If you are using forced air for heat and floor vents, consider locating a floor vent directly under the towel bar or hook where you will be hanging your wet towel to help dry the towel more quickly.

53. If you are considering an L-shaped counter, make sure the hardware does not extend out so far that it prevents the corner drawers from fully opening. See Lower Corner Cabinet Pitfall (page 115).

54. Check that the cabinet hardware and rosette (the decorative piece behind the knob, pull, or handle) are not too large for the cabinet stile (vertical outer edge of the cabinet). See Cabinet Door Rails and Stiles (page 232). Take the actual door front or a specification sheet for the door front with you when you select your hardware.

55. With bathroom wall space being taken up by showers, medicine cabinets, windows, doors, and so on, it is not uncommon to find there is no place to hang a bar or ring for hand towels or bath towels. Alternative options are a freestanding towel holder on your bathroom counter and storing bath towels rolled up in baskets.

56. Self-closing drawer runners will keep vanity drawers tightly closed.

57. When choosing wall coverings, faux paint, and paint, select ones that will not be adversely affected by humidity from showers. Some very

expensive wallpaper is made of delicate material that does not stand up well to humidity.

58. Take photos before the drywall goes in, and provide them to the trim carpenter to show where towel bars, art, and so on can be hung—this can prevent puncturing a pipe. During construction the plumber, electrician, or others may deviate from the plan, so a photo is best to record what is actually behind the wall. You don't want to puncture a water pipe when hanging a towel bar.

> **TIP: When specifying the height of your showerhead, realize there are two different heights: the actual height of the showerhead fixture where water is released, and the height of the plumbing where the shower arm is attached. Specify either the actual height of the showerhead extending from the shower arm or the height of the plumbing pipe that the shower arm will be affixed to.**

59. As you review floor plans during the architectural process, check what will be seen out of each window and door, and in each window and door. For instance, you don't want to look into a bedroom and see the toilet if the bathroom door is open.

60. Review your bathroom doors on your floor plans, making sure the water closet, linen closet, closet, bathroom, or other doors will not collide if opened simultaneously.

61. Study your floor plans and consider how much light from the bathroom will be cast on a person in bed. You may need to relocate the bed or change the direction the bathroom door swings.

62. If you want fixed shelves in your linen closet, think about what you will store on each shelf so the heights will accommodate your needs.

63. If you live in a humid climate or if the bathroom will be used for several baths or showers per day, avoid carpet on the bathroom floor. It will continually be damp, which leads to odors and mold. An option is to add a ceiling fan.

64. If the bathroom will be used by several people, supply plenty of towel storage space and a place to hang towels to dry.

65. Avoid white tile flooring with white grout, which shows shoe marks and hair, and requires constant maintenance. White or light-colored grout will become dingy-looking.

66. Avoid oddly shaped floors that won't let you use standard-size bath mats and rugs. Also allow room so that any door can be opened without moving your bath mat or rug out of the way.

67. To avoid towels spread all over, look for less visible areas to hang damp bath towels.

> **TIP: Handheld sprayers are convenient for bathing children and grandchildren, allow you to wash your hair in the bathtub, and are a great tool for cleaning the tub. They are also handy for seniors.**

BEDROOMS

The bedroom is the area of the home where you can retreat and recharge for the next day. It should be quiet and comfortable—and convenient. Does the location of the television work? Do you have adequate light to read in bed? Do you have to get up out of bed to turn on and off lights and fans? Do you have an easily accessible outlet to plug in your laptop? Is your telephone handy?

FORM TO USE
Bedroom Checklist (page 144)
Individual Room and Closet Fact Sheet (page 81)

HOW TO AVOID COMMON BEDROOM MISTAKES

1. Create a furniture plan when designing your bedrooms. Include the location of the television, making sure it can be seen from the bed. Provide your architect with photos and dimensions of furniture you plan to use in your bedrooms.

2. Plan window treatments so the curtain return has a place to hang when the curtains are open. (Potential mistakes include a window being too close to a side wall to fit a curtain rod or the fireplace hearth extending to the area where the curtain return hangs.)

> **TIP: For optimal health, the bedroom should be totally dark when you are sleeping, according to Dr. Mark Houston, a specialist in antiaging, hypertension, and internal medicine. Darkness promotes increased melatonin production, which can lower blood pressure, reduce cancer risk, improve cardiovascular function, and slow aging. So plan ahead for installation of window treatments that will provide total darkness while you sleep.**

3. If there will be windows on the headboard wall, locate the windows on each side of the headboard so they won't throw off the symmetry of the bedside tables, lamps, and headboard.

4. Be sure the headboard wall is long enough to fit the headboard and two bedside tables.

5. Check that outlets are placed in the right locations and there are enough outlets. Be sure the light switch on the wall above the bedside table is not randomly placed and does not interfere with the aesthetics. See Designing the Headboard Wall (page 100).

6. Make sure when the bedroom door to the bathroom is open, you like what you will see.

7. Count the number of individual window treatments you will open and close on a daily basis, and consider if there are too many individual windows.

8. When working with your audio/security person, pay close attention to where the security pad will be mounted on the wall. Compare it to your furniture plan. Also consider whether the lights on the pad will bother those sleeping. If it's located on a narrow wall, make sure it is centered.

9. Make sure the path from the bedroom door to the bathroom is not an obstacle course, with benches, coffee tables, or other furniture.

10. If someone makes urgent runs to the bathroom at night, consider the location of the bed relative to the toilet and the distance he or she will travel.

11. If you will have grown children or guests visiting who stay out late, locate your master bedroom away from the driveway so that headlights and vehicle noise do not disturb you.

12. Chose a quiet room for the area located directly above your bedroom.

13. If you want a fireplace in your bedroom, consider a raised fireplace so that you can view it from the bed. If placing it on a side wall, consider placing it on the side where the person who likes more warmth sleeps.

14. If you have a four-poster bed and television in a bedroom, make sure the bedposts do not interfere with watching the television.

15. Consider if you want your bedroom ceiling fan centered in the room or centered over the bed. A four-poster bed accentuates the fact that a ceiling fan is not centered over the bed.

16. If you have a favorite side of the bed, tell your architect early in the design process. One couple always had the man on the left side of the bed, closest to the bathroom. In their new home, he has to walk around the bed to reach the bathroom.

Designing the Headboard Wall

The wall area between the side of your headboard, the side of the bedside table, and below the top of your bedside table is a perfect place to locate some outlets and switches. Not only does it take away the unsightly light switches commonly placed on the wall above the bedside table, it also is a user friendly solution for the person in bed. Headboard Wall (below) shows how these outlets can be gracefully placed behind and beside a bedside table.

HEADBOARD WALL

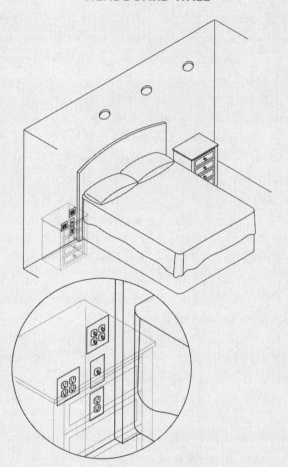

The outlet and light switches will need to be located in a vertical line with the top of the outlet faceplate or the top of a light switch plate three inches lower than the table top. A duplex outlet in this area will be handy for plugging in your laptop or heating pad. A fan control switch can be reached by someone lying down in bed. A light switch for the reading lights over your headboard and a light switch for the bedside table lamps are easily in reach. Bed linens protruding from the sides of the bed easily hide the outlets and switches.

A normal bedside table has three items that need to be plugged in: a lamp, a clock or clock radio, and a cordless phone base. However, a duplex outlet is usually installed, and you end up plugging in a plug extension. This may cause the bedside table to sit further out from the wall and items on your bedside table may end up falling between the table and the wall. Consider using a four-plex outlet behind the bedside table. If you have an oversized bedside table, specify that the wall outlet is placed closer to the edge of the bedside table near the headboard. This will allow you to reach the outlet more easily.

The light switch to the reading lights above the bed, to the lamps on each side of the bed, and to the ceiling fan located between the headboard and bedside table should each be a four-way switch. The switch on each side of the bed and the switch on the wall as you walk into the bedroom should all operate as a four-way switch.

Headboard and bedside table measurements will be needed when the electrician wires the bedrooms for the outlets and light switches.

If you use a landline for your telephone, have a telephone jack installed near each bedside table in the master bedroom. This will allow the telephone to be placed on either side of the bed or you can have two telephones, one on each bedside table.

If you will have windows on each side of the headboard, give special attention to the placement of those windows. Note the size of the headboard that will be placed between the windows, the placement of bedside tables in relation to the windows, and how window treatments will interact with bedside tables. You can see common pitfalls in window placement in the illustrations on page 101. In the left illustration, a window is placed behind the right bedside table only, so when the bedside tables are aligned horizontally, a large space is left behind the left bedside table—this can become a magnet for dropped objects such as eyeglasses and magazines. In the right illustration, windows are behind both bedside tables, but the headboard cannot fit between them, so it cannot fit flat against the wall.

The room behind or above the headboard wall should not be a kitchen, media room, laundry, staircase, or other room with a lot of noise.

NOTE: THE TABLE IS
MOVED AWAY FROM
THE WALL DUE TO
THE CURTAIN BEHIND
THE OTHER TABLE.

WINDOW
CURTAIN

NOTE: THE WALL SPACE IS
TOO NARROW BETWEEN
THE WINDOWS FOR THE
HEADBOARD TO FIT FLAT
AGAINST THE WALL.

BEDROOM CLOSETS

The bedroom closet should accommodate all your shoes, clothing, accessories, and other closet items. The more organized the space is for your belongings, the less time you will spend hunting for that perfect accessory or pair of shoes. Taking an inventory of your wardrobe and accessories is the only way to ensure you will have a place for everything—so the checklist is very extensive, covering every item you might want to store in this closet.

FORMS TO USE

Bedroom Closet Checklist (page 144)

Individual Room and Closet Fact Sheet (page 81)

HOW TO AVOID COMMON BEDROOM CLOSET MISTAKES

1. If one of you wears a size 46 or larger suit coat or jacket, install the hanging bar an inch further from the wall to ensure an oversized hanger will fit.

2. If one of you wears a tall shirt, suit, or jacket, measure the length of these and mount any double tier hanging bars far enough apart to accommodate.

3. If one of you wears shoes larger than a size 12, plan for extra length to accommodate the shoes.

4. If one of you is petite, discuss what standard measurements need to be adjusted, such as height of hanging bars, height of built-in drawers, and so on.

5. Create a list of all items that will need an outlet in the closet, such as a pants press, shoe buffer, and a clothes steamer. Discuss with your architect the location of these items.

6. Discuss with your architect how many hooks you will need for jackets or gently worn clothing.

7. Consider a motion sensor light that turns the closet light on and off as you enter and exit.

8. Tell your architect if you want a chair or other seating area in your closet.

9. A full-length mirror is a must either in the closet or bathroom. If you have space, consider a three-panel mirror that allows you to view yourself from behind.

10. Avoid fluorescent lighting in your closet, which distorts the true color of clothing.

11. Plan placement of a trash can so that you are not tripping on it.

12. Plan for dirty clothes storage whether in the closet or in the bathroom.

13. Telescoping rods are great for hanging clothing from the dry cleaner or for hanging clothing for packing.

14. If you are a frequent traveler, a packing area is a useful addition to a custom closet.

15. Placing the HVAC floor vent directly under an area in your closet to hang sweaty workout clothes or a wet swimsuit allows the forced air to help dry the items.

16. Whether your obsession is shoes, baseball caps, or ties, take an inventory and plan adequate storage space.

17. Skylights may fade clothes or other closet items. Discuss options to prevent direct sunlight.

BREAKFAST ROOM

As you design your breakfast room, first decide where you want your family to eat: at a table or a counter? Today's world has fewer and fewer traditional breakfast rooms and more breakfast areas. The breakfast area might be a nook near the kitchen with a breakfast table and chairs, an area with built-in upholstered benches (banquette seating), or a kitchen counter where the family gathers to enjoy meals. Other lifestyle questions to consider: Do you need a breakfast table for informal dinner parties? Will you use your laptop computer at the table? Will your children sit there to study?

FORMS TO USE
Breakfast Room Checklist (page 152)
Individual Room and Closet Fact Sheet (page 81)

HOW TO AVOID COMMON BREAKFAST ROOM MISTAKES

1. Create an exact furniture plan before chandeliers and sconces are hung. A buffet on the wall at the head of the table will shift the table inward, causing a chandelier hung in the center of the room to be off centered in relationship to the breakfast table. See Chandelier Placement Pitfall (page 105).

2. Work closely with your architect, builder, designer, and the HVAC subcontractor when placing HVAC vents. Consider furniture placement, curtains, rugs, and where people will be sitting.

3. Include the fringe of the rug when measuring the rug size for the room.

4. Discuss the direction of the sun during the meal hours when planning the location of the breakfast room windows and skylights. You don't want to have to wear sunglasses to eat breakfast.

5. Discuss the window treatment you plan to install with your architect and interior designer. If you have a banquette seating area, a motorized window shade might be the best option.

BUTLER'S PANTRY

A butler's pantry can serve three main purposes: an area between the kitchen and dining room used to serve meals and remove the dirty dishes; an area to store dishes, crystal, flatware, table linens, and so forth; and a bar. Your vision for the use of the butler's pantry is a lifestyle decision. Factors determining the size and shape of your butler's pantry include how many dishes, crystal pieces, and so on you have; how much entertaining you plan to do; and if the butler's pantry will be a bar.

FORMS TO USE

Butler's Pantry Checklist (page 153)

Individual Room and Closet Fact Sheet (page 81)

HOW TO AVOID COMMON BUTLER'S PANTRY MISTAKES

1. Determine what you will be plugging into an outlet when entertaining. Have an adequate number of outlets, located where you need them.

2. Make the top drawer an inch deeper inside than standard to prevent serving utensils from jamming when opening the drawer.

3. Plan serving tray storage by counting your trays and measuring the size, including handles and feet. Vertical storage is a popular choice. If you are storing silver trays, consider lining the storage area with silver cloth.

4. Plan stemware storage: measure the heights and the diameter of each piece so that you can determine how many will fit on a shelf and how many shelves you will need.

5. Measure the diameter of your dinner plates and let your architect and builder know the size. Make sure these measures are called out on your architectural plans.

6. If you own chargers (large decorative plates used under regular dinner plates), decide where you want them stored. Measure the diameter and tell your architect and builder so the shelf depth will be adequate.

7. Measure and inventory your serving pieces, making sure you have a place to store each piece.

8. Specify if you want a custom-designed drawer for your silver flatware and silver serving pieces. You can specify dividers within the drawers, and the drawers can be lined with silver cloth.

9. Measure the height of the coffeemaker you would use at a party, a large plate or tray you might store on a plate stand, or any other items that would be placed on your butler's pantry counter. Make sure your architect indicates on the plans the measurement you will need between the counter and the bottom of the upper cabinets so these items will properly fit.

10. If you will use a built-in trash can in the butler's pantry, make sure this is called out on the architectural plans. If you are using a freestanding can, make sure it has an open space to stand.

11. If you want locks on any of the china, silver, or crystal drawers or cabinets, have your architect note these on the architectural plans.

> **TIP: If the butler's pantry counter is deeper than the standard 24 inches, it will create a domino effect on any appliances under that counter. For appliances to be flush with the cabinet doors, your cabinetmaker will have to take into account the added depth.**

CONTROL ROOM

Control rooms are usually found in homes with sophisticated electronic control systems, which are used to operate everything from curtains, gas fireplaces, and lighting to HVAC and radiant heat systems. The components are mostly computer run, with one system that sets lighting, another that operates window curtains or shades, and another to turn on gas fireplaces. This sophisticated equipment needs to be kept at a certain temperature and humidity, and cannot be kept in the same room as the furnace.

Meet with the representative of each system you are buying, your architect, and your builder to design and decide the location for the systems in your control room. Each system has specific requirements that the architect and builder need to fully understand and plan for during the design process. Some of these specifications may be temperature, humidity, ventilation, fireproofing, and electrical power sources.

FORMS TO USE

Control Room Checklist (page 155)

Individual Room and Closet Fact Sheet (page 81)

HOW TO AVOID COMMON CONTROL ROOM MISTAKES

1. Provide your architect and builder with a specifications fact sheet for all control systems so they will know the temperature, humidity, ventilation, and electrical power requirements.

DINING ROOM

Will your dining room have more than one table, will the table be round or rectangular, and what other furniture will you use in your dining room? The table dimension illustrations (right, and page 105, left) show table size choices, and how many people each table size will seat. These and other questions in the checklist will help your architect know how to design this room.

FORMS TO USE

Dining Room Checklist (page 156)

Individual Room and Closet Fact Sheet (page 81)

HOW TO AVOID COMMON DINING ROOM MISTAKES

1. Before architectural plans are drawn, tell your architect the size and shape of your dining room table. This will guide your architect in designing the size and shape of the dining room.

2. Know the dimensions of your dining room rug before the initial floor plans are drawn so the room can be sized to fit your rug. (If you are having a custom rug made, this is not an issue.) Be sure to include the fringe.

SQUARE AND ROUND TABLE DIMENSIONS

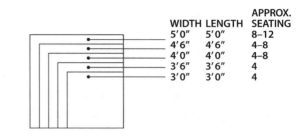

WIDTH	LENGTH	APPROX. SEATING
5'0"	5'0"	8–12
4'6"	4'6"	4–8
4'0"	4'0"	4–8
3'6"	3'6"	4
3'0"	3'0"	4

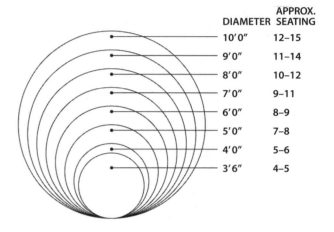

DIAMETER	APPROX. SEATING
10'0"	12–15
9'0"	11–14
8'0"	10–12
7'0"	9–11
6'0"	8–9
5'0"	7–8
4'0"	5–6
3'6"	4–5

3. Before the initial floor plans are drawn, give your architect photographs of any mirror, portrait, tapestry, and piece of art you will want hung in your dining room, with dimensions written on the back.

TIP: A fireplace in a dining room is lovely, but anyone seated near it may be ncomfortably warm during a dinner party. Even if you have gas logs that you turn off before you sit for dinner, the heat continues for a while. Try to locate a fireplace within your dining room so that it does not affect those seated for dinner.

4. Have a furniture plan before locating the chandelier or other lighting in the dining room. The

RECTANGULAR TABLE DIMENSIONS

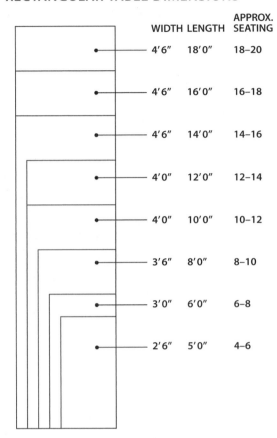

	WIDTH	LENGTH	APPROX. SEATING
	4' 6"	18' 0"	18–20
	4' 6"	16' 0"	16–18
	4' 6"	14' 0"	14–16
	4' 0"	12' 0"	12–14
	4' 0"	10' 0"	10–12
	3' 6"	8' 0"	8–10
	3' 0"	6' 0"	6–8
	2' 6"	5' 0"	4–6

CHANDELIER PLACEMENT PITFALL

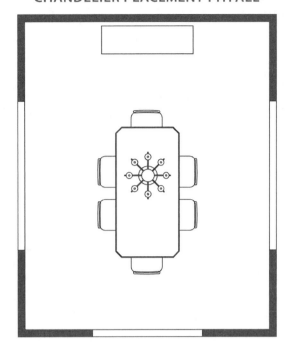

center of the room is not always the center of the dining room table, as you can see in the illustration, Chandelier Placement Pitfall (above, right). If a pair of doors will lead into the dining room, you may not be able to center the chandelier between the doors as well as on the table. A furniture plan will help you make these decisions.

5. Using the furniture plan as a guide, allow a minimum of 42 inches behind each dining chair to allow adequate space for a person to pass when someone is seated.

6. Discuss your furniture plan with your architect so that HVAC vents will not be placed where furniture will block air flow.

7. Make sure floor vents are not in the way of a rug.

8. Review your HVAC plans to make sure no floor vents are designated to go near windows that will cause your curtains to blow.

TIP: Having more than one entrance to a dining room will enhance the flow of guests at a party. If there is only one way in and out of the dining room, human traffic jams tend to occur.

DRIVEWAY

The shape and topography (the physical and natural features) of your property will greatly affect your driveway options. You'll also want to decide if you want a gate and call box, if you need a single or wider driveway, and where people will park.

FORMS TO USE

Driveway Checklist (page 157)

Individual Room and Closet Fact Sheet (page 81)

HOW TO AVOID COMMON DRIVEWAY MISTAKES

1. The gate to a driveway should be far enough off the street to allow a vehicle pulling a trailer to clear the street when stopping at the call box.

2. The call box for visitors should be easily accessible to the vehicle driver while sitting in the vehicle.

3. Make sure the electronic gate you choose can withstand the number of openings and closings it will receive day after day. If not, you will continually have maintenance issues.

4. Plan for household occupant parking, household employee parking, and visitor parking.

5. A porte cochere should be wide enough for two vehicles or the driveway should go around the porte cochere so cars don't get blocked in.

6. If you will have many vehicles in and out of your driveway on a given day, a single car driveway may not be adequate.

7. Plan where you will place trash cans for garbage pickup. Contact your Homeowner Association and municipality to find out what options you have.

8. Read your covenants and bylaws of the HOA to learn any mailbox requirements. Visit your local post office and find out rules for mail delivery in your area.

9. Avoid having your view obstructed by a driveway with cars parked in front of your home. Sometimes it makes sense to have parking along the side of the house.

10. Depending on the length of your driveway and sidewalks, place PVC pipe sleeves before the concrete is poured. This will allow you to run wires or pipes under the driveway for things such as sprinkler systems and invisible dog fences if you want them later.

11. Locate your driveway so that routine delivery trucks or fire trucks will not strike limbs when passing under trees.

12. Curbs need to be low enough so that cars can pass over them without striking the bottom of the car.

13. Plan for the location of electric meters, water meters, and natural gas meters if you plan to have a gate on your driveway and a secured yard. Be sure they are aesthetically placed.

14. Not all driveways give access to your back yard. Identify any large items for your backyard that need to be placed before building your home, such as hot tub, large boulders used in landscaping, and large transplanted trees.

> **TIP: Visit your local post office to find out what options you have for mail delivery. Some delivery routes require mailboxes on the street. Other routes allow mail to be delivered through a mail drop on the door.**

ENTRY FOYER

The entry foyer gives your guests the second impression of your home, after they have viewed the front of your home as they are approaching the front door. The entry foyer should be warm and inviting. A chair in the entry foyer is nice in case a guest needs to sit down. It is convenient to have a chest or table near the front door to set down deliveries while signing for them.

The size and shape of your entry foyer is a personal decision. Some are large and formal while others are small and informal. Some run toward the back of the home, others run side-to-side. Some are located at one end of the home; others are located in the center of the home. The location of the entry foyer will evolve as the design of your home is determined. If you have a particular vision for your entry foyer, share that with your architect.

If you entertain large groups, a spacious entry foyer will accommodate many guests arriving or departing at once. Also a spacious entry foyer with many rooms flowing from it allows guests to flow from one room to another without a human traffic jam.

The coat closet is an important element. Having an ample-size closet to hold guests' coats sets a nice tone for your home. A good rule of thumb is that your coat closet should hold as many coats as you can seat guests at your dining room table. Obviously, the climate where you live will influence how often you use your coat closet.

A luxurious option for your entry foyer is a fireplace welcoming your guests into your home on a frigid night.

FORMS TO USE

Entry Foyer Checklist (page 158)

Individual Room and Closet Fact Sheet (page 81)

HOW TO AVOID COMMON ENTRY FOYER MISTAKES

1. Create a furniture plan for the entry foyer and share this with your architect. Make sure a fully opened door does not bump furniture.

2. If you plan to have double doors, pay close attention to the width of the doors. Generally with double doors, you open only one of the doors on a daily basis.

3. It is lovely to walk into a home and instantly hear music. Consider having stereo speakers in your entry foyer.

4. Once framing is in place and you have a furniture plan, decide the exact locations of the security pads, light switches, outlets, HVAC vents, chandeliers, and sconces. Take into account the addition of crown molding, cornices on windows and other decorating or construction parts that may affect centering items.

5. Depending on the location of the coat closet, consider putting your security pad and speaker volume control inside the closet. Generally, the front door is not the door you use to enter and exit your

The Hallways of Your Home

Plan for ample-sized hallways in your home. Standard hallways measure 3 feet 6 inches to 4 feet 3 inches in width. A hallway less than 4 feet wide creates the feeling of being in a maze. A wider hallway evokes a feeling of expansiveness and allows for the placement of a narrow chest or table. When visiting friends' homes, measure the width of their hallways to get an idea of the width that feels best for you.

home. On the occasions when you do, you can turn the alarm on or off from inside the coat closet. It's also nice to adjust the individual volume control for the entry foyer speakers from inside the coat closet. This keeps unattractive items from cluttering the walls.

6. Any glass panels near exterior doors need to be countered by security measures such as a glass-break sensor with an alarm or decorative iron over the glass, so that a burglar cannot break the glass, reach in, and unlock the door.

7. When in doubt, go larger with your coat closet.

8. For convenience, install a three-way light switch in a convenient location so you can easily turn off foyer or outside lights without having to walk to the front door every evening before bed.

9. The stairstep depth and the riser height ratio should be standard and consistent on all steps. If they are not, people going up and down your stairs will have an awkward gait. Also, if the depth of each step is too shallow, the toes of shoes will leave marks on the risers.

10. If the landing before the first step down a staircase does not extend out from the railing, when you walk by the area, your peripheral vision gives you a feeling that you are about to fall down the steps.

EXERCISE ROOM

Your approach to the design of your exercise room revolves around the amount of equipment and the weight and size of the equipment you will use. Another factor is whether this room may be converted into a bedroom at a later date. An exercise room can be simple with a single cardio machine or an elaborate one that resembles the local fitness center. You'll want to consider your needs carefully to create the exercise room that fits your lifestyle.

FORMS TO USE

Exercise Room Checklist (page 159)
Individual Room and Closet Fact Sheet (page 81)

HOW TO AVOID COMMON EXERCISE ROOM MISTAKES

1. Meet with experts and your trainer, if you have one, to design a floor plan for your exercise/ fitness room. Give this to your architect at the beginning of your design process.

2. For all equipment, request specification sheets indicating the dimensions, weight, electrical specifications, and placement requirements. Record this information on, or attach it to, the Individual Room and Closet Fact Sheet for the exercise room.

TIP: Be aware of the noise and vibration generated by exercise equipment. Ask your architect to specify additional sound and vibration insulation. Also, when reviewing your floor plans, identify any rooms that might be affected by the noise or vibrations and discuss this with your architect.

3. Specify on the floor plans and the framing plans where reinforcement is needed for hanging exercise equipment from the ceiling or wall (such as a punching bag, chin-up bar, or ballet bar) and for placing heavy equipment on the floor. Sometimes the floor needs to be reinforced to handle the weight load.

4. Determine the size of your stretching area by the number of people who will be using the area to stretch at the same time.

5. Determine the size and height of a jump rope area. Will more than one person jump rope at the same time?

6. Once there is an equipment floor plan showing equipment in place, identify which pieces need an outlet.

TIP: Natural light increases your training drive, according to Charles Poliquin, a strength coach to Olympic and professional athletes. He suggests you allow as much natural light as possible in your exercise room, whether from windows or skylights.

7. Let your architect know if you want a closet, built-in cabinets, open shelves, or a piece of furniture to store all small exercise equipment.

8. If the exercise room gets western sun and you tend to work out in the late afternoon, extra AC ventilation may be needed to keep it cool.

9. Carefully position wall sconces or can lights so that light will not shine directly into your eyes when you are on your back using equipment or stretching.

10. If you will have massages in this room, plan where the table will be set up and, if you own the table, where you will store it.

11. Discuss with your architect proper ventilation or an air purifier system for the room, especially in a humid climate.

12. If a treadmill is positioned with the back of the treadmill close to the wall, if the user missteps, he or she could be thrown into the wall and injured.

13. If you plan to watch television while using exercise equipment, make sure that the noise from the equipment will not overpower the sound from the television. Consider purchasing equipment that comes with an attached television monitor and

headphone jack. If you choose this option, determine where the machine will be placed in your exercise room so that the cable or DirecTV connector and electrical outlets will be properly located.

14. Too much glare and direct sunlight from windows and skylights can be an annoyance when working out. Discuss types of window treatments that will maximize sunlight but cut the glare. And if you use a television or DVD player, position it so that sunlight won't obscure the screen.

15. Allow for an extra room for the addition of new equipment.

EXTERIOR FRONT ENTRY

Some front doors are located on the front of the house; others are on the side; still others require you to walk through a courtyard. Some have steps leading up or down. Perhaps you have to cross a bridge to reach the entrance, or maybe a screened-in front porch, an open porch, or a covered walkway area. Often the style of the home you want dictates or influences the exterior front entry to your home.

FORMS TO USE
Exterior Front Entry Checklist (page 160)
Individual Room and Closet Fact Sheet (page 81)

HOW TO AVOID COMMON EXTERIOR FRONT ENTRY MISTAKES

1. Every front door should have some sort of covering to protect guests from rain, even if it is a deep doorjamb area. This will also protect the front door and reduce door maintenance.

2. If your home has a circular driveway and a porte cochere in the front of a home, the driveway should be wide enough for two vehicles or you should have an alternative driveway around the porte cochere so vehicles will not get blocked in.

3. If your family has many vehicles or you expect many visitors to your home, consider making the entire driveway wide enough for two cars to prevent cars from being blocked in.

4. Give your architect photos of tables, benches, chairs, or other furniture you want to use at your front door, with dimensions written on the photo.

5. If you will use planters at your front door, measure and photograph them and share this information with your architect. If you are shopping for planters, take the floor plans with you so that you can make sure they will fit the desired area.

6. Plan a faucet near every porch or entry way, aesthetically placed, so the area can be hosed off and plants can be watered.

7. If you plan to use a drip system for planters, discuss this with the architect so that it can be part of the plumbing and architectural plans.

8. An outlet or outlets should be aesthetically placed near the front door for lighted Christmas decorations. You will also need an outlet for your blower, electric hedge trimmers, electric edger, and other equipment.

9. Consider the age of most of your guests and home occupants. If they will not be able to maneuver steps or if they use a wheelchair, have an alternative way to enter your home.

10. If you plan to use gas lanterns, inform your architect. Once you receive your plans, make sure that is noted on the plumbing plans.

FAMILY ROOM

The family room may also be called the den, the keeping room, or the gathering room. The size and location in your home are two of the most important decisions to make.

FORMS TO USE
Family Room Checklist (page 161)
Individual Room and Closet Fact Sheet (page 81)

HOW TO AVOID COMMON FAMILY ROOM MISTAKES

1. If the ceiling joists are installed perpendicular instead of parallel to the drop-down screen of your television, the screen will not retract. Meet with your communications expert and architect to identify any specific framing needs.

2. If you plan to have a television in your family room that will be seen by those in the kitchen and breakfast room, discuss the location of the television with your communications expert and architect.

3. Make sure when reviewing electrical plans that the outlet and the television cable, DirecTV connector, or satellite connector are in the correct location.

4. Spend time designing your built-in bookcase, noting any outlets or television connections. You may need additional outlets for a lamp or clock.

5. Confirm that the dimensions shown on the elevation plans for a television in the bookcase are correct.

6. Make sure the floor outlets are correctly located on the electrical plans and the outlet is connected to a conveniently located light switch.

7. Review the electrical plan and make sure outlets that connect to light switches are shown.

8. Review the furniture plan with your architect and look for any furniture that may be bumped by a door.

9. Make sure the rug you plan to use will fit the room. Provide the dimensions, including the fringe. Do not forget about the baseboard and shoe mold measurement.

10. Review the furniture plan and check that outlets, chandeliers, sconces, light switches, vents, and speakers are shown in the correct location.

11. When reviewing the furniture plans, make sure floor or baseboard vents will not interfere with furniture placement or your rug, and that when the air is flowing, the curtains will not blow or balloon out.

SIZING ART FOR SPACE ABOVE MANTEL

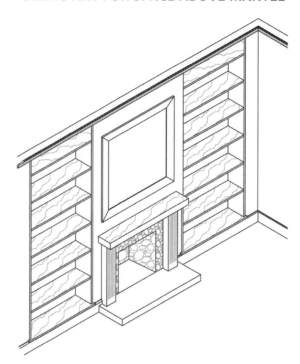

12. Discuss window treatment designs with your architect and interior designer to find out if what you want will work. Pay particular attention to the curtain return when curtains are open.

13. Provide measurements of items you plan to display on your bookcases to ensure they will fit. Include an inventory of books and book measurements.

14. If you plan to mount a flat-screen television over the mantel, find out the suggested maximum height for viewing.

15. If you have a family portrait or piece of art you want to hang above the mantel, measure it carefully so that enough space is allowed between the top of the mantel and the crown molding. (See illustration above.)

GARAGE

The number one question to ask yourself about your garage is what you will store there. Although garages are predominantly used for vehicles, without careful planning, hobbies, collectibles, and plain old junk may end up in the garage, with the vehicles parked outside.

FORMS TO USE

Garage Checklist (page 162)

Garage Vehicle Checklist (page 164)

Garage Item Storage Checklist (page 165)

Individual Room and Closet Fact Sheet (page 81)

HOW TO AVOID COMMON GARAGE MISTAKES

1. Based on the sizes of the vehicles you drive, plan a garage door opening wide enough to avoid knocking off side mirrors.

2. For aesthetic purposes, even if you have different size vehicles, keep all garage doors the same size.

3. If you keep a storage or other rack on top of your car, select a taller garage door to avoid damaging the item you're carrying or damaging the garage if you forget about the rack.

> **TIP: Many security companies advise limiting the number of doors entering your home. If you can enter your home from the garage, they often advise against having an exterior door in the garage. However, if any of your family members frequently leaves the house through the garage, it will be inconvenient to open and close the garage door each time. An exterior door would be a better solution.**

4. If you add columns outside your garage door, allow adequate space to back out before the driver turns the steering wheel to avoid the front corners of the vehicle striking the column.

5. If you do not want someone to be able to look through a window and see if your vehicle is parked in the garage, avoid windows on your garage door or garage walls. Make sure any windows are high enough to prevent someone from seeing through them, or install a window covering.

6. If you live in a cold climate, having a hot/cold faucet in the garage is an inexpensive luxury; be sure faucets are installed away from vehicle doors and do not block the area you use to walk around your vehicles.

> **TIP: For a basketball goal in the garage area, make sure the glass windows on your garage door or any window on your garage will not be in harm's way.**

7. The drains in the garage floor must be lower than the garage floor. If you have grooves cut to the drain, make sure the drain is lower than the grooves.

8. If you plan on storing your trash and recycle bins in your garage, give your architect the dimensions and number of trash and recycle cans.

9. If you will have more than one door from the garage into your home, you will want buttons to operate the garage door at each location.

10. Decide the order of the garage door opening buttons that are placed on the wall by the door leading into your home, and tell your architect and builder. When the garage doors are being installed, discuss the order with the installer.

11. If you have large parties, consider adding a couple of 220V outlets in the garage for the caterers to use for their ovens.

KITCHEN

Your lifestyle will dictate many of the choices you make involving your kitchen. Are you a gourmet cook or do you rarely cook? Do you entertain often or do you rarely have visitors in your home?

Designing Your Kitchen and Pantry

When designing the layout of your kitchen, kitchen pantry, and butler's pantry, use the Kitchen Item Storage Checklist (page 177) to help you identify the items you will need to store. Once you have checked the items, decide if you want them stored in the kitchen, the pantry, or the butler's pantry. On the checklist, fill in the preferred storage location (kitchen, kitchen pantry, butler's pantry, or other). Next fill in the precise storage location.

Possibilities for precise storage are cabinets above the counter, cabinets below the counter, drawers below the counter, on top of the counter, on top of the island, cabinets below the island, drawers below the island, on a pot rack, drawers under the counter, and open shelves above the upper cabinets. With this information in hand, you can sketch where you want drawers and cabinets and note what you want stored in each. Measure the height of the largest item you plan to store in the drawer so you can specify the interior height of drawers.

The Kitchen Cabinet Layout Checklist (page 171) is a great tool for determining the design of your kitchen cabinets. This checklist will help clarify where you want drawers and where you want cabinet doors. Additionally, it will help you determine what goes where in your kitchen and plan the layout of your kitchen cabinets.

The Kitchen Island Checklist (page 174) focuses on how you plan to use your island, the components that will be part of the island, and the many shapes for kitchen islands. The Kitchen Appliance Checklist (page 175) lists potential appliances found in a kitchen, and the Kitchen Plumbing Checklist (page 176) lists potential plumbing fixtures found in a kitchen. Check any that apply.

FORMS TO USE

Kitchen Checklist (page 169)

Kitchen Cabinet Layout Checklist (page 171)

Kitchen Island Checklist (page 174)

Kitchen Appliance Checklist (page 175)

Kitchen Plumbing Checklist (page 176)

Kitchen Item Storage Checklist (page 177)

Individual Room and Closet Fact Sheet (page 81)

HOW TO AVOID COMMON KITCHEN MISTAKES

1. Create a work triangle in the kitchen between the sink, stove, and refrigerator. This does not have to be a perfectly shaped triangle, but avoid having one of these appliances on opposite sides of the island. The triangular relationship between these three areas will create a functioning kitchen.

2. Do not place an ice maker or an under-counter beverage refrigerator within the kitchen triangle, because someone getting ice or a beverage will interfere with meal preparation.

3. Avoid having a wall or short wall next to the refrigerator or freezer that will prevent the door from opening a full 180 degrees to allow removal of shelves or drawers for cleaning.

4. Choose a refrigerator or ice maker that makes the type or shape of ice you desire.

5. If you have a large family or often have house guests, consider two microwaves.

6. Pay attention to the height specified for a microwave on your elevation plan. It is difficult to read the controls on microwaves located below the counter and bending over may be difficult for seniors or those with back issues. Microwaves installed too high can be dangerous when removing hot items.

7. Follow the manufacturer's specifications regarding the height of wall ovens. If a wall oven is too high, you may burn your arm when removing hot dishes. If it is installed too low, you will find

yourself stooping to check the item in the oven and to remove it. Heights vary depending on the size oven you select.

8. Early in the design process, tell your architect what size wall oven you want. Consider the size of your cookie sheet, pizza stone, and other baking items when deciding the size. Realizing you want a larger oven later in the design process may involve redesign of your kitchen, which will be expensive and could delay your job.

9. Early in the design process, determine the number of burners you want on your range or stove top. Again, adding a larger range or stove top later in the process can get complicated.

10. If you have a preference as to which side of the sink the dishwasher should be placed on, tell your architect early in the design process.

11. If you want two sinks, one larger than the other, when ordering you can specify whether the larger sink is on the right or left side, and whether the disposal is on the smaller sink or the larger sink.

12. A too shallow sink and a faucet spout placed too high will cause water to splash out of the sink.

13. If you will have a vegetable sink in your kitchen, it makes sense to have a vegetable refrigerator drawer next to it.

14. Some farmhouse sinks are designed with the front edge of the sink lower than the kitchen counter. When washing dishes, you are more likely to get splashed.

15. With a self-rimming sink or an under-mounted sink, allow adequate space in front of the backsplash for cleaning. (Refer back to Faucet/Backsplash Relationship, page 94.)

16. When specifying the location of a pot filler faucet, consider the height of the pot you will be

POT FILLER PLACEMENT OVER COOKTOP

PLUMB POT FILLER AT GROUT LINE AND/OR CENTERED ON TILE

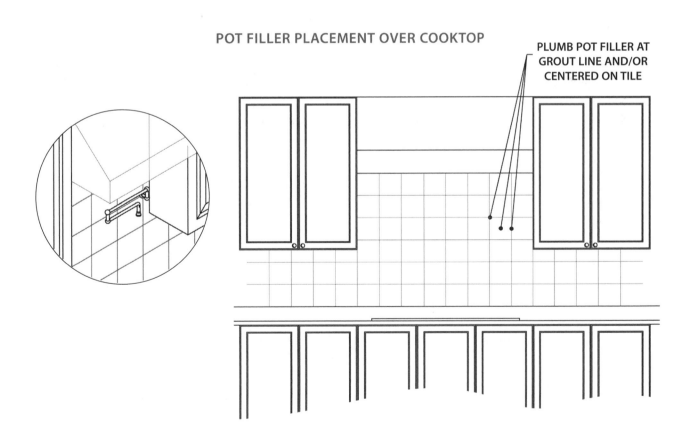

filling. The faucet should clear the top of the pot so you don't have to tilt the pot to fit it under the faucet.

17. For aesthetic purposes, the faucet should be centered at the grout line and/or centered on the tile. See Pot Filler Faucet Placement over Cooktop (page 113).

TIP: In a double sink, place the disposal in the sink closest to the dishwasher so you can load the dishwasher without getting both sinks dirty.

18. Select a disposal with enough horsepower to handle the amount of waste your family generates.

19. Specify on the architectural plans how to turn on your disposal: a switch on the wall or in the cabinet below, a push button on the counter or rim of the sink, or manually for a batch feed disposal. Make sure your preference is specified on the architectural plans.

20. A large kitchen should have two areas for garbage. Locate a trash compactor, trash bin, or compost container next to or near the sink for convenience when scraping plates or preparing food. A large kitchen should have two areas for garbage.

21. If possible, a warming drawer should be located in the vicinity of the breakfast area or dining table.

22. Do not position appliances where the doors will collide if both are open at the same time, as illustrated in Appliance Door Collision Pitfall (right).

23. Discuss the height of family members with your architect when positioning exhaust fan hoods. It is extremely painful to hit your head on the corner of an exhaust fan hood.

24. It is more convenient if everyday dishes, glasses, and flatware are stored near your dishwasher.

25. If you raise the height of the kitchen counters, you will need to raise the height of the upper cabinets so that standard size items such as a blender

or canister set will fit between the bottom of the upper cabinet and the counter. You also want to be able to comfortably reach items in the higher upper cabinets.

26. The top of your upper cabinets can go to the ceiling, stop short of the ceiling to create an open area between the top of the cabinets and the ceiling, or go to a furdown, a finished structure above kitchen cabinets. If you have decorative accessories you want displayed above the cabinets, measure those items and specify the amount of open space needed.

27. Take a cookbook inventory so you will have enough shelf space to accommodate your cookbooks. Also measure the various sizes.

28. To prevent kitchen utensil drawers from jamming, request that the inside depth of the top drawers throughout the kitchen be one-fourth to half an inch deeper than standard measurements.

29. The minimum distance between a kitchen counter and an island, when two appliances are opposite each other, is 48 inches.

30. Vertical tray storage is a great way to store trays, large cutting boards, a pizza stone, a pizza

APPLIANCE DOOR COLLISION PITFALL

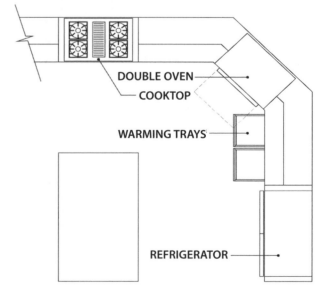

DOUBLE OVEN
COOKTOP
WARMING TRAYS
REFRIGERATOR

paddle, and barbecue boards. Measure the size and count the number of items you plan to store in a vertical tray storage cabinet. Be generous with space as they fill up quickly.

> **TIP: In many cases, the standard measurements for kitchen cabinets have not caught up with the trend toward oversized dinner plates. To avoid having cabinet doors that will not fully close, take the time to measure your plates and give those measurements to your architect or cabinetmaker.**

31. Avoid storing heavy items such as pots, pans, and dishes in a very wide, very deep drawer. The weight can put too much strain the drawer glides, eventually causing a malfunction. It is better to have two medium-sized drawers than one extremely large one.

32. To operate a pull-out shelf in a lower cabinet, both cabinet doors need to be fully open. The inside of the cabinet doors will end up with scratches and grooves in the door from trying to pull the shelf out without fully opening the cabinet door. Drawers are a better solution.

33. If you have two counters meeting in a corner, a drawer or dishwasher will not open fully if it is blocked by large hardware on another drawer or an oven door handle. It also may not open fully if the stiles, the vertical part of the cabinet, are not wide enough or if an appliance sticks out. Lower Corner Cabinet Pitfall (above, right) shows a drawer that will not open because a dishwasher extends too far.

34. The direction of the door swing on cabinets needs special attention. A cabinet door that opens in the wrong direction will cause great frustration.

35. Having a toe kick on the island will make standing at the island more comfortable.

36. For practical purposes, it is best not to run

LOWER CORNER CABINET PITFALL

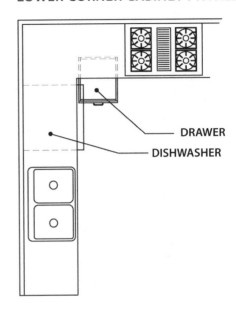

the counter between two sinks. Although having the counter run between double or triple sinks looks great, it is normal to move a running faucet between the two sinks, which would cause the water to run off the counter and onto the person at the sink. The sink divider should be lower than the counter. See Kitchen Sink Divider Pitfall (page 116).

37. Dark granite counters look beautiful when perfectly clean. However, keeping a darker counter streakless will involve additional maintenance. Lighter-colored granite requires less maintenance.

38. If cooking with natural gas is important, make sure that natural gas is available where you will build your home.

39. If you have a window over your kitchen sink and will use shutters for window treatments, make sure the space between the windowsill and the height of the kitchen faucet will allow the shutter to open.

40. Select a floor color that does not show every crumb or every scuff mark.

41. Avoid light-colored grout on the floors, which will look dingy over time.

42. Instead of cluttering your backsplash and

KITCHEN SINK DIVIDER PITFALL

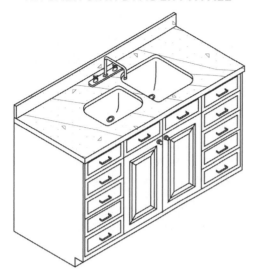

47. Make sure the kitchen light switches will be aesthetically placed. Identify the lights you want attached to the same gang plate, those switches that need to be three- or four-way, the order of a gang of switches, and the ones that need dimmers.

48. Avoid having light switches in too many locations.

49. You may want a light over the kitchen sink on a separate switch if you like to leave it on at night.

50. Have a broom closet near the kitchen.

TIP: I recommend a toe kick of 4 to 4½ inches. If you will have drawers as part of your toe kick, that will dictate the height. A vent in the toe kick area will also affect the height. Some cabinets are designed to look like furniture, and the toe kick area will be determined by that design.

island with exposed outlets, consider a strip of outlets under the bottom of the upper cabinets and under the overhang of the top of the island. Make sure this will pass code inspection for your area.

43. A halogen strip or puck lights gives a more pleasing light than fluorescent lights for under-cabinet lighting.

44. Specify that all under-cabinet lights be connected and turned on by a light switch. Having to reach under each cabinet to turn on lights individually is frustrating.

45. If you are having an open shelf above the upper cabinets, adding halogen strips adds a wonderful lighting touch.

46. Indicate on the architectural plans if you have a recessed can light you want centered over the sink or over the island, so you will avoid ending up with a joist, sprinkler pipe, sprinkler head, or HVAC vent or equipment that will prevent it from being centered.

TIP: If kitchen counters are too high, the appliances may end up lower than the counter height, as the height range for appliances is limited.

KITCHEN PANTRY

The kitchen pantry can be a large room, a walk-in closet, or a part of the kitchen cabinets. Which use is best for you? Will it be used solely for food and dry goods? Will it double as your broom closet? Will you store your small appliances on the shelves? Will you store serving pieces on the shelves? Will you store large bags of dog food?

FORMS TO USE

Kitchen Pantry Checklist (page 182)
Kitchen Item Storage Checklist (page 177)
Individual Room and Closet Fact Sheet (page 81)

HOW TO AVOID COMMON KITCHEN PANTRY MISTAKES

1. Request adjustable shelves to give storage flexibility.

2. Have some shelves deep enough for a case of water or soda, or other case item.

3. Request that your pantry shelves have a center support every three feet to prevent sagging in the middle.

4. For a window or skylight in your pantry, plan a window treatment to prevent sunlight from shining directly on food items.

5. Decide where you want to store your mop, broom, and so on. If it's in the pantry, make sure the specific location is spelled out on your floor plans.

6. Have a designated place for all items you plan to store in your pantry. Refer to the Kitchen Item Storage Checklist (page 177).

7. Request a couple of outlets in the wall behind the shelves to plug in items that need charging such as a handheld vacuum, screwdriver, and flashlight.

8. If you use a water dispenser, designate an area on the floor and an outlet for the power source.

9. For aesthetic reasons, try to avoid fluorescent lights in walk-in pantries.

10. If larger cabinet doors in your kitchen will serve as your pantry, plan a recessed can light near the cabinet doors to illuminate the items inside.

LAUNDRY ROOM

The main decisions to make regarding the design of your laundry room include the size, location in your home, whether you want a crafts or sewing section in the room, and how many laundry rooms and washing machines and dryers you will have.

FORMS TO USE

Laundry Room Checklist (page 184)
Individual Room and Closet Fact Sheet (page 81)

HOW TO AVOID COMMON LAUNDRY ROOM MISTAKES

1. Plan the location of washer and dryer outlets so the plug will reach the outlet.

2. Dryers have either three-prong or four-prong plugs; make sure the planned outlets are compatible with the one on your dryer. You may need to change the plug on your washer or dryer.

3. Take your floor plans with you if you are buying a new washer and dryer to ensure that the direction of the door swing is correct.

4. Mounting the washer and dryer outlets on the wall just under the top of the unit makes it easier to unplug them than reaching down to the standard location.

5. Check the architectural plans for the width and height of the laundry room doorway to make sure the opening will accommodate the units. In particular, clearing the doorway when stacking a washer and dryer in a small laundry closet can be problematic.

6. The dryer vent should be located on the wall directly behind the dryer, not on a side wall, where the vent hose would prevent the dryer from being pushed back against the wall.

7. If you use a dryer vent box in the wall behind the dryer so the dryer will fit snugly against the back wall, it must line up exactly with the vent on the dryer.

8. For side-by-side washer and dryers, add a shelf 8 to 12 inches deep just above the back of the washer and dryer to hold oversized laundry detergents with spouts. The shelf surface can be made of the same material as your laundry room counters.

9. Allow an adequate area to work when folding clothes or doing projects.

10. Make sure any cabinets over the washer and dryer do not extend out so far that you could hit your head on them.

11. Specify that the cabinet shelves are adjustable. With so many different sizes of laundry products on the market, having the flexibility of adjusting the shelf height is invaluable.

12. Plan an oversized drawer, to store cleaning rags and towels.

TIP: If you will use your laundry room for caterers when entertaining, consider a disposal on your sink. However, if you will pour dirty mop bucket water down that sink, or use it for flower arranging or cleaning muddy boots, a disposal isn't a good idea.

13. If storing your mop inside a broom closet, consider having the closet lined with a waterproof surface so a damp mop does not damage the interior of the closet.

14. If you have a dog or participate in activities that require hosing off, a tiled area with a drain and faucet with sprayer in the laundry room will be a lifesaver.

15. The ease of filling a mop bucket in the laundry room sink is determined by the depth of the sink and the shape of the faucet. A large, deep, single sink with a swivel faucet and sprayer are great choices.

16. A spray nozzle comes in handy. For a tiled shower area for bathing the dog and rinsing items, consider locating it near the sink so that a wall-mounted handheld shower can serve both areas. Another option is a commercial high-pressure sprayer.

TIP: If you will have front-load washers and dryers on a pedestal base or a stackable washer and dryer, tell your architect, builder, and cabinetmaker— the height of those appliances will affect the height of the upper cabinets.

17. In a tiled area, install a hanging bar so you can air dry items. Additionally, you can hang ironed items on the bar.

18. A drain in the floor under the washing machine will prevent flooding should the washer malfunction or hoses break.

19. Specify 220 volt plugs if you plan to have a refrigerator and freezer in the laundry room.

20. For a refrigerator or freezer, make sure no wall or counter will prevent you from opening the doors at least 180 degrees so that you clear the door shelves when storing larger items and can easily remove shelves and drawers for cleaning.

21. Check the location of a fold-down ironing board on the architectural plans. Can both a left-handed and right-handed person use it? Make sure an outlet for the iron is specified.

22. Specify an outlet in the electrical plans if you will have an electric five-gallon water dispenser or a sewing machine.

23. If you have a large family and a multilevel home, install a laundry chute to save time and steps.

24. If you air dry many of your clothes, a ceiling fan in the laundry room will hasten the process.

LIBRARY

The function of your library will greatly influence the design process. Your library may be a room in your home for the family to gather, with walls full of bookcases, and perhaps a desk. Your library may be a part of the master suite or on another level entirely. If it will be used as an office, you will need to take many more details into account, and will need the Office Checklist (page 194).

FORMS TO USE
Library Checklist (page 186)
Office Checklist (page 194) if it will be used as an office
Individual Room and Closet Fact Sheet (page 81)

HOW TO AVOID COMMON LIBRARY MISTAKES

1. Tell your architect your rug size, including fringe, so the library will accommodate it.

2. Once you receive the floor plans from your architect, create a furniture plan that includes the location of all equipment such as printers, fax machines, hard drives, routers, and televisions; this helps determine the location of built-ins, floor outlets, wall outlets, computer wiring, cable connections, and telephone jacks.

3. Use the furniture plan to identify the location of ceiling fans, fireplaces, televisions, stereo equipment, computers, telephones, electrical outlets, and phone jacks as they relate to your furniture and rug.

4. To give your library a more aesthetically pleasing look, store office equipment inside a credenza or in a closet—but allow proper ventilation.

5. Designate a few outlets used by lamps to be connected to the light switch, so you can turn on lights from a light switch as you walk into the room.

6. If your desk telephone is not wireless, you will need a telephone jack. If you will place your cordless phone base in your library, you will need both an outlet and a telephone jack to operate it.

7. Plan both a phone jack and an electrical outlet for the fax machine location.

8. Have adequate outlets, phone jacks, and computer wiring for all office equipment.

9. Give your architect all computer wiring needs and computer outlet needs.

10. Have an easily accessible outlet to plug in a laptop computer while sitting at your desk or in your favorite chair.

11. Have ample light on books on the bookcase so you can read the book titles. You can use either specific bookcase lighting fixtures or wall wash–type lighting, a fixture such as a recessed can light, or track lighting.

12. If you will have stereo equipment in the library, plan adequate lighting on the equipment so that you can read the control knobs.

13. Provide adequate lighting on the library desk, especially if you work at your desk.

14. Have enough outlets and surge protection for stereo equipment.

15. Bookcases often have lamps, clocks, and other items requiring an outlet. Specify the location for outlets to be installed within the bookcase shelves.

16. Plan outlets for a lighted globe or a lighted world map mounted on the wall.

17. Work out television location and wiring needs with your architect during the design process.

18. Identify to your architect anything that will be hung on the walls: family portrait, hunting trophies, fishing trophies, family crest, writing board, world map, or other.

19. Work with your designer regarding window treatments in the library; consider a pocket behind the bookcase for a return or sliding panels to cover windows.

20. Have adequate AC ventilation, particularly if this room will receive western sun.

21. Inventory your books, including the number of books of each size, so bookcase shelves will be the proper size.

22. If you want built-in file drawers, tell your architect how many letter- and legal-size hanging files you will need to store.

23. If you want to hang a family portrait or piece of art above the mantel, allow room between the top of the mantel and the crown molding. (See illustration, page 110.)

LIVING ROOM/GREAT ROOM

Historically, the living room has been a formal gathering room, reserved for Christmas or when guests visit. As our society has become less formal, this room is either left out of a home or combined with the great room. Today's living room/great room is larger and has numerous rooms adjacent to it. The family will flow through the living room/

great room as they move about the home. Determine if you want the traditional room or a more informal one.

FORMS TO USE

Living Room/Great Room Checklist (page 188)
Individual Room and Closet Fact Sheet (page 81)

HOW TO AVOID COMMON LIVING ROOM/ GREAT ROOM MISTAKES

1. If you entertain, have at least two entrances to prevent a bottleneck created by people trying to enter and exit through one doorway.

2. Give your architect photos of portraits and art, including measurements, to ensure a proper fit.

3. When reviewing the furniture plans, make sure floor or baseboard vents will not interfere with furniture placement or rugs, and that the air flow won't make the curtains blow or balloon out.

4. If any items on the mantel require electricity, have an outlet installed on the mantel.

5. If you have an heirloom clock or other decorative item to be displayed on the mantel, make sure the mantel shelf is deep enough to hold the item.

6. Measure any family portrait or piece of art to be hung above the mantel, so enough room is allowed between the top of the mantel and the crown molding. (Refer back to illustration, page 110.)

7. Use a furniture plan to carefully plan for a spotlight to hit the center of the coffee table and for a chandelier to be centered over the seating area.

MECHANICAL ROOM

The mechanical room is home to the "mechanics" that operate a home. Commonly these include the water heaters, furnaces, security system, and various cutoff valves. If your home is more sophisticated, you may have an integrated home automation

system, radiant heating system, air purifier system, water purifier system, lighting system, and sound system. The number of systems and the amount of space dedicated to each system will determine the size of this room.

FORMS TO USE

Mechanical Room Checklist (page 189)
Individual Room and Closet Fact Sheet (page 81)

HOW TO AVOID COMMON MECHANICAL ROOM MISTAKES

1. Allow space for servicing of equipment in a mechanical room.

2. Know the municipality codes in your area regarding sizes allowed for mechanical rooms.

3. Have a cost analysis done comparing a ventless water heater and a tank water heater. Tell your architect if you will use a tankless water heater, so it can be specified on the architectural plans.

4. Determine the savings on your water bill if you add a recirculating hot water pump to your tank or tankless water heater, producing instant hot water at any faucet and reducing the amount of water the household wastes.

5. Install a drain in the floor of your mechanical room in case the water heater malfunctions.

6. Meet with your architect, builder, and the representative for each system you plan to purchase, to identify requirements and specifications needed to install each system in the mechanical room.

MEDIA ROOM

Some homes have rooms that are dedicated solely to being a media room; others have rooms that combine media equipment with the features of the family room or playroom. If you will be combining your "media" with another room, fill in the checklist for both rooms.

FORMS TO USE

Media Room Checklist (page 190)

Individual Room and Closet Fact Sheet (page 81)

HOW TO AVOID COMMON MEDIA ROOM MISTAKES

1. Stadium seating is best in the media room when you have several rows of seating. Consider the size of the chair backs in the media room and the height of the second and third row, if applicable.

2. Plan some dim lighting so that guests can move about when the lights are turned out and the movie is playing. For stadium seating, have any steps illuminated.

3. Have a powder room or a bathroom on the same level as the media room.

4. Plan adequate floor outlets if you will have a popcorn wagon, portable sundae counter, or lighted candy counter.

5. Depending on the size of the media room and its proximity to the bar or kitchen, you may want a mini-kitchen.

6. If the media room is located above or below the kitchen area, consider a dumbwaiter to send food and beverages to and from the kitchen.

7. Have a designated area for storing your movie collection.

8. Avoid locating the media room next to a room with noisy equipment such as a laundry room, mechanical room, or exercise room.

MORNING KITCHEN

A morning kitchen is often used in a larger home that has the master bedroom located away from the kitchen or on a different level than the kitchen, or in a home with a guest suite. This allows you to make morning coffee and prepare a simple breakfast within the master suite or allows a guest to do the same without waking anyone in the home. The morning kitchen can be as simple as a counter with a coffeemaker on top and a mini-refrigerator below, or it can be a mini-kitchen in a room.

FORMS TO USE

Morning Kitchen/Counter Checklist (page 191)

Individual Room and Closet Fact Sheet (page 81)

HOW TO AVOID COMMON MORNING KITCHEN MISTAKES

1. An open morning kitchen counter in a bedroom is not aesthetically pleasing, so place it in the hallway or off the master bedroom or guest bedroom. A small room with a door would be the ideal location.

2. Place the mini-refrigerator or ice maker far away from the bed or in a room with a door that can be closed, so occupants do not hear the motor clicking on and off or the sound of ice falling and the water supply filling back up.

3. Appliances emit a lot of heat; if they are in an enclosed cabinet, plan proper ventilation.

4. Determine which small appliances will need outlets and specify an adequate number of outlets and their locations. Appliances may include a coffeemaker, coffee bean grinder, juicer, blender, toaster, and toaster oven.

5. Identify what dishes, beverage ware, flatware, utensils, linens, trays, serving pieces, food, and so on you will store in the morning kitchen and plan adequate storage.

6. A dishwasher drawer (a separate drawer that lets you run a small load) is a luxury for the morning kitchen if you can afford it.

MUDROOM

A mudroom is usually the first room you encounter when you enter your home from the garage or side door. The materials used on the floor are selected to withstand wear and tear, and often the floor has a drain for easier cleaning. The mudroom also serves as an area for household members to organize what they need to take with them when they leave the house. If children live in the house, it is a great place to put backpacks to take to school the next day. You can have school-type lockers installed or cubbies made. If your home is located in an area with mud, snow, or sand, or you have young children who love to get dirty, a mudroom is perfect.

FORMS TO USE

Mudroom Checklist (page 192)

Individual Room and Closet Fact Sheet (page 81)

HOW TO AVOID COMMON MUDROOM MISTAKES

1. When designing the layout, plan pieces of furniture or a built-in counter on which to set down items you are carrying into your home, and a place to sit down to put on or take off shoes or boots.

2. If you live in a ski area and people will be coming in and out with ski equipment, plan a convenient way to store skis, ski boots, and other ski equipment. Include outlets for boot warmers.

3. If anyone in your home is a hunter, plan a temporary area, safely out of the reach of children, for guns to be placed after a hunt. This could be in a hunting closet or other area with a door that locks.

4. If anyone in your home fishes, plan a place for fishing poles, tackle box, waders, and other equipment to be put after a day of fishing.

5. Plan enough hooks for coats, jackets, hats, and scarves.

6. Avoid floor material that will show footprints and every speck of dirt.

7. If people will track in mud or snow, a drain in the floor will help keep the floors clean, and a faucet and hose can be used for hosing off the floor.

8. Make sure you have an area for a hanging mirror or fixed mirror to check your appearance before leaving.

9. Create an area in the mudroom to place clothes going to the dry cleaner.

TIP: Lockers or cubbies are a great tool for a family to stay organized. Designate one for each child as well as each parent.

NURSERY

One of the first decisions involving a nursery is whether this room will later become the baby's bedroom or another room. You'll want to consider the points on the Nursery Checklist when designing your nursery.

FORMS TO USE

Nursery Checklist (page 193)

Individual Room and Closet Fact Sheet (page 81)

HOW TO AVOID COMMON NURSERY MISTAKES

1. Create a furniture plan with ample wall space for all baby furniture and baby equipment. If you already own the baby furniture, photograph it, write the measurements on the back of the photo, and give this information to your architect at the beginning of the design process.

2. Tell your architect the types of equipment that will need an outlet and where they will be located.

3. Discuss future uses for the nursery with your architect, and identify any work that should be done during construction in preparation. For example, if the nursery will become a bedroom, you will want electric outlets on what will be the headboard wall and a light switch. If the nursery will become an office, you will want computer wiring and phone jacks.

4. Make sure a HVAC vent will not blow directly toward the baby's bed.

OFFICE

In today's world, it is not uncommon for all adults to need an individual home office. Do you want a small office off the kitchen or master bedroom? Do you want separate offices, or can you share one? Do you want a library in your home that will serve as an office for all? Do you want a library and multiple offices, or can the library double as an office for one of you?

FORMS TO USE

Office Checklist (page 194)

Individual Room and Closet Fact Sheet (page 81)

HOW TO AVOID COMMON OFFICE MISTAKES

1. If your desk will be in front of a window, consider what outsiders will see when looking in. Consider a longer desktop so that items such as computer monitors can be out of sight from outside. Another option is to raise the height of the windowsill.

2. Have an outlet easily accessible for your laptop computer power.

3. Identify where equipment requiring an outlet will be located, and confirm that the outlets are noted and in the proper location. In some cases, a surge protector strip can provide power to several pieces of equipment located in the same area.

4. Tell your architect your computer wiring needs.

5. Locate your office equipment so that the noise generated from office equipment, such as a fax machine and printer, does not disturb people in nearby rooms.

6. Decide if you need a floor outlet and discuss the location with your architect. (You will want this floor outlet connected to a light switch.)

7. Tell your architect if you need a phone jack and where you need it. (Any jack that may be used with a cordless phone base should have an outlet next to it.)

8. If you prefer not to see office equipment, store the equipment in a closet or a credenza. Allow proper ventilation for the heat generated by the equipment. Don't forget outlets.

TIP: Consider a bar-height desk as an alternative to the traditional-height desk. The bar height allows you to stand and work at your desk or sit on a bar stool, and allows more drawer space.

9. Identify the location of all desks and provide adequate lighting for all desks.

10. Too much glare or direct sunlight shining into your office will be distracting when working at your desk and will make it difficult to use a computer. Choose screens that block out the glare but still allow you to see out, or some other window treatment.

11. If your office is subject to the western sun, additional AC vents may be needed to keep the room cool.

12. Tell your architect if you need a window to look out while sitting at your desk.

13. If you plan to use a freestanding desk, give a photo or catalog picture with dimensions to your architect at the initial phase of the design process. Make sure the desk will fit through the hall and door leading to the office and that it will fit in the room.

14. For rugs, give a photo and dimensions (including fringe) to your architect at the initial phase of the design process.

15. Tell your architect how many letter- and legal-size hanging files you will need. Built-in drawers that can accommodate both letter- and legal-size hanging files work best.

PLAYROOM/GAME ROOM

When you hear the word "playroom," what vision comes to mind? A room to gather in with your children and their toys and games? Or a game room with a pool table and other games, a bar, and a big screen television? Discuss the various approaches to using this room with your architect, and determine what is right for you. Keep in mind that the playroom can begin as a room for young children and their toys and later be converted into a game room with toys for adults.

FORMS TO USE

Playroom/Game Room Checklist (page 196)
Individual Room and Closet Fact Sheet (page 81)

HOW TO AVOID COMMON PLAYROOM/ GAME ROOM MISTAKES

1. Have a powder room or bathroom on the same level as the playroom.

2. A furniture plan showing the exact measurements of game tables and furniture will help prevent chandeliers or pendant light fixtures from being wired off center.

3. Whatever game table you plan to install, find out the manufacturer's suggested total area required, and tell your architect.

4. A long narrow shelf along the wall near a game table is a perfect place for people to set drinks. This shelf can also be wide enough to set bar stools under it.

5. If the playroom/game room is located above or below the kitchen, consider a dumbwaiter from the kitchen to the playroom/game room.

POOL HOUSE

You can take several approaches when designing your pool house: open air, semi-enclosed structure, or totally enclosed. The size and shape of your property along with HOA and municipal codes will limit what you can ultimately build.

FORMS TO USE

Pool House Checklist (page 197)
Individual Room and Closet Fact Sheet (page 81)

HOW TO AVOID COMMON POOL HOUSE MISTAKES

1. Work out a detailed storage plan for typical pool items that will need storing, such as towels, rafts and floats, furniture cushions, and pool-cleaning equipment.

2. Include a bathroom in your pool house so wet swimmers don't need to walk inside the house to use the bathroom.

3. Have an outside and inside entrance for the bathroom. This will prevent wet bodies from tracking through the pool house to the bathroom.

PORCH, PATIO, DECK, AND BALCONY

Identify the number of porches, patios, decks, and balconies you would like in your new home, and where you want them located. Fill in forms for each porch, patio, deck and balcony, and identify the sheet by the name of the room it is attached to.

FORMS TO USE

Porch, Patio, Deck, and Balcony Checklist
(page 198)
Individual Room and Closet Fact Sheet (page 81)

HOW TO AVOID COMMON PORCH, PATIO, DECK, AND BALCONY MISTAKES

1. Every porch, patio area, deck, and balcony should have a faucet, to water plants and hose off the area.

2. Think about all outlet needs and the location of the outlets.

3. If your porch, deck, or balcony will have a curb, have adequate openings so that water and debris run off when you hose off the area.

4. If water on your porch, deck, or balcony will run off and disturb the area below, install a drain, with the top of the drain lower than the floor.

5. If you have children, grandchildren, or pets that you want to be able to prevent from leaving the porch or deck, have a gate that matches the railing.

6. Depending on the height of your porch, deck, or balcony, the municipality in which you are building will dictate if a railing is needed and the height of such railing.

7. If you use your porch, patio, deck, and balcony late in the afternoon, be aware of the angle the sun sets so you can position these areas to avoid too much direct sun or sun in your eyes.

8. Plan for a place to store the furniture cushions. Consider a built-in seated area that lifts up for storage.

9. If you will use propane heaters on the porch, find out the recommended height of the ceiling for the propane heater.

10. Consider ceiling-hung portable electrical heating systems in addition to or instead of using a standing propane heater.

11. If you will use a spray mist cooling fan, plan for a water source.

12. Plan dry firewood storage and ways to keep it from getting wet.

POWDER ROOM/HALF BATH

The size of your home, the number of levels, your budget, the number of children in your home, and the number of household staff will determine the number of powder rooms you will need. (The term powder room and half bath are used interchangeably.)

Preferably, each level of your house should have a powder room. If you have children, a less formal powder room near the family living area is a luxury, and if you have household staff, consider a powder room designated for them. If you want more than one powder room, create a fact sheet for each powder room.

FORMS TO USE

Powder Room/Half Bath Checklist (page 200)
Individual Room and Closet Fact Sheet (page 81)

HOW TO AVOID COMMON POWDER ROOM MISTAKES

1. Look at your house plans to see if you will view the toilet when the powder room door is left open. If so, a quick solution may be to hinge the door on the other side or flip the direction of the door swing.

2. Identify any decorative accessories in your powder room, such as a lamp or lighted magnifying mirror that will need an electrical outlet.

3. If you have a household staff or children, a second powder room will allow the formal powder room to be used only by guests.

4. If you entertain guests in your game or media room on a different level than your formal powder room, plan a third powder room convenient to the game or media room.

5. For a multilevel home, plan a bathroom or powder room on each level.

SAFE ROOM

The three most common reasons for a safe room today are safety from weather, from intruders, and from attack. Make sure your safe room meets FEMA residential specifications, which can be found on the FEMA website (www.fema.com). Among other things, you'll want the door to open outward, with three hinges mounted with three-inch screws and a

Important Items for Your Safe Room

- Breathing machines rated N95 or better
- Cell phone charger cord
- Duct tape
- Emergency first aid kit
- Flashlight, extra batteries
- Food for minimum of 72 hours
- Medicines needed for minimum of 72 hours
- Pillows, blankets, sleeping bags
- Portable radio, extra batteries
- Water for minimum of 72 hours

heavy duty strike plate that cuts deep into the door frame; solid core or steel doors; and reinforced sheeting in the walls or steel walls.

FORMS TO USE

Safe Room Checklist (page 201)

Individual Room and Closet Fact Sheet (page 81)

HOW TO AVOID COMMON SAFE ROOM MISTAKES

1. Hire a security consultant to advise you on the needs and specifications for your safe room.

2. Make sure your safe room meets FEMA specifications.

3. Locate the safe room in your basement or in the interior of your home on the first floor, in the center of your home for easy access. An exterior safe room should be close to the door you will exit.

4. Specify an outlet for cell phone battery charging.

5. Wire the room for a telephone landline.

6. The door to the safe room should open outward to prevent an intruder from kicking in the door.

7. The safe room should be large enough for the maximum number of people who are regularly in your house.

8. Discuss with your consultant, the architect, and the builder, the pros and cons of having a generator for the safe room.

TIP: Ask your insurance agent if you will receive a discount on your home insurance for having a safe room.

SPECIALTY ROOM

A specialty room is a room representing an activity and the equipment accompanying that activity, generally something for which you have a great passion. This room tends to be personal and the person whose passion is represented thinks of this room as "mine." A golfer may have a practice putting green. A fly fisherman might escape to this room to tie flies. A potter may have a potter's wheel and shelves exhibiting pottery.

FORMS TO USE

Specialty Room Checklist (page 202)

Individual Room and Closet Fact Sheet (page 81)

HOW TO AVOID COMMON SPECIALTY ROOM MISTAKES

1. Consider the nature of the specialty and determine the size and shape of the room based on those needs.

2. Besides giving the architect photos and dimensions of trophies or other items you want displayed in the specialty room, allow space for future items.

3. Because of the weight of some trophies, discuss with your architect and builder how to make sure the trophy will be secure when mounted.

WINE ROOM

Wine rooms come in all shapes and sizes and hold different quantities of wine. The checklist will help you clarify your vision.

FORMS TO USE

Wine Room Checklist (page 203)

Individual Room and Closet Fact Sheet (page 81)

HOW TO AVOID COMMON WINE ROOM MISTAKES

1. Realize that wine bottles are not uniform in size. Racks can be individual squares or individual diamond shapes with the bottle neck and cork sticking out. Another option for racks is large X-shapes with numerous bottles of wine fitting into one opening. Wine can be mounted sideways in a rack with the label showing.

2. Make plans for storing larger size wine bottles such as magnums.

3. If you serve wine or drinks in your wine room, a sink is important.

4. The wine room should have a separate lock and key from the home. Depending on how rare, expensive, or extensive your wine collection is, you will want the room secure. Consider a separate security code.

5. Many wine rooms are nothing but floor-to-ceiling and wall-to-wall wine racks. Allow space if you want to display personal items, such as corks, labels, books on collecting wine, and so on.

6. Make the area larger than you think you will need; a common complaint about wine rooms is that they do not hold enough bottles of wine.

7. To make sure furniture can be moved into the wine room, present a furniture plan during the design process, to make sure that your furniture will fit into the room. Entrances to some wine rooms are narrow and not always moving-friendly.

Tip: If you have an extensive and expensive wine collection, install a temperature rise sensor to alert you if the temperature or humidity in the wine room rises above a safe level that could spoil the wine. The proper temperature for wine is 55 to 75 degrees and the humidity needs to be less than 80 percent.

Apartment Area Checklist

Approximate size _____ One or two story? _____

Location in the home or will it be a detached dwelling? Explain. _____

If in the home, where in the home do you want the apartment area located? Explain. _____

_____

Circle the intended use of your apartment.

Rental property   Housing for guests   Housing for nanny   Housing for caretaker

Housing for elderly relative   Other _____

Circle the rooms you want in your apartment area.

Bedroom (how many?) 1 2 3   Bathroom (how many?) 1 2 3

Powder room   Living area   Dining area   Mini-kitchen   Full kitchen

Other rooms _____

Circle the appliances you want in your apartment area.

Washer/dryer (stackable or individual?)   Refrigerator/freezer combo   Individual refrigerator

Individual freezer   Range   Stove top   Oven   Microwave   Oven/microwave combination

Disposal   Trash compactor   Other _____

What are your apartment electrical outlet needs? List uses. _____

_____

Do you want any of the following?

YES   NO
❑   ❑   Separate security system
❑   ❑   Utilities metered separately from the main house
❑   ❑   Ability to lock apartment area off from the house
❑   ❑   Separate HVAC zone
❑   ❑   Built-ins*
❑   ❑   Ceiling fan*
❑   ❑   Computer wiring*
❑   ❑   Fireplace*
❑   ❑   Security alarm pad*
❑   ❑   Stereo equipment*
❑   ❑   Stereo speakers*
❑   ❑   Telephone jacks*
❑   ❑   Televisions*

*Fill in the relevant information on the corresponding Entire-Home Selections form in Chapter 12.

Attic Checklist

How will you use your attic? _____

How much attic space will you need? _____

Do you want your attic space over your garage, over your home, as many places as possible? _____

Do you want any of the following?

YES	NO	
❑	❑	More than one entrance to your attic—explain. _____
❑	❑	Closets within the attic area—if so, will they be climate controlled? _____
		Approximate dimensions of each closet_____
		What will you store in the attic closets? _____
❑	❑	Cedar-lined closets—if so, will they be climate controlled? _____
		Approximate dimensions of each closet_____
❑	❑	Rods for off-season clothing in your attic—if so, how many feet of hanging rods will you need? _____
❑	❑	Plastic bins for storage—if so, how many? _____ Dimensions of the storage bins? _____
❑	❑	Shelves for plastic bins or other items—if so, what will be the dimensions of each shelf and how many shelves? _____
❑	❑	Flooring added to your entire attic or to a particular area—if so, explain. _____
❑	❑	A three-way light switch in your attic (one switch in the attic, one switch at the bottom of the stairway). Explain. _____
❑	❑	Motorized ventilation system
❑	❑	HVAC system located in the attic
❑	❑	Vents in the soffits and ridge of the roof
❑	❑	Insulated tent installed over your fold-down stairway to prevent air from escaping
❑	❑	The option of turning your attic into living space in the future

What are your attic electrical outlet needs? List uses. _____

Is it important for you to enter your attic through a door, rather than a fold-down stairway, if you have a two-story home?

Explain. _____

How wide and long do you need your attic opening to be if using a fold-down staircase? _____

Will you need a heavy-duty fold-down stairway due to the weight of household occupants and the weight of items that will be stored in the attic? _____

Will you store any extra-heavy items in your attic that may require additional floor reinforcement? If so, what type of items?
_____

How much space in your attic will need to be illuminated by lights? _____

What kind of lighting fixtures do you want in your attic? _____

Will you use rolled, blown, or other type of insulation in the attic? _____

Bar Checklist

Approximate room size _____ Location in the home _____

How often will you use your bar? Explain. _____

Do you want a bar area you can stand in and serve from, or a walk-up counter against a wall? _____

Circle the shape of the bar counter you want.

Single straight counter   Two parallel counters   L-shaped counter   U-shaped counter   Counter on four sides

How many feet of counter space will you need? _____

What type of material do you want for your bar counter and splash? _____

Will your bar be a combination bar and room, complete with chairs, sofa, and fireplace as well as a bar and bar stools? Explain.

_____

How many bar stools do you want placed at your bar? _____

Do you want any of the following?

YES   NO
❏   ❏   Seating on both sides of a bar counter
❏   ❏   Wet bar—if so, hot and cold water or just cold water? _____
❏   ❏   Wine sink to chill wine, water bottles, soda cans and other beverages—if so, will it just be a sink with a drain or
                also have a faucet? _____

Circle how you want your sink mounted.

Below the counter   Self-rimming above the counter   Vessel sink on top of the counter

Do you want your faucet mounted into the counter or into the wall? _____

Circle the appliances you will use in your bar.

Mini-refrigerator   Wine chiller   Ice maker   Refrigerator drawer   Glass washer   Dishwasher drawer

Built-in blender   Built-in professional coffeemaker   Disposal   Hot water dispenser

Other _____

Will you apply fronts to your appliances to match your cabinets or will you have stainless, black, or other colored appliance

fronts? Explain. _____

What type material and finish will you have on your cabinets? Wood, stainless, or other? Explain.

_____

Circle the small appliances that you will operate in your bar.

Blender   Coffeemaker   Juicer   Frozen drink machine   Other _____

Will you use a portable margarita or daiquiri machine or have one built into your bar? Explain. _____

What are your bar electrical outlet needs? List uses. _____

Do you want upper and lower cabinets or just lower cabinets? Explain. _____

If you want lower cabinets, how many drawers do you want? _____

Do you want any of the following?

YES   NO
❏   ❏   Glass fronts on any of the cabinet doors—explain. _____
❏   ❏   Lighting underneath the upper cabinets
❏   ❏   Lighting inside the cabinets, if having glass on the cabinet doors
❏   ❏   Toe kick illuminated
❏   ❏   Built-in trash can in your bar (see Under-Cabinet Trash Storage, page 90)
❏   ❏   Self-closing drawer runners

Do you want your upper cabinets to go to the ceiling, go to a furdown, or have an open shelf? Explain.

_____

If an open shelf, do you want lighting above the upper cabinets? _____

Will you store glasses inside a cabinet, in a drawer, or on an open shelf? Will stemware hang from a rack above the counter?

Explain. _____

Circle how you will store your hard liquor.

On the counter   On an open shelf   In a drawer behind a cabinet door   In a cabinet above the counter

Other _____

Circle how you plan to store your wine bottles. (See Wine Storage Options, page 91.)

In a wine chiller   In a vertical line in the upper cabinet   In a horizontal line in the upper cabinets

In a horizontal line in the island   In a vertical line in the cabinets below the counter   In a drawer

Behind a cabinet door above the counter   Behind a cabinet door below the counter

Other _____

How many bottles of wine will you store? _____

Do you have any of the following?

YES   NO
❏   ❏   Wine decanter that will need a custom location
❏   ❏   Wine opener needing special mounting or installation
❏   ❏   Magnums or other large size bottles to display in your bar—if so, how many? _____ What are the dimensions
              of the bottles? _____

YES	NO	
❑	❑	Collectibles you want to display in your bar, such as miniature bottles, sports team memorabilia, and so on—explain _____
❑	❑	Ceiling fan*
❑	❑	Computer wiring*
❑	❑	Fireplace*
❑	❑	Stereo speakers*
❑	❑	Telephone jacks*
❑	❑	Televisions*

*Fill in the relevant information on the corresponding Entire-Home Selections form in Chapter 12.

Basement Checklist

Circle the intended use(s) of your basement.

Unfinished storage area   Playroom   Media room   Another finished-out level in the house

Other _____

Would you like to reach the basement from inside your home or will you have an exterior door? Explain.

_____

Is the land on which you plan to build a slope, allowing windows, or will the basement be entirely underground? Explain.

_____

Do you have plans to finish out the basement? Explain. _____

If used for storage:

Will you have one large open area or smaller areas with closets? Explain your vision.

_____

Will the walls, ceiling, and floors be finished out? _____

Will you have a cedar closet, gun closet, gun safe, or other type storage? _____

If finished out as another level in your home:

What rooms do you want in your basement? List. _____

What closets do you want in your basement? List. _____

If future plans call for finishing it out:

What preliminary plumbing and electrical work do you want done? Explain. _____

What are your basement electrical outlet needs? List uses.

_____

_____

Bathroom Checklist

Which bathroom does this checklist represent? _____

Approximate room size _____ Location in the home _____

How many people will share this bathroom? _____ If a master bathroom, do you want to share it with your partner or do you

want two completely separate bathrooms? _____

If separate master bathrooms, do you want to share a shower, tub, water closet, or linen closet? Explain.

_____

Vanity

Circle the combination you want in this bathroom.

One vanity/one sink   One vanity/two sinks   Two separate vanities with one sink each

Do you want a standard vanity counter or one that looks like a piece of furniture? _____

What height and length do you want this vanity counter? _____

What material will you use for this vanity counter? _____

Do you want any of the following?

YES	NO	
❏	❏	Seated makeup area—if so, a standard chair height or a bar stool height? _____
❏	❏	Separate vanity for seated makeup area
❏	❏	Natural light for this seated makeup area
❏	❏	Cabinets above the vanity counter (see Cabinets Above Vanity Counter, page 93)
❏	❏	Drawers or cabinet doors in the lower cabinets—if so, which? _____
❏	❏	Drawer below the cabinets under the sink (see Drawers Underneath Cabinet Doors, page 93)
❏	❏	Self-closing drawer runners
❏	❏	Tilt drawer under the sink
❏	❏	Outlet in drawer for hair dryer
❏	❏	Pull-out trash can built into the vanity (See Under-Cabinet Trash Storage, page 90)
❏	❏	Decorative freestanding trash can
❏	❏	Wall-mounted magnifying mirror—if so, will it be a lighted mirror? _____

Do you want drawers on both sides of the kneehole for makeup area or on just one side? _____

Do you want a combination of drawers and cabinet doors below your counter or mostly drawers? _____

Use the Bathroom Storage Item Checklist (page 140) to assist you in determining your drawer and cabinet needs.

Will you have a fixed mirror above the vanity or a decorative hanging mirror? _____ If a fixed mirror, do you want it

framed with stone, tile, wood, or other type of framing? _____

Will you want your electrical outlets mounted in the splash, on the mirror, or on the wall in this bathroom? Explain.

_____

(Depending on the bathroom layout and for a medicine cabinet, the splash or mirror may be your only options.)

What are your vanity counter outlet needs? List uses.

_____

_____

_____

Drawers you may want: **nail** (manicure and pedicure products), **hair accessory** (clips, ponytail holders, headbands), **electric hair products** (hair dryer, electric rollers, flattening iron), **female products, tooth care products, hair color products, hair products** (shampoo, conditioner, hair spray), **makeup, first aid products, lotions and sunscreen products,** and **miscellaneous items.**

Sink/Faucet

Circle your preference for this bathroom sink.

Under-mounted   Self-rimming   Counter vessel   Pedestal   Prefabricated counter with sink a part of the counter

What size, shape, depth, and color sink do you want? _____

Do you want any of the following?

YES   NO
❏   ❏   Soap pump dispenser at this sink
❏   ❏   Hot water dispenser at this sink
❏   ❏   Water purifier

Do you want the faucet in this bathroom mounted in the counter or in the wall? _____

Do you want a one-lever faucet that controls temperature and flow of water or do you want a faucet with two separate

controls for the temperature and flow of water? _____

Shower/Tub

Approximate size of bathroom shower? _____

Do you want any of the following?

YES   NO
❏   ❏   Shower
❏   ❏   Tub
❏   ❏   Shower/tub combination

YES NO

❑   ❑   Tile pieces going all the way to the ceiling and covering the ceiling—if so, explain.

_____

❑   ❑   Tile pieces only going partially up the wall
❑   ❑   Bench—if so, shape and size of the bench? _____

Do you want to use a piece of slab on the bench and bench skirt or stone/tile pieces? _____

❑   ❑   Steam shower—if so, one head or two? _____
❑   ❑   Jetted sprays on this shower walls—if so, how many and height of each?_____
❑   ❑   Heated towel bar—if so, will it be electric heated, water heated, or a radiator-type heater?

_____

❑   ❑   Towel-warming drawer
❑   ❑   Radiant heat on this bathroom floor, shower walls, shower floor, bench, bathtub deck, or other. List.

_____

❑   ❑   Fogless mirror in this shower
❑   ❑   Waterproof speakers or a waterproof radio _____
❑   ❑   Shower shelves built into the wall or attachable fixtures—if so, what dimensions and how many?

_____

❑   ❑   Grab bars
❑   ❑   Drying off area between this shower and this bathroom
❑   ❑   Specialty tub—if so, circle the type: Infinity   Soaking   Jetted   Mood lighting   Other _____
❑   ❑   Handheld sprayer for this tub
❑   ❑   Window by this tub
❑   ❑   Indented area along the tub deck wall to hold a tier rack of candles.

Will you use a prefabricated shower or use granite, marble, travertine, quartz, other tile pieces, or glass for the walls? _____

If using stone, will it be honed or tumbled? _____

Will the showerhead be wall mounted, ceiling mounted, or mounted as a handheld? Will you have a handheld along with a

wall- or ceiling-mounted showerhead? _____

What height do you want the actual showerhead? _____

What height do you want the handheld showerhead mounted at? _____

Do you want the shower walls to be glass, stone, or glass and stone combination? Explain.

_____

Do you want this tub in a tub deck or freestanding? _____ If in a tub deck, will it be under mounted or

self-rimming? _____ (See Bathtub Mount Options, page 95.)

Will there be a step beside the tub deck? What material do you want for this tub deck and tub skirt? Explain.

_____

Does the direction this tub faces matter to you? _____

What size and shape tub do you want? _____

Will this tub faucet be deck mounted, wall mounted, or floor mounted? _____

Do you want the tub area cantilevering out from the home? _____

Do you want a single faucet and handle that controls water flow and temperature, or do you prefer two knobs to control flow

and temperature? _____

Circle the type of tub drain you want.

Fixed strainer   Up-and-down lever to strainer

Turn knob on strainer? _____

Shower Door/Curtain

Circle the type shower door you want in this bathroom.

Sliding door   Swinging door   Shower curtain

Circle your shower door preference.

Clear glass   Frosted glass   Glass with etching   Other _____

Do you want this shower door to swing 180 degrees, both inside and outside the shower, or do you prefer

a sliding shower door? Explain. _____

How many shower door hinges will you use? _____ (The size and weight of the shower door are factors.)

Do you want your shower door large enough to accommodate a wheelchair? _____

Water Closet/Toilet

Do you want any of the following?

YES	NO	
❑	❑	Water closet or portioned wall to hide the toilet. If portioned wall, would it be a short wall or go to the ceiling?
❑	❑	Bidet and urinal
❑	❑	Window in this water closet or by the toilet if no water closet
❑	❑	Taller toilet seat
❑	❑	Padded toilet seat
❑	❑	Heated toilet seat
❑	❑	Quiet-close toilet seat
❑	❑	Recessed magazine rack near this toilet
❑	❑	Recessed toilet paper holder

YES   NO
❏   ❏   Wall-mounted telephone
❏   ❏   Ledge behind the toilet (see page 96)
❏   ❏   Storage cabinet above the toilet

Linen Closet

Circle how you plan to store your towels.

Linen closet   Rolled up in a basket   Rolled up on wall-mounted hanger   Rolled up in a cubbyhole

Hanging on a towel bar   Folded on open shelves   Folded in a drawer   Other _____

Will the linen closet have adjustable shelves? _____ If not, what distance do you want between shelves? _____

What height do you want the first shelf from the floor? _____

What distance do you want between the top shelf and the ceiling? _____

Will you store your dirty clothes in the linen closet? _____ If so, in a laundry basket, in a store-bought hamper, or a custom-

built area within your linen closet? Explain. _____

Medicine Cabinet

Do you want a medicine cabinet? _____

If so, do you want a prefabricated or custom-built medicine cabinet? _____

Where do you want it located? Side wall next to sink, wall in front of sink, other? _____

If you have two sinks in this bathroom, do you want two medicine cabinets? _____

Do you want an electrical outlet in the medicine cabinet for charging a toothbrush or razor? _____

Do you want to be able to lock this medicine cabinet? _____

Miscellaneous

Do you want any of the following?

YES   NO
❏   ❏   Hidden towel bar hook to hang damp towels to dry
❏   ❏   Massage table—if so, would you need a place to store a massage table? _____
❏   ❏   Ballet bar area off this bathroom—if so, how large an area? _____
❏   ❏   Scale in this bathroom
❏   ❏   Shampoo bowl in this bathroom—if so, would you want it in a closet part of the vanity counter? _____
                 Will you need to store the shampoo chair or would you leave it out? _____

138

YES	NO	
❑	❑	Manicure table and chair in your bathroom area that will need to be stored
❑	❑	Exterior door to this bathroom
❑	❑	Exterior shower off this bathroom
❑	❑	Appliances in your bathroom such as mini-refrigerator
❑	❑	Area rug or bath mat to use in this bathroom—if so, keep in mind the standard measurements for rugs unless they are custom made. Also make sure any door near the rug will be able to clear it.
❑	❑	Wainscoting in your bathroom—if so, will the material be stone or tile? _____
❑	❑	Ceiling fan*
❑	❑	Computer wiring*
❑	❑	Fireplace*
❑	❑	Stereo equipment*
❑	❑	Stereo speakers*
❑	❑	Telephone jacks*
❑	❑	Televisions*

*Fill in the relevant information on the corresponding Entire-Home Selections form in Chapter 12.

What material will you use for your bathroom baseboards?_____

What design and what height? _____ (If you have a stone floor in your bathroom, a matching stone baseboard is a nice complement.)

Do you want any of the following?

YES	NO	
❑	❑	Mirrored walls—if so, any etching on the mirror? _____
❑	❑	Floor-to-ceiling mirror in either this bathroom or closet
❑	❑	Mirror with three sides that lets you see your back

Stone

If this bathroom will have stone counters, what will be the thickness and design of the edge?

_____

What height will the backsplash be behind the sink and the tub? _____

Will it be made of the same material as the tub deck? _____

Will there be a decorative detail on the top edge? _____

Bathroom Storage Item Checklist

Number of Towels

Fill in the number of each type towel you will be storing.

_____ Bath sheets   _____ Hand towels

_____ Bath mats   _____ Washcloths

_____ Bath towels   _____ Other _____

_____ Beach towels

What items do you plan to place on top of your bathroom counter? _____

_____

Do any of these items require electrical outlets? List. _____

Makeup

Will you store your makeup in a drawer, on the counter, or other? Explain. _____

_____

Hair Items

Place a check in the appropriate column to indicate where you will be storing these items.

Item	Drawer	Closet	Linen Closet	Medicine Cabinet
Bobby pins				
Comb				
Conditioners				
Curling iron				
Hair brush				
Hair clips				
Hair color				
Hair color tools				
Hair dryer				
Hair rollers				

Item	Drawer	Closet	Linen Closet	Medicine Cabinet
Hair spray				
Headbands				
Heated rollers				
Ponytail holders				
Shampoo				
Shower cap				
Straightening iron				
Styling serums				
Other _____				
Other _____				

Will you want an electrical outlet in a drawer for a hair dryer? _____

Lotions

Will you store your lotions on the counter, in a cabinet, or in a drawer? _____
If in a drawer, measure bottles and make sure the inside of the drawer is tall enough.

Medicine/First Aid

Will you have a medicine cabinet to store medicine and first-aid items, or will you store those items on a shelf or in a drawer?

Explain. _____

Do you want a lock on the medicine cabinet, cabinet, or drawer? Explain. _____

_____

Miscellaneous Items

Place a check in the appropriate column to indicate where you will be storing these items.

Item	Drawer	Closet	Linen Closet	Medicine Cabinet
Cleaning items				
Contact lens products				
Cotton balls				
Electric razor				
Electric toothbrush				
Female products				
Heating pad				
Hot water bottle				
Ice packs				
Nail care products				
Perfume				
Shave kit				
Shaving products				
Shoe cleaning supplies				
Sunscreens				
Swabs				
Tissue				
Toilet paper				
Travel makeup bags				
Other _____				
Other _____				

Bedroom Checklist

Which bedroom _____

Approximate room size _____ Location in the home _____

Size of bed? _____ Number of beds? _____ Number of occupants in this bedroom? _____

If a couple, on which side of the bed does each prefer to sleep? _____

If a couple, which person prefers to be closest to the bathroom door? _____

Do you prefer the headboard wall to have windows or be a solid wall? _____

Will you have oversized bedside tables? If so, what are the dimensions? _____

Do you want recessed can lights for reading over the headboard? If so, how many? _____

Circle how you will store your television.

Flat screen wall-mounted   Drop down from ceiling screen   Inside an armoire   Pop up out of furniture

Corner wall-mounted   Freestanding stand   Bookcase shelf   On top of a piece of furniture   Other_____

What are your bedroom electrical outlet needs? List uses. _____

_____

Do you want any of the following?

YES NO
❏   ❏   Sitting area—if so, list the furniture you want in that seating area.
_____
_____

❏   ❏   Area for a baby crib
❏   ❏   To mount a canopy or crown over the headboard
❏   ❏   Built-ins*
❏   ❏   Ceiling fan*
❏   ❏   Computer wiring*
❏   ❏   Fireplace*
❏   ❏   Security alarm pad*
❏   ❏   Integrated Home Automation Monitor *
❏   ❏   Stereo equipment*
❏   ❏   Stereo speakers*
❏   ❏   Telephone jacks*
❏   ❏   Televisions*
❏   ❏   Balcony, porch, or patio off this bedroom—if so, which? _____
❏   ❏   Open area for yoga, stretching, sit-ups—if so, how large an area? _____

*Fill in the relevant information on the corresponding Entire-Home Selections form in Chapter 12.

Bedroom Closet Checklist

Fill out this checklist for each bedroom closet, noting whose bedroom this closet is in. (See Appendix 2, pages 354–355, for some standard closet measurements.)

Person using closet _____ Room_____

Check the type of closet
- ❑ Man's closet
- ❑ Woman's closet
- ❑ Man's and woman's closet combined
- ❑ Child's closet

Personal female data: Height _____ Weight _____ Shoe size _____ Dress size _____ Pant size _____ Coat size _____

Circle: Petite   Regular   Tall   Left-handed   Right-handed

Personal male data: Height _____ Weight _____ Shoe size _____ Shirt size _____ Pant size _____ Coat size _____

Circle: Regular   Tall   Left-handed   Right-handed

Do you want to enter this closet from the bathroom, bedroom, or both? _____

Preferred closet ceiling height? _____

Do you want a single door or double doors to enter this closet? _____

Will you use a closet consultant? _____ If so, will the consultant build and install the closet? _____

Will your closet be designed by your architect and built by your builder's carpenter? _____

Do you want any of the following?

YES	NO	
❑	❑	This closet on a separate alarm system from the house
❑	❑	This closet door to lock—if so, key in knob, dead bolt, or other? _____
❑	❑	Safe in your closet—if so, built into the floor or wall, or freestanding? _____
		Approximate size of safe_____
❑	❑	Window
❑	❑	Skylight
❑	❑	Hidden closet off your closet—if so, how large? _____
❑	❑	Cedar closet within your closet—if so, how large? _____
❑	❑	Open closet rods of clothing
❑	❑	Closet rods built into an area behind cabinet doors
❑	❑	Double and single tier hanging rods
❑	❑	Open shelves—if so, how many?_____ Length and depth? _____
❑	❑	Shelves to be located behind cabinet doors—if so, how many? _____
❑	❑	Adjustable shelves
❑	❑	Bank of drawers—if so, how many drawers? _____ (Number and size of the drawers will be determined by the information you fill in on the attached pages.)

YES	NO	
❑	❑	The top couple of drawers to be able to lock
❑	❑	Counter above a bank of drawers where you can place your purse or wallet, charge your cell phone, camera battery, and so on
❑	❑	Island
❑	❑	Peninsula
❑	❑	Area to pack a suitcase on the island or peninsula
❑	❑	Seated area built into the island or peninsula or other area
❑	❑	Three-way folding mirror in your closet
❑	❑	Stackable washer and dryer in your closet
❑	❑	Fold-down ironing board
❑	❑	Motorized hanging system as used at dry cleaners
❑	❑	Second floor above your closet to store off-season clothing
❑	❑	Pull-down seasonal clothing closet rod system that allows you to store one closet rod above the other
❑	❑	Motion sensor that turns lights on and off as you enter your closet
❑	❑	Ladder attached to a rail to reach the upper shelves and cabinets
❑	❑	Furniture in your closet—if so, list. _____
❑	❑	Trash can built into the island, peninsula, or other area in your closet
❑	❑	Custom-built place for empty hangers to be stored
❑	❑	Ceiling fan*
❑	❑	Computer wiring*
❑	❑	Fireplace*
❑	❑	Stereo speakers*
❑	❑	Telephone jacks*
❑	❑	Televisions*

*Fill in the relevant information on the corresponding Entire-Home Selections form in Chapter 12.

What are your closet electrical outlet needs? List uses. _____

_____

Will you store your luggage in your closet? If so, please provide a photo of the entire collection you want to store with some

dimensions. _____

Do you prefer drawer hardware or a drawer front with half moon cut out to use to open? Discuss.

_____

Do you have a shoe shine, steamer, or pant press machine that needs an outlet? If so, where in your closet do you want these

located? _____

Do you currently use and want to continue to use any special storage mechanisms for hats, gloves, purses, shoes, jewelry, scarves, belts, ties, and so forth? If so, please describe and provide a photo with dimensions.

_____

Do you plan to store shoes, sweaters, hats or other items in boxes? If so, count the boxes, take measurements of the boxes, and

list here. _____

_____

Dirty Clothes

How and where do you want to store dirty clothes? Built-in holder, laundry basket, freestanding dirty clothes hampers, other?

_____

Do you want to be able to separate hand wash, machine wash, and dry cleaning?_____

Do you want to be able to separate colors for machine washing? _____

Any special needs or information not covered:

_____

_____

Circle those items you wish to store in your closet.

Ski clothes   Hunting clothes   Fishing clothes   Winter coats   Luggage   Cameras

Hunting shoes/boots   Ski boots/helmet   Waders   Other _____

Women's Clothing

Fill in the quantity for each item. Mark whether you want it stored in a drawer, on a shelf, or on a hanger. For those items to be stored on a hanger, write in the number of feet of hanging rod space needed per item (see Clothing and Closets in Appendix 2, page 354–355) and check off whether they will be hanging folded or unfolded.

Item	Quantity	Drawer	Shelf	On a Hanger	Length of Hanging Rod Space	Hanging on Hanger	Folded on Hanger
Athletic socks							
Blazers							
Bras							
Casual pants							
Casual socks							
Cocktail dresses							

Item	Quantity	Drawer	Shelf	On a Hanger	Length of Hanging Rod Space	Hanging on Hanger	Folded on Hanger
Dress pants							
Dress suits							
Dress T-shirts							
Dressy long-sleeved blouses							
Evening gowns							
Fur coats							
Gym shorts							
Hiking socks							
Hosiery							
Hunting clothing							
Hunting socks							
Jeans							
Lightweight jackets							
Long-sleeved workout T-shirts							
Long underwear							
Pajamas							
Panties							
Pantsuits							
Panty hose							
Rain, wind jackets							
Short-sleeved casual blouses							
Short-sleeved workout T-shirts							
Shorts							
Ski clothing							
Ski socks							
Slips							
Sweaters							
Sweatshirts							
Tennis/golf shorts							
Turtlenecks							
Winter jackets							
Winter long coats							
Other _____							

Fill in the approximate number of each.

_____ Casual boots	_____ Hiking boots
_____ Casual shoes	_____ Hunting boots
_____ Cowboy boots	_____ Sandals
_____ Flat dress shoes	_____ Short dressy boots
_____ Flip-flops	_____ Slippers
_____ Golf shoes	_____ Tall boots
_____ High-heeled shoes	_____ Workout shoes

_____ Other _____

How would you like to store your shoes: in the original shoe box on a flat shelf, in a plastic shoe box on a shelf, in a drawer with a glass front, on a pull-out shelf, on a slanted board underneath hanging clothes, or other? Explain.

_____

_____

Women's Accessories

Fill in the approximate number of each.

_____ Casual belts	_____ Scarves
_____ Dress belts	_____ Shawls
_____ Handbags	_____ Winter scarves
_____ Handkerchiefs	_____ Other _____

How do you store each of the above items? Drawers, boxes, plastic tubs?

_____

Will hair accessories such as headbands, rubber bands, and barrettes be stored in your closet or in your bathroom?

_____

Men's Clothing

Fill in the quantity for each item. Mark whether you it stored in a drawer, on a shelf, or on a hanger. For those items to be stored on a hanger, write in the number of feet of hanging rod space needed per item (see Clothing and Closets in Appendix 2, pages 354–355) and check off whether they will be hanging folded or unfolded.

Item	Quantity	Drawer	Shelf	On a Hanger	Length of Hanging Rod Space	Hanging on Hanger	Folded on Hanger
Athletic socks							
Casual pants							
Casual T-shirts							
Dress pants							
Dress shirts							
Dress socks							
Dress T-shirts							
Gym shorts							
Hiking socks							
Hunting clothing							
Hunting socks							
Jeans							
Lightweight jackets							
Long johns							
Long-sleeved casual shirts							
Long-sleeved workout T-shirts							
Pajamas							
Rain, wind jackets							
Short-sleeved casual shirts							
Short-sleeved workout T-shirts							
Shorts							
Ski clothing							
Ski socks							
Sport coats							
Suits							
Sweaters							
Sweatshirts							
Tennis/golf shorts							
Turtlenecks							
Underwear							
Winter jackets							
Winter long coats							
Other _____							

Men's Shoes

How do you prefer to store your shoes? _____

Fill in the approximate number of each.

____ Casual boots   ____ Golf shoes

____ Casual shoes   ____ Hiking shoes

____ Cowboy boots   ____ Hunting boots

____ Cross-training shoes   ____ Rubber boots

____ Dress boots   ____ Running shoes

____ Dress shoes   ____ Slippers

____ Flip-flops   ____ Tennis shoes

____ Other _____

How would you like to store your shoes: in the original shoe box on a flat shelf, in a plastic shoe box on a shelf, in a drawer with a glass front, on a pull-out shelf, on a slanted board underneath hanging clothes, or other?

_____

_____

Men's Accessories

Fill in the approximate number of each.

____ Ascots   ____ Dress belts

____ Bow ties   ____ Handkerchiefs

____ Casual belts   ____ Jewelry/watches

____ Cummerbunds/tux ties   ____ Pocket squares

____ Other _____

How do you plan to store these accessory items? In a drawer, plastic box, or tub? _____

Storage for Hats, Gloves, and Glasses/Goggles (Women's or Men's)

Hats

Fill in the approximate number of each.

_____ Baseball caps   _____ Ski hats

_____ Cowboy hats   _____ Other _____

_____ Dress hats

How do you plan to store the above items? In original boxes, on a shelf, in a plastic box? _____

Gloves

Fill in the approximate number of each.

_____ Casual gloves   _____ Ski gloves

_____ Dress gloves   _____ Other _____

_____ Hunting gloves

How do you plan to store the above items? In original boxes, on a shelf, in a plastic box? _____

Glasses/Goggles

Fill in the approximate number of each.

_____ Hunting glasses   _____ Ski goggles

_____ Motorcycle goggles   _____ Sunglasses

_____ Prescription glasses   _____ Other _____

How do you plan to store the above items? In original boxes, on a shelf, in a plastic box? _____

Any special needs or information not covered:

_____

_____

_____

_____

_____

Breakfast Room Checklist

Approximate room size _____ Location in the house _____

Do you want a separate room for your breakfast room or an open area as part of the kitchen?

_____

Do you want a table and chairs or a banquette? _____ If a banquette, do you want

two parallel benches, a U-shaped bench, a straight bench on one side of the table and chairs on the other, an L-shaped bench,

or a semicircular bench? _____

Do you want storage under your banquette bench? _____ If so, do you want a lift-up seat, drawers, or cabinet doors?

_____

Do you want part of the banquette under a window? _____

What shape of table do you want for your breakfast room? _____

How many people do you want to seat? _____

What are your breakfast room electrical outlet needs? List uses.

_____

_____

_____

_____

Do you want any of the following?

YES NO
❑   ❑   Built-ins*
❑   ❑   Fireplace*
❑   ❑   Stereo speakers*
❑   ❑   Telephone jacks*

*Fill in the relevant information on the corresponding Entire-Home Selections form in Chapter 12.

Butler's Pantry Checklist

Approximate room size _____ Location in the house _____

Will you use your butler's pantry for storing silver, china, crystal, and entertaining pieces, or will it be a work area to use when entertaining in the dining room or both? Explain.

_____

_____

Will the butler's panty be a separate room or a hallway with counters on one side or both sides? Explain.

_____

Will you have upper and lower cabinets? _____ If having upper cabinets, do you want glass on your cabinet doors? _____

If so, do you want the interior of the cabinet illuminated? _____

Will the upper cabinets go to the ceiling or the furdown, or have an open area between the top of the cabinet and the ceiling?

Explain. _____

If you have an open area, what height do you want the space between the top of the cabinet and the ceiling? _____

Do you want that area illuminated? _____

Do you want any of the following?

YES   NO
❑   ❑   Lights underneath the upper cabinets
❑   ❑   Vertical tray storage area
❑   ❑   Area for large bulky size serving pieces
❑   ❑   Silver closet—if so, do you want a lock on the door? _____
❑   ❑   Silver cloth lined drawers—if so, do you want a lock on the drawer? _____
❑   ❑   Sink—if so, what size? _____

Circle any appliances you will want in your butler's pantry.

Warming drawer   Oven   Dishwasher   Wine chiller   Ice maker   Other _____

Will the butler's pantry also serve as a bar? _____

What are your butler's pantry electrical outlet needs? List uses.

_____

_____

What type of material will you want for your counter? Explain. _____

Will you want your butler's pantry counter to have extra depth? _____ If so, discuss with your architect and builder how the extra depth will affect appliances.

If having upper cabinets over the counter, do you want extra distance between the counter and the bottom of the upper cabinet to accommodate taller items such as a large coffeemaker, decorative items you will place on the counter, and so on?

Explain. _____

Circle any that you will use that will use an electric outlet in your butler's pantry.

Coffeemaker   Espresso maker   Blender   Crepe maker   Other _____

Do you want any of the following?

YES	NO	
❑	❑	Ceiling fan*
❑	❑	Computer wiring*
❑	❑	Stereo speakers*
❑	❑	Telephone jacks*

*Fill in the relevant information on the corresponding Entire-Home Selections form in Chapter 12.

Control Room Checklist

Approximate room size _____ Location in the house _____

Exterior door _____

Will your control room have a dual function and also serve as a safe room? _____

What systems will be installed in your control room? Circle.

Air purifier   Audio controls   Gas log fireplace controls   HVAC controls   Lighting system

Radiant heated floor and surface controls   Security controls   Motorized window controls

Other _____

What are your control room electrical outlet needs? List uses.

_____

_____

Type of system _____ System name _____

Basic system specifications _____

Are you attaching a specification sheet for this system? _____

Type of system _____ System name _____

Basic system specifications _____

Are you attaching a specification sheet for this system? _____

Type of system _____ System name _____

Basic system specifications _____

Are you attaching a specification sheet for this system? _____

Dining Room Checklist

Approximate room size _____ Location in the house _____

Do you want any of the following?

YES   NO
❑   ❑   Square room
❑   ❑   Rectangular shaped room

Do you want a formal or informal dining room? _____

Do you want a dining room/breakfast room combination? _____

Do you want your dining room to be an open area or in a separate room? _____

Do you prefer your dining room to be located in the front, side, or back of your house? _____

What shape of dining room table(s) do you plan to use? _____

How many people do you plan to seat at your dining room on a daily basis? _____

How many people do you plan to seat when table leafs are in place? _____

How many chairs do you want to place away from the table and around the wall in your dining room? _____

Will you use a sideboard? _____ If so, will it be located at the long end of the table or to the side of the center of

the table? _____ Just one or one at each end or side? _____

Will you have art, a portrait, mirror, or other to hang in this room? _____

Do you have a rug for this room? _____ If so, measure the dimensions including any fringe and include those on the
room fact sheet.

Do you want the ability to close off the dining room through pocket doors, French doors, or other type doors?

_____

What are your dining room electrical outlet needs? List uses.

_____

Do you want any of the following?

YES   NO
❑   ❑   Built-ins*
❑   ❑   Ceiling fan*
❑   ❑   Fireplace*
❑   ❑   Stereo speakers*
❑   ❑   Telephone jacks*

*Fill in the relevant information on the corresponding Entire-Home Selections form in Chapter 12.

Driveway Checklist

Circle the type of driveway you want.

Circular with two entrances from the street   Circular with one entrance from the street

Noncircular with one entrance from the street   Turnaround area of the driveway   Other _____

Do you want a single-car or double-car width driveway? _____

What type of driveway material do you prefer? Asphalt, concrete, washed rock, pavers, pebbles, other? Explain.

_____

Do you want lampposts or other lighting along the driveway? If so, explain. _____

On average, how many vehicles will be parked at your home during the day? _____ Overnight? _____

Number of parking spots at the front of the house _____ On the side of the house _____ Near the garage _____

Is there a hazard along your driveway that will need a curb or guard rail? If so, what type of safety barrier do you want? Explain.

_____

If you have an apartment on your property, where do you want the occupants to park?

_____

Do you own a boat, camper, bus, hunting vehicle, trailer, or other vehicle that will need to be parked on your property?
List and explain your plans.

_____

Do you want a porte cochere? _____ If so, will it be located at the front of the home or side? _____

Would it be wide enough for one or two cars? _____

Do you want any of the following?

YES	NO	
❑	❑	Electronic gate at driveway
❑	❑	Electronic foot traffic gate
❑	❑	Special parking needed for household staff
❑	❑	Mailbox at the street, if not, where? _____

Entry Foyer Checklist

Approximate room size _____ Location in the house _____

What rooms would you like connected to your entry foyer? List.

_____

Will your entry foyer be square, rectangular, circular, or another shape? _____

Will your entry foyer be located in the center of your home or at one end? _____

Will your entry foyer run toward the back of your home or side-to-side? _____

Do you want a single or double front door? _____

What are your entry foyer electrical outlet needs? List uses.

_____

Do you want any of the following?

YES	NO	
❑	❑	Staircase in the entry foyer
❑	❑	Screen door
❑	❑	Coat closet—if so, how many? _____ What size(s)? do you want? Explain.

_____

❑	❑	Jamb switch on the coat closet door
❑	❑	Fireplace*
❑	❑	Security alarm pad*
❑	❑	Stereo speakers*
❑	❑	Telephone jacks*

*Fill in the relevant information on the corresponding Entire-Home Selections form in Chapter 12.

Exercise Room Checklist

Approximate room size _____ Location in the house _____

Circle the pieces of equipment you will use.

Treadmill   Elliptical trainer   StepMill   FreeClimber   Bicycle   Other _____

List weight machine equipment. _____

Will you have free weights? _____ If so, how many total pounds? _____ Number of racks and rack dimensions?

_____

Circle any type of equipment you want in your exercise room.

Pilates   Workout bench   Workout seat   Padded exercise mat (how large?) _____   Other _____

Circle any wall-mounted equipment you will use.

Ballet bar (how long?) _____   Chin-up bar   Punching bag   Other _____

Will you want to be able to jump rope in this room? _____

Circle any small equipment you will need stored.

Medicine ball   Stability ball   Jump rope   Tubes   Balancing board   Other _____

Do you want mirrors on the wall? _____ Which walls? _____

What are your exercise room outlet needs? List uses.

_____

_____

Do you want any of the following?

YES	NO		YES	NO	
❏	❏	Additional air conditioning vents	❏	❏	Furniture in this room—if so, list.
❏	❏	Air purifier system			_____
❏	❏	Built-ins*	❏	❏	Half bath
❏	❏	Ceiling fan*	❏	❏	Humidifier
❏	❏	Computer wiring*	❏	❏	Security alarm pad*
❏	❏	Exterior door to this room	❏	❏	Stereo equipment*
❏	❏	Fireplace*	❏	❏	Stereo speakers*
❏	❏	Five-gallon water dispenser	❏	❏	Telephone jacks*
❏	❏	Full bath in this room—if so, fill out a Bathroom Checklist (page 134).	❏	❏	Televisions*

*Fill in the relevant information on the corresponding Entire-Home Selections form in Chapter 12.

Exterior Front Entry Checklist

Do you want the main door to your home to be on the front of your home or will it be on the side? Explain.

_____

Circle the type flooring you want at the front exterior entry.

Brick   Slate   Tile   Concrete   Other _____

Do you want any of the following?

YES   NO

❑   ❑   Porch at your front door—if so, how large a porch and what shape?

❑   ❑   Porte cochere at the front door—if so, do you want it wide enough for two cars to fit under it or an additional
            driveway outside the porte cochere for cars to pass? _____

❑   ❑   Enter your front door by passing through a courtyard—explain. _____

❑   ❑   Steps leading up to your "front" door—if you have steps and a porch, what type of railing do you want?

            _____

❑   ❑   Special lights along the steps

❑   ❑   Removable grate in the exterior floor at the front door for wiping off snow or mud

❑   ❑   Potted plants that will need a built-in drip system by the front entry area

❑   ❑   Faucet near your front door to hose off the area and for watering plants—if so, will you need a drip water system
            to keep them watered? _____

❑   ❑   Columns at your front door

❑   ❑   Any awnings over your front door

❑   ❑   Screened-in front porch leading to your front door

❑   ❑   Mail drop into your house (check with U.S. Postal Service to make sure it is allowed)

❑   ❑   Hanging lantern

❑   ❑   Mounted lantern—if so, do you want brick, slate, tile, or other flooring at the exterior front entry area? _____

❑   ❑   Special architectural elements—if so, describe. _____

❑   ❑   Bench or pair of benches or other furniture located at your front entry—if so, list, and provide photos with dimensions.

            _____

What kind of lighting do you want around the exterior front door: gas or electric? _____

Circle the kind of light fixture you want.

Lanterns   Hanging lantern   Light on a post   Other _____

What are your exterior front entry electrical outlet needs? List uses.

_____

_____

Family Room Checklist

Approximate room size _____ Location in the house _____

Is your vision of your family room an open room off the kitchen or a separate room with four walls? Explain.

_____

What furniture do you want in your family room?

_____

_____

Do you envision your family room as a family room/playroom combination? Explain.

_____

What are your family room electrical outlet needs? List uses.

_____

_____

Do you want any of the following?

YES NO
❑ ❑ Built-ins*
❑ ❑ Ceiling fan*
❑ ❑ Computer wiring*
❑ ❑ Fireplace*
❑ ❑ Stereo equipment*
❑ ❑ Stereo speakers*
❑ ❑ Telephone jacks*
❑ ❑ Televisions*

*Fill in the relevant information on the corresponding Entire-Home Selections form in Chapter 12.

Garage Checklist

Approximate size _____ Location _____

Will you want your garage attached to your home by a door, attached to your home by an enclosed and covered walkway, attached to your home by an open covered walkway, or entirely detached from the home? Explain.

_____

_____

Do you want a totally enclosed garage with a garage door in front, a covered garage with no garage door and open sides, or a covered garage with a garage door and side walls that have openings into a courtyard? Explain.

_____

_____

Do you prefer that the garage doors are on the front of the house, the side of the house, or behind the house?

_____

If you have more than one vehicle, do you want an individual garage door for each vehicle, a double garage door, or a

combination of a double door and single doors? Explain. _____

_____

What height and width do you want your garage door(s)? _____

Do you want your garage to be hidden from the street by the position on the lot or behind landscaping?

_____

What are your garage electrical outlet needs? List uses.

_____

_____

Will any of your vehicles need a battery tender or need to be charged, requiring an outlet? _____

Do you want any of the following?

YES	NO	
❑	❑	Storage space for garbage bins inside your garage—if so, number and dimension of bins? _____
❑	❑	Custom-built area outside the garage to hold the garbage and recycle bins
❑	❑	Storage space for recycle bins in your garage—if so, how many and what size bins? _____
❑	❑	Decorative hardware affixed to your garage door
❑	❑	Exterior door leading out of your garage
❑	❑	Wood workshop off the garage—if so, explain. _____
❑	❑	Climate control room in your garage for a dog, attached to an exterior dog run
❑	❑	Walk-in storage closets—if so, what sizes and what will be their uses? _____
❑	❑	Doggy door into your garage

YES	NO	
❏	❏	Tiled dog bath area in your garage
❏	❏	Climate-controlled garage
❏	❏	Heated garage—if so, radiant floor heat, wall-mounted system, or other? _____
❏	❏	Any appliances in the garage—if so, list. _____
❏	❏	Sink in your garage
❏	❏	Any design or special paint on your garage floors
❏	❏	Any special treatment to your garage walls
❏	❏	Car stops in your garage
❏	❏	A place to store tables and chairs that are used for entertaining—if so, size of area, how many tables and chairs? _____
❏	❏	Wall-mounted code panel on the outside of your garage for opening your garage—if so, where will you want it mounted? _____
❏	❏	Basketball goal mounted around your garage area—if so, where and what type of mount? _____
❏	❏	Work counter—if so, how deep and how wide? _____
❏	❏	Any professional tool or auto equipment that will be placed in your garage: tool drawer on wheels, air compressor, and so on—if so, list here, measure, and fill them in on your Individual Room and Closet Fact Sheet. _____
❏	❏	Drains in the garage floor—if so, how many drains and location of each? _____
❏	❏	Ability to wash your car inside your garage—if so, do you need the lower portion of your walls to be waterproof?
❏	❏	Hot and cold water faucets
❏	❏	Commercial-type car wash power sprayer
❏	❏	Built-ins*
❏	❏	Ceiling fan*
❏	❏	Computer wiring*
❏	❏	Fireplace*
❏	❏	Stereo equipment*
❏	❏	Stereo speakers*
❏	❏	Telephone jacks*
❏	❏	Televisions*

*Fill in the relevant information on the corresponding Entire-Home Selections form in Chapter 12.

Circle your choice for the area above your garage.

Open vaulted ceiling   Flat ceiling   Attic space   Finished-out room   Other _____

How tall do you want your garage ceilings? _____

Do you want concrete, brick, or another surface for your garage floor? _____

If concrete, do you want a painted floor or other design applied to the concrete? _____

Do you want windows in your garage door, windows in your garage wall, or a skylight? _____

Garage Vehicle Checklist

Item	Number of Vehicles	Make and Model	Battery Tender Needed?	Stored on a Trailer?	Dimensions of Trailer	Ceiling Mounted Remarks
ATVs						
Bicycles						
Boat						
Canoe						
Cars						
Golf carts						
Jet ski						
Kayak						
Motorcycle						
Riding lawn mower						
Snowmobile						
Trucks						
Other _____						

For garage measurements, see Appendix 2 (page 353).

Garage Item Storage Checklist

Item	In Cabinet	On Open Shelf	In Closet	In Garage Attic	On Garage Wall	Open Area in Garage	Drawer in Garage	Hang from Ceiling
Lawn Tools								
Chain saw								
Fertilizer								
Fertilizer spreader								
Push lawn mower								
Rake								
Shovel								
Wheelbarrow								
Other_____								
Gardening								
Flowerpots								
Garden hoses								
Hand tools								
Potting soil								
Power tools								

Item	In Cabinet	On Open Shelf	In Closet	In Garage Attic	On Garage Wall	Open Area in Garage	Drawer in Garage	Hang from Ceiling
Sprayers								
Sprinklers								
Other ____								
Car Supplies								
Car cover								
Car washing supplies								
Gas can								
Jumper cables								
Snow chains								
Snow tires								
Tire air compressor								
Other ____								
Paint Supplies								
Paint								
Paint brushes								

(Garage Item Storage Checklist, continued)

Item	In Cabinet	On Open Shelf	In Closet	In Garage Attic	On Garage Wall	Open Area in Garage	Drawer in Garage	Hang from Ceiling
Paint bucket								
Paint rollers								
Plastic covering								
Roller pans								
Solvents								
Other____								
Barbecue Supplies								
Butane tank								
Charcoal								
Grill								
Grill cooking utensils								
Wood chips								
Other____								
Picnic Supplies								
Blanket								

(Garage Item Storage Checklist, continued)

Item	In Cabinet	On Open Shelf	In Closet	In Garage Attic	On Garage Wall	Open Area in Garage	Drawer in Garage	Hang from Ceiling
Candles								
Folding chairs								
Folding table								
Ice chest								
Picnic basket								
Other ____								
Tools								
Hand power tools								
Hand tools								
Level								
Nails/screws								
Tool chest								
Other ____								

Kitchen Checklist

Approximate room size _____ Location in the house _____

Do you want your kitchen open to other rooms or do you prefer that it be an entirely separate room? Explain.

_____

Do you want your kitchen located on the front, side, or back of your home? _____

Do you want a window in front of your kitchen sink? _____

Will you need a broom closet in your kitchen or do you prefer a laundry room nearby to store brooms, mops, and so on?

_____

When you walk into your home, do you set your keys, purse, or packages down on the kitchen counter? _____

If so, would you prefer to have a small office area just off the kitchen to set down keys, purse, sunglasses, and so on, leaving

the kitchen counter clear? _____

Do any of the following describe your lifestyle?

YES	NO	
❑	❑	When your family is home, everyone gathers in the kitchen.
❑	❑	Homework is done at the island.
❑	❑	When friends stop by, everyone gathers in the kitchen.
❑	❑	You pay bills, use a laptop, open mail, and so on at your kitchen counter or island or a desk area in the kitchen.
❑	❑	You entertain often—if so, with dinner parties, cocktail parties, brunches, card games, or other? How frequently? Usual number of guests? Explain. _____
❑	❑	You have parties catered—if so, when having a large party, does the caterer set up in the garage? _____
		If so, do you need a 220-volt outlet in the garage for extra ovens or warming devices? _____

What are your kitchen electrical outlet needs? List uses.

_____

_____

Does your family eat at the island or breakfast table or in the dining room? _____

If your family eats at the island or kitchen counter, do you want a raised ledge for eating and using bar stools or do you want

the island to be one height and use counter height bar stools? _____

Do you currently have a desk area in the kitchen? If so what works in your current desk area and what does not?

_____

_____

Will you hang a three-tier basket for fruits and vegetables? Explain. _____

Will you mount your knives on the wall, store in a drawer, or store in a knife block? _____

Do you want your shelves and drawers lined in silver cloth? Explain. _____

Do you want a lock on your silver closet and a separate alarm system? Explain. _____

If using a pot rack, will there be lights on the pot rack that will need a power source? _____

How do you prefer to store your damp dishtowels? On an exposed towel bar or hook or a slide-out towel bar located within a

cabinet door? Explain. _____

Do you want any of the following?

YES   NO
❑   ❑   Ceiling fan*
❑   ❑   Computer wiring*
❑   ❑   Fireplace*
❑   ❑   Stereo equipment*
❑   ❑   Stereo speakers*
❑   ❑   Telephone jacks*
❑   ❑   Televisions*

*Fill in the relevant information on the corresponding Entire-Home Selections form in Chapter 12.

Kitchen Cabinet Layout Checklist

Height of counter? _____ Depth of counter? _____

Height of island? _____ Dimensions of island _____ Shape of island _____

Distance between counter and bottom of upper cabinets? _____

Depth of upper cabinet shelves? _____

Do you want adjustable shelves? _____ Circle your preference of the type of finish on your shelf clips.

Brass   Stainless   Acrylic   Other _____

Circle the type of material you want on your cabinets.

Wood   Stainless   Glass and wood   Glass   Plastic   Other _____

Circle the type of finish you want on your cabinets.

Stain   Paint   Faux paint   Pickle   Other _____

Explain. _____

What style of cabinet front do you plan to use? Flush mount cabinet door and drawers or an overlay cabinet door and drawers?

_____

Do you want the area below your counter to be drawers or cabinet doors or mixture? _____ Provide a rough drawing of your vision for this area. If you know what you want to store in a drawer and in a cabinet, list that information.

How high will the upper cabinets extend? To the ceiling/crown molding, leave an opening between top of upper cabinet and

ceiling, or to the furdown. Explain. _____

If having an open area between the upper cabinet and ceiling, what height do you want for the open shelf? _____

If applicable, what height will the furdown be? _____

How tall do you want the actual inside storage space in the drawer? _____

What type of counter surface will you use? Explain. _____

How thick do you want the counter edge and what type edge design? _____

Will you have an under-mount, self-rimming, or tile-mounted kitchen sink? _____

How high of a toe kick do you want? _____

How do you want to use the lower corner cabinet area? Pull-out corner drawers, cabinet door with shelves that swing out from

a pole, or other. Explain. _____

Do you want any of the following?

YES NO

❑   ❑   Panels that match the cabinets on your appliances

❑   ❑   Trash compactor—if so, more than one? _____

❑   ❑   Custom trash can in a cabinet drawer (see Under-Cabinet Trash Storage, page 90)

❑   ❑   Recycle drawer. Explain. _____

❑   ❑   Cabinets above the refrigerator—if so, do you want them flush with the front of the refrigerator or set back so you can place things on top of your refrigerator? _____

❑   ❑   Pot rack in the wall or hanging from the ceiling. Will it have can or rope lights built into it? Explain. _____

❑   ❑   Oversized drawer to store pots and pans

❑   ❑   Tilt drawer in front of the sink

❑   ❑   Custom dividers for utensils or flatware inside any drawer

❑   ❑   The inside of your drawers laminated

❑   ❑   Under-cabinet flip-down television

❑   ❑   Wood-burning pizza oven in your kitchen

❑   ❑   Your dishwasher raised from the floor

❑   ❑   Drawer for pet food

❑   ❑   Custom-designed drawers such as a spice drawer, drawer to hold china, drawer to hold flatware. If so, list the number of place settings and dimensions of china pieces. Also list individual flatware pieces—indicate the total number and the length of each piece. _____

❑   ❑   Open vertical shelves to store plates

❑   ❑   Vertical storage cabinet or drawer for cookie sheets, muffin tins, cutting boards If so, create a list with dimensions.

❑   ❑   Vertical storage cabinet for trays—if so, how many trays? _____ What is the dimension of the largest tray, including handles? _____

❑   ❑   Special area for telephone books—if so, explain. _____

❑   ❑   Shelves to store cookbooks—if so, how many shelves? _____ Will the cookbooks be stored on open shelves or behind cabinet doors? _____ How many cookbooks? _____ Range of cookbook dimensions? _____

❑   ❑   Special storage system for table cloths

❑   ❑   Baskets for storing potatoes, onions, and other vegetables—if so, where would you store the baskets? _____ How many baskets and what are the basket dimensions? _____

❑   ❑   Built-in desk as part of the kitchen cabinets—if so, what size desk? _____ Do you want shelves above, computer monitor and hard drive, hanging file, drawer, counter height, or desk height? Explain. _____

What will you be placing on the kitchen counters? List.

_____

_____

Will you store your coffee cups and mugs stacked in a cabinet, hanging on hooks, or other? _____

How do you plan to hang your dish towels? Pull-out bar inside a cabinet, on a towel bar, a hook or other?

_____

Will your microwave be built into an upper or lower cabinet? _____ Will you have more than one? _____

Will you have a cutting board inset into the counter, a freestanding piece of furniture with cutting board top, or other?

_____

Will you have a custom drawer or custom open slots for wine bottles? _____ How many bottles would you want to

store in this area? _____ (See Wine Storage Options, page 91)

Kitchen Island Checklist

Will you have one, two, or three islands? _____ If more than one island, you will need to fill out this checklist for each.

Do you want any of the following?

YES	NO		YES	NO	
❑	❑	One continuous counter height	❑	❑	Stainless top
❑	❑	Two counter heights, one part counter height, one part bar height	❑	❑	Standard counter height—if not, how high do you want the island? _____
❑	❑	Built-in island with cabinets, drawers, and so on below	❑	❑	Sink on island—if so, for washing dishes, vegetable washing, or bar sink? _____
❑	❑	Movable island on wheels	❑	❑	Stove top on island
❑	❑	Piece of furniture for island	❑	❑	Island surface with no equipment
❑	❑	Butcher block for island			
❑	❑	Marble top or marble section of island for pastry or bread making			

Do you want any of the following below your island counter?

YES	NO		YES	NO	
❑	❑	Trash compactor	❑	❑	Juice refrigerator
❑	❑	Dishwasher	❑	❑	Wine chiller
❑	❑	Dishwasher drawers	❑	❑	Wine bottle storage (see Wine Storage Options, page 91)
❑	❑	Refrigerator drawers			
❑	❑	Recycle cabinets	❑	❑	Tray storage
❑	❑	Custom trash pull-out cabinet (see Under-Cabinet Trash Storage, page 90)	❑	❑	Cookbook shelves
			❑	❑	Open shelves for decorative items
❑	❑	Microwave			

(If you want a sink on the island and will use it to wash dishes, you will need a dishwasher or dishwasher drawers next to the sink below the island.)

If you have a stove top on your island, will you want an exhaust system that rises out of the counter or a vented exhaust system?

Explain. _____

Will the island be used for seating? _____ Counter or bar height stools? _____ How many stools? _____

Do you prefer drawers or cabinet doors for storage space below your island? _____ Will there be special cabinet or drawers sizes to accommodate specific items being stored? List items and note dimensions below or on a separate sheet.

_____

_____

What are your kitchen island electrical outlet needs? List uses. _____

_____

Do you want a strip of outlets hidden under the island top? _____

Kitchen Appliance Checklist

Do you want any of the following?

YES   NO

❑   ❑   One individual refrigerator and one individual freezer (2 pieces)

❑   ❑   Two individual refrigerators and two individual freezers (4 pieces)

❑   ❑   One unit, refrigerator/freezer combination (Refrigerators are available in many different door widths. Make sure if selecting a wider door that it will clear the island.)

❑   ❑   Dishwasher—if so, how many? _____ Left or right side of sink? _____
Location for second dishwasher _____

❑   ❑   Disposal—if so, how many? _____ Which side of sink(s)? _____ (If you have a double or triple sink, the disposal should be located on the same side as the dishwasher.)

❑   ❑   Trash compactor—if so, how many? _____ Location(s) _____

❑   ❑   Wall oven—if so, how many? _____ Size(s) _____

❑   ❑   Oven/microwave combination

❑   ❑   Range with oven below—if so, how many burners? _____ Gas or electric? _____ Griddle, grill, or other options? _____

❑   ❑   Stove top only, no oven below—if so, how many burners? _____ Gas or electric? Griddle, grill, or other options? _____

❑   ❑   Self-cleaning oven

❑   ❑   Warming drawers—if so, how many? _____ Location(s) _____

❑   ❑   Microwave—if so, how many? _____ Location(s) _____

❑   ❑   Under-counter ice maker—if so, clear or frosted ice, size and shape? _____ Location _____

❑   ❑   Freestanding large ice maker—if so, clear or frosted ice, size and shape? _____
Location _____

❑   ❑   Wine chiller—if so, under-counter or full standing size? _____ Location _____

❑   ❑   Exhaust fan—if so, ceiling mounted or pop up from counter? _____

❑   ❑   Built-in professional coffeemaker—if so, location _____

❑   ❑   Built-in deep fryer—if so, location _____

❑   ❑   Built-in blender base—if so, location _____

❑   ❑   Built-in mixer base—if so, location _____

❑   ❑   Compact entertainment center or fold-up television under kitchen cabinet—if so, location _____

Kitchen Plumbing Checklist

Which of the following do you want in your kitchen?

YES	NO	
❑	❑	Single sink
❑	❑	Double sink
❑	❑	Triple sink
❑	❑	Farmhouse sink
❑	❑	Sink faucet, flow control, and temperature control all in one
❑	❑	Sink faucet and two handles
❑	❑	Water purifier
❑	❑	Sprayer attached to sink faucet
❑	❑	Sprayer not attached to faucet
❑	❑	Commercial sink sprayer
❑	❑	Pot filler faucet near stove—if so, exact location _____
❑	❑	Disposal—if double or triple sink, which side gets the disposal? Explain. _____
❑	❑	Soap dispenser at kitchen sink
❑	❑	Hot water dispenser at kitchen sink
❑	❑	Ice maker, part of freezer
❑	❑	Individual under-counter ice maker
❑	❑	Freestanding large ice maker
❑	❑	Built-in professional coffeemaker
❑	❑	Refrigerator door front ice and water dispenser

If you will have more than one kitchen sink, for each additional sink, list the type of sink and the type of faucet. Indicate if you want a spray nozzle, soap dispenser, hot water dispenser, disposal, or any other option.

_____

_____

_____

_____

❑ Check if you have any specification forms attached.

Kitchen Item Storage Checklist

Items	Preferred Storage Location	Precise Storage Location
Basic Items		
Canister set		
Can opener		
Cheese grater		
Cookbooks		
Cutting boards		
Knives		
Paper towel holder		
Pot lids		
Pots and pans		
Pyrex dishes		
Roasting pans		
Salad spinner		
Thermos		
Tupperware, plastic ware		
Baking Items		
Baking utensils		
Cake decorating items		
Cake pans		
Cookie sheets		

Items	Preferred Storage Location	Precise Storage Location
Cupcake pans		
Measuring cups		
Mixing bowls		
Rolling pin		
Sifter		
Cleaning Products		
Mop, broom, dust pan, bucket		
Rags		
Vacuum bags		
Cloth Goods		
Aprons		
Cloth napkins, rings		
Dish towels		
Placemats		
Pot holders		
Table cloths		
Dry Goods		
Garbage bags		
Paper products (napkins, paper towels, and so on)		
Plastic cups, Styrofoam cups		
Plastic wrap, plastic food storage bags, foil		

Items	Preferred Storage Location	Precise Storage Location
Entertaining Pieces		
Bowls		
Cake stands		
Casserole dishes		
Casserole holders		
Coffee service		
Pitchers		
Platters		
Tea set		
Trays		
Everyday Dishes/Flatware		
Coffee cups, mugs		
Dishes		
Flatware		
Glasses		
Steak knives		
Tea cups		
Food Items		
Baking items (vanilla, baking soda, and so on)		
Beverages (sodas, juices, water)		
Beans (dried)		

Items	Preferred Storage Location	Precise Storage Location
Bread		
Canned goods		
Cereal		
Coffee, filters, tea bags		
Flour, sugar		
Fresh fruits and vegetables		
Pasta, rice		
Snacks (cookies, crackers, chips, and so on)		
Spices		
Vinegars, oils		
Vitamins		
Wine		
Small Appliances		
Blender		
Bread machine		
Can opener		
Cappuccino maker		
Coffeemaker		
Deep fryer		
Food processor		

Items	Preferred Storage Location	Precise Storage Location
Griddle		
Ice cream maker		
Juicer		
Mixer		
Rice cooker		
Slow cooker		
Toaster, toaster oven		
Miscellaneous		
Batteries		
Coupons		
HVAC filters		
Light bulbs		
Recipe drawer, box, or folder		
Shopping bags, grocery sacks		
Tools		
Warranty information		
Other _____		
Other _____		
Other _____		
Other _____		
Other _____		

Kitchen Pantry Checklist

Which of the following fits the description of the type of kitchen pantry you want in your home?

YES NO
☐   ☐   Butler's pantry combined with working pantry
☐   ☐   Part of the kitchen cabinets
☐   ☐   Simple walk-in-closet-type pantry with shelves against the wall
☐   ☐   Working pantry with work space area
☐   ☐   Working pantry, butler's pantry, and laundry room combined

Approximate room size _____

If working pantry, do you want any of the following?

YES NO
☐   ☐   Island—if so, approximate size and shape _____
☐   ☐   Pot rack above island
☐   ☐   Sink—if so, type and size of sink _____
☐   ☐   Commercial sprayer
☐   ☐   Disposal
☐   ☐   Trash compactor
☐   ☐   Trash can—if so, built-in or freestanding? _____
☐   ☐   Pull-out cabinet trash drawer
☐   ☐   Ovens
☐   ☐   Refrigerator or freezer—if so, which? _____
☐   ☐   Upper and lower cabinets with doors
☐   ☐   Drawers
☐   ☐   Open shelves
☐   ☐   Small storage closet for a broom, mop, vacuum, other cleaning items in the pantry
☐   ☐   Area with hooks to hang household keys
☐   ☐   Windows or skylights

If walk-in pantry with shelves, do you want any of the following?

YES NO
☐   ☐   Adjustable shelves
☐   ☐   Storage for a broom, mop, vacuum, other cleaning items in the pantry—if so, you will need an area for these to hook onto the wall or stand on the floor.
☐   ☐   An area with hooks to hang household keys

Circle any items you will store in your pantry that will require an outlet to charge.

Handheld vacuum   Electric screwdriver   Flashlight   Other _____

What are your kitchen pantry electrical outlet needs? List uses.

_____

_____

Do you have a particular shape in mind? Explain. _____

_____

How many shelves do you need? _____

Distance from ceiling for shelves to begin? _____

Distance from floor for shelves to begin? _____

What size shelves do you need: height, depth, and width? _____

_____

_____

_____

Discuss with builder the maximum width of shelves to avoid sagging.

If you have baskets or bins to place on the shelves, what are the dimensions of those items?_____

_____

_____

_____

Fill in the Kitchen Item Storage Checklist (page 177), checking any items that will be stored in the pantry.

Laundry Room Checklist

Approximate room size _____ Location in the house _____

How much cabinet and counter space do you need? Explain. _____

How large of a clothes folding area do you want? _____

Circle those that apply to how you want to use your laundry room.

Strictly for laundry   Overflow for caterers when entertaining   Storing serving pieces for entertaining

Storing silver   Gift wrapping   Flower arranging   Sewing   Dog washing   Pet's room   Crafts

Bulk item storage   Storage lockers for each child   Other _____

How many washing machines? _____ How many dryers? _____

Circle any of the following you want in your laundry room.

Dishwasher   Oven   Disposal   Trash compactor   Refrigerator   Freezer   Refrigerator/freezer combo

Refrigerator for storing fresh flowers   Desk area   Skylight   5-gallon water dispenser   Fold-down ironing board

Other _____

On a copy of the Blank Comment Form (page 18), fill in any comments to discuss with your architect on any item circled.

What are your laundry room electrical outlet needs? List uses.

_____

_____

List items you will store in your laundry room.

_____

_____

Do you want any of the following?

YES   NO
❑   ❑   More than one laundry room in your home—if so, where will the others be located? _____
❑   ❑   Stackable washer and dryer or single units
❑   ❑   Front-loading washer and dryer
❑   ❑   Top-loading washing machine
❑   ❑   Washer and dryer on a pedestal
❑   ❑   Large drawer to store clothing to be ironed
❑   ❑   Large drawer to store clothing to be washed—or will you need an area to store a laundry basket for dirty clothes?

                  _____

❑   ❑   Large drawer to store washed and folded clothes for each member of the household

YES	NO	
❏	❏	Mesh drying rack for drying sweaters—if so, do you want a special place to store it? Explain. _____ Include dimensions of the drying rack. _____
❏	❏	Island or peninsula
❏	❏	Drain under your washing machines in the laundry room floor
❏	❏	Sink—if so, size, single, double, or triple? _____
❏	❏	Sprayer on your sink—if so, a commercial sprayer? _____
❏	❏	Tiled area to wash a dog, to hang clothing to dry, and so on
❏	❏	Drawer to store cleaning rags, car washing and drying towels, or dog drying towels
❏	❏	Drawer to store dry pet food—if not, where and how will your store the food? _____
❏	❏	Area for a pet's bed, food, and water
❏	❏	Dutch door to a laundry room so that a pet cannot get out
❏	❏	Storage space for brooms, mops, a vacuum, or buckets
❏	❏	8- to 12-inch open shelf just above your nonstacked washer and dryer
❏	❏	Recycle bins in your laundry room—if so, how many? _____
❏	❏	Hanging pot rack in your laundry room
❏	❏	Powder room off the laundry room
❏	❏	Upper and lower cabinets
❏	❏	Lights under the upper cabinets. Will your upper cabinets go to the ceiling, stop short of the ceiling creating an open area, or go to a furdown? _____ If open area, will you want rope lights or a halogen strip of lights to light that area? _____
❏	❏	Ceiling fan*
❏	❏	Computer wiring*
❏	❏	Stereo speakers*
❏	❏	Telephone jacks*
❏	❏	Televisions*

*Fill in the relevant information on the corresponding Entire-Home Selections form in Chapter 12.

Library Checklist

Approximate room size _____ Location in the house _____

Will your library be a working office or more of another room to enjoy in your home? Explain.

_____

What pieces of furniture do you want to use in your library? For example, do you want a seating area with sofa(s) and chairs or just a couple of chairs for visitors to sit by the desk? List.

_____

Will you have a two-sided desk with a kneehole on each side that needs to be positioned so that two people can work at the desk?

_____

Circle any office equipment you want in the library.

Printer   Fax   Hard drive   Computer monitor   Other _____

Circle where will you want your office equipment stored.

In a closet   Inside the credenza   On top of the credenza   On top of the desk   Other _____

How much file storage space will you need? Explain.

_____

What are your library electrical outlet needs? List uses.

_____

_____

Circle the appliances you want in your library.

Mini-refrigerator   Wine cooler   Other _____

For a built-in bookcase, do you want floor-to-ceiling shelves or cabinets and drawers in the lower portion? Explain.

_____

Number of books and size of shelves? _____

Do you want any of the following?

YES	NO	
❑	❑	Built-in desk
❑	❑	Freestanding piece of furniture for a desk
❑	❑	Two-sided desk with kneeholes on both sides
❑	❑	Built-in credenza
❑	❑	Freestanding piece of furniture for a credenza
❑	❑	Standard height or bar height built-in desk

YES NO

❑ ❑ Built-in file drawers—if so, what size: legal, letter, or combination? _____

❑ ❑ Metal file cabinets—if so, how many and what are the dimensions? _____

❑ ❑ Built-in hanging file drawers—if so, where would you want them located: in a closet, in a cabinet under a bookcase, under a windowseat, or other? _____ Will you want letter, legal, or combination? _____

❑ ❑ File storage closet—if so, approximate size? _____

❑ ❑ Office equipment closet—if so, approximate size? _____

❑ ❑ Conference table—if so, to seat how many? _____

❑ ❑ Conference videoing or other specific electronic needs. List. _____

❑ ❑ Writing board on the wall

❑ ❑ World map or any other item that needs mounting on the wall and electric power—explain. _____

❑ ❑ Lighted globe that needs an outlet

❑ ❑ Wet bar within the library—if so, do you want it open or hidden behind cabinet doors? _____

❑ ❑ Specific memorabilia collection to display or store—explain. _____

❑ ❑ Display area for hunting, fishing, or other trophies. List trophies and how you want them displayed. _____

❑ ❑ Rug to be used in your library—if so, provide dimensions including fringe. _____

❑ ❑ Exterior door to your library

❑ ❑ Built-ins*

❑ ❑ Ceiling fan*

❑ ❑ Computer wiring*

❑ ❑ Fireplace*

❑ ❑ Stereo speakers*

❑ ❑ Stereo equipment*

❑ ❑ Telephone jacks*

❑ ❑ Televisions*

*Fill in the relevant information on the corresponding Entire-Home Selections form in Chapter 12.

Living Room/Great Room Checklist

Approximate room size _____ Location in the house _____

What shape do you want the living room? Explain. _____

Do you want a formal living room or a living room/great room combination? Explain.

_____

What rooms do you want flowing to and from the living room? List.

_____

Will you have any built-in bookcases in your living room? If so, will you have any outlet needs within the bookcase shelves?

_____

Will you want special bookcase lighting? _____

What are your living room electrical outlet needs? List uses.

_____

Will you want to be able to close off the living room with doors?_____ If so, pocket doors, French doors, or other type of

doors? _____

Do you want any of the following?

YES	NO	
❑	❑	Ceiling fan*
❑	❑	Computer wiring*
❑	❑	Fireplace*
❑	❑	Stereo speakers*
❑	❑	Telephone jacks*
❑	❑	Televisions*

*Fill in the relevant information on the corresponding Entire-Home Selections form in Chapter 12.

Mechanical Room Checklist

Approximate room size _____ Location in the house _____

Circle the equipment you want in the mechanical room.

Air purifier   Water purifier   Water softener   Hot water heater   Radiant heating system   Security system

Humidifier   HVAC   Other _____

Circle which control systems for your home will be located in the mechanical room.

Audio controls   HVAC system controls   Gas fire log controls   Lighting controls   Radiant heat controls

Security system controls   Window treatment motorized controls   Other _____

Are there any municipal codes limiting the size and use of the mechanical room? Explain. _____

Do you want an exterior door to the mechanical room? _____

If you will have an exterior door, do you want a separate security system? _____

Will the mechanical room also serve as a safe room and/or a control room? _____

Will you use it as a storage room? If so, what do you plan to store in the mechanical room? List.

_____

_____

_____

_____

Will you want extra ceiling, floor, and wall insulation to cut down on the noise generated from the mechanical room? Explain.

_____

What are your mechanical room electrical outlet needs? List uses.

_____

_____

Will you want a drain in the floor of your mechanical room in the event your water heater leaks? _____

Do you want any of the following?

YES   NO
❏   ❏   Computer wiring*
❏   ❏   Security alarm pad*
❏   ❏   Telephone jacks*
❏   ❏   Televisions*

*Fill in the relevant information on the corresponding Entire-Home Selections form in Chapter 12.

Media Room Checklist

Approximate room size _____ Location in the house _____

Will this room be solely a media room or will it serve as a multipurpose media room, playroom, and game room? Explain.

_____

If this will be a multipurpose room, identify the rooms represented, such as media, game, and playroom, and fill in the checklists for each of those rooms, noting on the checklist that these are part of the media room.

If solely a media room, how many people do you want to seat? _____

What type of furniture do you want in this room? Sofas, reclining chairs, other? Explain. _____

_____

What size movie screen do you want to use? _____

What type of material will you use for the counter? _____

How and where do you want to store your video and DVD collection? Explain._____

What are your media room electrical outlet needs? List uses.

_____

_____

Do you want any of the following?

YES   NO

❑   ❑   Counter with a sink, cabinets above and below—if so, how long? _____
❑   ❑   Curtain to open and close in front of the movie screen
❑   ❑   Glass candy display case that resembles one at the movie theater
❑   ❑   Media room consultant
❑   ❑   Popcorn wagon
❑   ❑   Powder room or half bath nearby
❑   ❑   Stadium seating
❑   ❑   Windowless room
❑   ❑   Sprayer for your sink
❑   ❑   Soap dispenser
❑   ❑   Mini-kitchen with sink, microwave, mini-refrigerator, or other appliances
❑   ❑   Ceiling fan*
❑   ❑   Computer wiring*
❑   ❑   Fireplace*
❑   ❑   Stereo equipment*
❑   ❑   Stereo speakers*
❑   ❑   Telephone jacks *
❑   ❑   Televisions *

*Fill in the relevant information on the corresponding Entire-Home Selections form in Chapter 12.

Morning Kitchen/Counter Checklist

If you want more than one morning kitchen/counter, fill out a copy of this checklist for each one.

Location: _____

Do you want a small room that you can close off or an open counter? _____

Approximate size of a small room? _____ Approximate length of a counter? _____

What are your morning kitchen electrical outlet needs? List uses.

_____

_____

Do you want any of the following?		
YES	NO	
❏	❏	Cabinets above the counter
❏	❏	Cabinets below the counter
❏	❏	Pull-out trash can built into the lower cabinets
❏	❏	Mini-refrigerator
❏	❏	Full-size refrigerator
❏	❏	Wine chiller
❏	❏	Microwave
❏	❏	Dishwasher
❏	❏	Dishwasher drawer
❏	❏	Built-in coffeemaker
❏	❏	Warming drawer
❏	❏	Sink
❏	❏	Hot water dispenser
❏	❏	Soap dispenser
❏	❏	Spray nozzle

Which small appliances will you use?		
YES	NO	
❏	❏	Coffeemaker
❏	❏	Tea maker
❏	❏	Coffee bean grinder
❏	❏	Toaster
❏	❏	Bagel toaster
❏	❏	Toaster oven
❏	❏	Juicer
❏	❏	Blender
❏	❏	Other _____

Will you need storage for any of the following?		
YES	NO	
❏	❏	Dishes—if so, list type and number. _____
❏	❏	Utensils—if so, list type and number _____
❏	❏	Barware—if so, list type and number _____
❏	❏	Napkins
❏	❏	Trays
❏	❏	Dry food items
❏	❏	Beverages—if so, what type? _____
❏	❏	Knives—if so, stored in a knife block or in a drawer?_____
❏	❏	Cutting board
❏	❏	Other _____

Mudroom Checklist

Approximate room size _____ Location in the house _____

If your home is on a ranch, near a ski slope, near a beach, or near a lake you may want custom-built areas in the mudroom to hold specialized equipment for family members and guests. Circle any items requiring custom storage space in the mudroom.

Guns   Hunting equipment   Skiing equipment   Beach equipment   Fishing equipment   Other _____

Circle the door(s) you want to lead into the mudroom.

Door from the garage   Door on side of your home   Door on front of your home   Back door

What are your mudroom electrical outlet needs? List uses.

_____

_____

Do you want any of the following?

YES   NO

❑   ❑   Built-in lockers or cubbyholes—if so, how many lockers and/or how many cubbyholes? Explain.
_____

❑   ❑   Storage bins or baskets to fit into cubbyholes or shelves—explain.
_____

❑   ❑   Metal lockers to store backpacks, school lunches, signed forms for school, and other items—if so, how many metal lockers? _____

❑   ❑   Any pieces of furniture in your mudroom—if so, what pieces?
_____

❑   ❑   Built-in bench or a freestanding bench or chair in the mudroom to sit on when putting on or removing shoes or boots.

❑   ❑   Built-in counter

❑   ❑   Heated mudroom

❑   ❑   Bins and baskets for storing items—if so, how many and what are the dimensions?
_____

❑   ❑   Handheld faucet sprayer and a waterproof floor with a drain to make cleaning easier

❑   ❑   Fixed mirror for that last-minute appearance check

❑   ❑   Coat closet, a row of hooks, or both for hanging coats and jackets—explain.
_____

❑   ❑   Storage closets—if so, what will you store in them? List.
_____

❑   ❑   Ceiling fan*

❑   ❑   Computer wiring*

❑   ❑   Stereo speakers*

❑   ❑   Telephone jacks*

*Fill in the relevant information on the corresponding Entire-Home Selections form in Chapter 12.

Nursery Checklist

Approximate room size _____ Location in the house _____

How close to the master bedroom do you want the nursery located? _____

What furniture will you have in the nursery: baby bed, changing table, armoire, chest of drawers, day bed, chair, other? List.

_____

Will the nursery eventually become a bedroom or some other type room such as a closet, office, or study? Explain and fill in a

checklist for the particular room it will become. _____

Will the nursery have a bathroom attached? _____ If so, fill in a copy of the Bathroom Checklist (page 134).

Will the nursery need a closet? _____ If so, fill in a copy of the Bedroom Closet Checklist (page 144).

Circle any equipment you will have in the nursery.

Baby monitor   Baby camera   Sound monitor   Humidifier   Air purifier   Sound machine

Heated wipes dispenser   Other _____

What are your nursery electrical outlet needs? List uses.

_____

_____

Is there a need for multiple baby beds? If so, how many? _____

Do you want any of the following?

YES   NO
❑   ❑   Ceiling fan*
❑   ❑   Computer wiring*
❑   ❑   Stereo equipment*
❑   ❑   Stereo speakers*
❑   ❑   Telephone jacks*
❑   ❑   Televisions*

*Fill in the relevant information on the corresponding Entire-Home Selections form in Chapter 12.

Office Checklist

Approximate room size _____ Location in the house _____

How will you use your office: for household/personal use, for a home-based business, or for an outside job?

_____

Do you want a large office, a small office, or a built-in desk area against a wall in another room (for example, in a family room near the kitchen)? Explain.

_____

How much desktop space do you want for a built-in desk? _____

How much closet space do you want in your office? Explain.

_____

How much file storage space do you need? Explain.

_____

Circle any special office needs associated with your job.

Equipment   Brochures   Samples   Files   Other _____

Circle the type of office equipment will you be using.

Printer   Fax   Copier   Hard drive   Monitor   Postage machine   Mailing machine   Paper cutter

Other _____

Where do you see your office equipment located: in a closet, inside a credenza, on top of a credenza, on top of a desk, or in a closet? Explain. _____

What are your office electrical outlet needs? List uses.

_____

_____

Do you want any of the following?

YES	NO	
❑	❑	Built-in desk
❑	❑	Freestanding furniture desk
❑	❑	Two-sided desk with kneeholes on both sides
❑	❑	Built-in credenza
❑	❑	Freestanding credenza
❑	❑	Standard height or bar height built-in desk
❑	❑	Built-in file drawers—if so, what size: legal, letter, or combination? _____
❑	❑	Metal file cabinets—if so, how many and what are the dimensions? _____

YES   NO

❑   ❑   Built-ins for bins, cubbyholes, or shelves in your office—if shelves, will they be open or behind cabinet doors?
_____

❑   ❑   Custom gift wrap area
❑   ❑   Bulletin board or whiteboard hung in your office—explain. _____
❑   ❑   Exterior entry to your office—if so, will you need a separate alarm system? _____
❑   ❑   Ceiling fan*
❑   ❑   Computer wiring*
❑   ❑   Fireplace*
❑   ❑   Security alarm pad*
❑   ❑   Stereo equipment*
❑   ❑   Stereo speakers*
❑   ❑   Telephone jacks*
❑   ❑   Televisions*

*Fill in the relevant information on the corresponding Entire-Home Selections form in Chapter 12.

Playroom/Game Room Checklist

Approximate room size _____ Location in the house _____

Explain how you will use this room: will it serve as a multipurpose room, strictly a playroom, or strictly a game room?

_____

What furniture do you want in your playroom/game room? List?

_____

_____

Circle the games you will use in your game room.

Pool   Ping-Pong   Foosball   Shuffleboard   Dartboard   Pinball   Other _____

Circle the game tables you want in your game room.

Card table   Craps table   Blackjack table   Other_____

What are your playroom/game room electrical outlet needs? List uses.

_____

_____

Do you want any of the following?

YES   NO
❑   ❑   Bar—if so, fill in the Bar Checklist (page 130)
❑   ❑   Built-in bookcases or shelves
❑   ❑   Window seat
❑   ❑   Storage cabinets or closets
❑   ❑   Snack counter with microwave, sink, mini-refrigerator
❑   ❑   Popcorn wagon
❑   ❑   Sundae counter
❑   ❑   Dumbwaiter to kitchen, if applicable
❑   ❑   Ceiling fan*
❑   ❑   Computer wiring*
❑   ❑   Fireplace*
❑   ❑   Stereo equipment*
❑   ❑   Stereo speakers*
❑   ❑   Telephone jacks*
❑   ❑   Televisions*

*Fill in the relevant information on the corresponding Entire-Home Selections form in Chapter 12.

Pool House Checklist

Approximate size of the pool house _____

Will your pool house be a freestanding structure or connected to the house? Explain

_____

Do you want an open-air pool house or one with doors? Explain.

_____

Do you want one big open room with mini-kitchen counter, full kitchen, guest bedroom(s), his and hers full baths, one unisex

bath, a powder room, coat closet, bedroom closet(s) or other? List. _____

_____

Fill in the bathroom, kitchen, closet, family room, game room or any other appropriate room checklist for the rooms you want in your pool house.

Will your pool house also serve as a game room? If so, what game tables will you use? List.

_____

If including a bathroom or powder room, do you want an exterior entrance as well as an interior entrance?

_____

Do you want a fire pit outside your pool house area? _____

Do you want a sauna or steam room in your pool house? _____

Will you have a storage area for pool supplies, patio furniture cushions, and other pool items inside your pool house?

_____

Will you have a security system for your pool house? _____

Do you want any of the following?

YES	NO	
❏	❏	Ceiling fan*
❏	❏	Computer wiring*
❏	❏	Fireplace*
❏	❏	Security alarm*
❏	❏	Stereo equipment*
❏	❏	Stereo speakers*
❏	❏	Telephone jacks*
❏	❏	Televisions*

*Fill in the relevant information on the corresponding Entire-Home Selections form in Chapter 12.
If your pool house will be enclosed with a bathroom, kitchen, bedroom, and so forth, fill out the appropriate checklists for those specific rooms.

Porch, Patio, Deck, and Balcony Checklist

How many porches, patios, decks, and balconies would you like, in what locations, and what approximate sizes? Explain.

_____

Do you want any of the following? If so, write out to the side if it is for a porch, patio, deck, or balcony.

YES	NO	
❑	❑	Screened-in porch
❑	❑	Multilevel deck
❑	❑	Retractable motorized screen
❑	❑	Faucet near the porch, patio, deck, and balconies for watering plants and hosing off the area
❑	❑	Drip system for watering plants
❑	❑	Drain in the middle of your porches, patios, or balconies
❑	❑	Spray mist cooling system—if so, plan for an electric outlet and water connection.
❑	❑	Portable heating system—if so, will it require an outlet, natural gas connection, or a butane tank? _____
❑	❑	Fire pit in the patio area
❑	❑	Outdoor fireplace on a porch, patio, or deck
❑	❑	Grilling area on your porch, patio, or deck
❑	❑	Built-in grill
❑	❑	Built-in serving areas around a grill
❑	❑	Built-in benches
❑	❑	Hot tub
❑	❑	Area to store cushions—explain. _____
❑	❑	Any awning on your porches or balconies—explain. _____
❑	❑	Protective storm panels around your porches, covered patios, or balconies—explain. _____

Will you have a frozen drink machine at a party and place it on the porch or patio? If so, you will need an appropriate outlet.

Explain. _____

Will you use gas or electricity for lanterns? Explain. _____

What are your electrical outlet needs? List. _____

_____

What are your Christmas decoration needs for the porches, patios, decks, and balconies? See Exterior and Interior Christmas Lights and Decorations Checklist (page 262) for possibilities.

_____

_____

_____

What type of floor will you use on this porch, patio, or balcony? Explain. _____

What type of wood do you want to use for your deck? Explain. _____

Do you want any of the following? If so, write out to the side if it is for a porch, patio, deck, or balcony.

YES   NO
❏   ❏   Ceiling fan*
❏   ❏   Computer wiring*
❏   ❏   Fireplace*
❏   ❏   Stereo speakers*
❏   ❏   Telephone jacks*
❏   ❏   Televisions*

*Fill in the relevant information on the corresponding Entire-Home Selections form in Chapter 12.

Powder Room/Half Bath Checklist

If more than one powder room or half bath in your home, copy this page and fill in for each room.

Approximate room size _____ Location in the house _____

Who will be the primary users of this room? _____

What are your powder room/half bath electrical outlet needs? List uses.

_____

_____

Do you want any of the following?

YES	NO	
❑	❑	Sitting area within the powder room
❑	❑	Taller toilet and padded seat
❑	❑	Water closet within the powder room
❑	❑	Full-length mirror

Do you want the sink built into a piece of furniture, on a pedestal, mounted in a corner, or in a built-in counter?

_____

Will you use a fixed or decorative hanging mirror over sink? _____

Will you use a chandelier, sconce, recessed can, or other lighting? List.

_____

Safe Room Checklist

Approximate room size _____ Location in the house _____

Circle the dangers you want your safe room to protect against.

Tornados   Other natural disasters   Intruders   Home invasion   Terror threats   Kidnapping

Abusive family member   Other _____

Will you use your safe room to store valuables? _____

Will your safe room have dual purposes such as being the master closet and safe room, laundry room and safe room, bathroom and safe room, or other combination? Explain.

_____

_____

Will you purchase a prefabricated safe room or have one custom built? _____

How many people would likely gather in the safe room at one time? _____

Do you want your safe room accessible from inside the home or away from the home, such as a prefabricated room buried in your yard for tornado protection? _____

What are your safe room electrical outlet needs? List uses.

_____

Do you want any of the following?

YES	NO	
❑	❑	Air filtration system
❑	❑	Fireproof protection
❑	❑	Generator for power
❑	❑	Heavy-duty strike plate cut deep into the door frame
❑	❑	Open shelves or cabinets with shelves to store emergency products
❑	❑	Safe room door behind a hidden door
❑	❑	Security alarm keypad
❑	❑	Security consultant for planning your safe room
❑	❑	Steel doorjamb
❑	❑	Telephone landline
❑	❑	Three-inch screws and three hinges
❑	❑	Video monitor to see what is going on outside the door or other areas of your home

Specialty Room Checklist

Approximate room size _____ Location in the house _____

Circle the type of specialty you want represented in your specialty room.

Golf   Fishing   Fly-fishing   Hunting   Crafts   Other _____

What shape do you envision for this room? (For example, if golf, perhaps you want it long and narrow for a putting area.)

_____

Will the display cases need special locks? Explain. _____

Do you have special closet or storage needs? Explain._____

What are your specialty room electrical outlet needs? List uses.

_____

_____

Are there any special electrical needs? _____

Do you want any of the following?

YES   NO
❏   ❏   Exterior entrance
❏   ❏   Special trophies that need to be mounted such as hunting and fishing trophies
❏   ❏   Special display cases for trophies or memorabilia
❏   ❏   Built-ins*
❏   ❏   Ceiling fan*
❏   ❏   Computer wiring*
❏   ❏   Fireplace*
❏   ❏   Stereo speakers*
❏   ❏   Telephone jacks*
❏   ❏   Televisions*

*Fill in the relevant information on the corresponding Entire-Home Selections form in Chapter 12.

Wine Room Checklist

Approximate room size _____ Location in the house _____

Circle the type of wine room you envision.

Small walk-in closet   Room with chairs   Room with a dining table   Room with seating plus a dining table

Other _____ Explain. _____

How many bottles of wine do you want to store? _____

Do you want your wine stored with the bottom of the bottles against the wall and the neck of the bottlse sticking out, or

stored with the bottles parallel to the wall with the label exposed? _____

What are your wine room electrical outlet needs? List uses.

_____

_____

Do you want any of the following?

YES	NO	
❑	❑	Section of the wine storage case that locks
❑	❑	All sections of wine behind caged type doors that lock
❑	❑	Special mounted wine opener
❑	❑	Decanter in a stand
❑	❑	Temperature riser sensor
❑	❑	Humidity level sensor
❑	❑	Ceiling fan*
❑	❑	Computer wiring*
❑	❑	Fireplace*
❑	❑	Sink
❑	❑	Stereo speakers*
❑	❑	Telephone jacks*
❑	❑	Televisions*

*Fill in the relevant information on the corresponding Entire-Home Selections form in Chapter 12.

6 Ceilings, Doors, Floors, Lighting, Walls, and Windows

The six basic parts of almost every room are the ceilings, doors, floors, lighting, walls, and windows. At the end of this chapter, you'll find a Ceilings, Doors, Floors, Lighting, Walls, and Windows Checklist. Once you begin filling in this checklist, file it in Binder 4.

As you make decisions regarding ceilings, doors, floors, lighting, walls, and windows, record these on the appropriate Individual Room and Closet Fact Sheet (page 81) and file it in Binder 4. If you need further explanation on the options and questions on the checklist, ask your architect or interior designer for opinions and suggestions.

CEILING OPTIONS

Some homes have flat ceilings that are the same height throughout the house, while other homes have a mixture of ceiling styles and heights. A home may have flat ceilings in most rooms with a cathedral ceiling in the living area, a domed ceiling in the entry foyer, and a vaulted ceiling in the master bathroom. The style home you want will influence which style ceiling will work in your home. Though you may not have answers to these questions, you will know some of the questions to ask when meeting with your architect. In Ceiling Shapes (page 210), you'll see examples of dropped, cathedral, tray, vaulted, domed, and shed ceilings.

Once you have determined the styles and heights of the ceilings you want in your home, then you need to decide what kind of ceiling material you want to use. The most common is sheetrock, which can be smooth or textured. Depending on the type of material, an array of options for the finishes and special treatments can be applied to the ceiling.

FORMS TO USE

Ceilings, Doors, Floors, Lighting, Walls, and Windows Checklist (page 212)
Individual Room and Closet Fact Sheet (page 81)

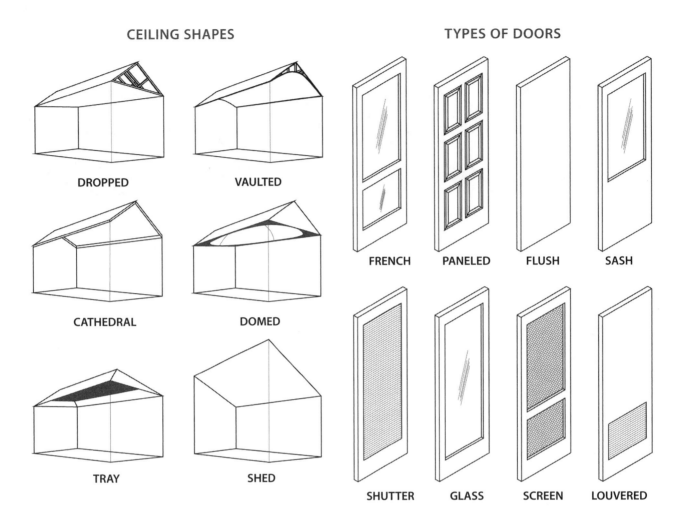

CEILING SHAPES

DROPPED

VAULTED

CATHEDRAL

DOMED

TRAY

SHED

TYPES OF DOORS

FRENCH   PANELED   FLUSH   SASH

SHUTTER   GLASS   SCREEN   LOUVERED

TIP: Ceilings should be no lower than nine feet tall. In today's market, higher ceilings will help with resale. A home with eight-foot ceilings is harder to sell.

DOOR OPTIONS

The three main types of doors in a home are the front door, other exterior doors, and the interior doors. A typical three-bedroom, three-bath home will have about twenty doors. Properly placed doors, the swing of the door, the type of door, and the type of interior door opening are all important in the overall aesthetics and function of a home.

Dutch doors are split horizontally, letting you open either the top half or the bottom half, and a pocket door is an interior door that slides into a "pocket" in the wall.

Common types of doors are French, paneled, flush, sash, shutter, glass, screen, and louvered, which you'll find illustrated in Types of Doors (above). Interior Door Openings (page 207) illustrates eight common types of doors: single, double, pocket, sliding, double swing, double pocket, Dutch, and bifold.

You can learn the terms for different parts of a door in the Door Components illustration (page 207), which will be useful in planning your home. And in the illustration on page 208, you'll see examples of decorative windows—fanlights, side panels,

INTERIOR DOOR OPENINGS

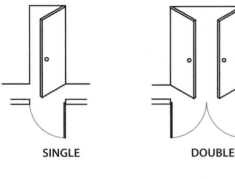

SINGLE   DOUBLE

POCKET   SLIDING

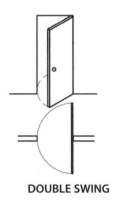

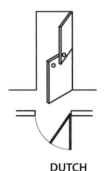

DOUBLE SWING   DOUBLE POCKET

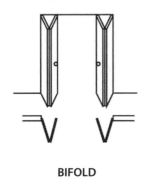

DUTCH   BIFOLD

DOOR COMPONENTS

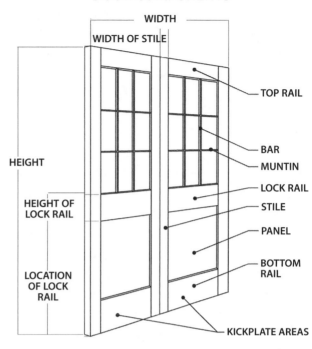

WIDTH
WIDTH OF STILE
TOP RAIL
BAR
MUNTIN
HEIGHT
LOCK RAIL
STILE
HEIGHT OF LOCK RAIL
PANEL
BOTTOM RAIL
LOCATION OF LOCK RAIL
KICKPLATE AREAS

and transoms—that can be positioned above or beside interior or exterior doors.

FORMS TO USE

Ceilings, Doors, Floors, Lighting, Walls, and Windows Checklist (page 212)
Individual Room and Closet Fact Sheet(page 81)

FRONT DOOR

The first tactile experience a visitor to your home will have is touching the front door or knocker. A solid, heavy, and beautiful front door and the entry hardware on that door give the feeling of quality and stability, making a lasting impression.

EXTERIOR DOORS

Exterior doors come in many shapes and sizes, and the number varies from house to house. You have many choices of materials to use on your doors. Doors off the back of a home often have glass in the door for a view of the backyard and patio. If you entertain on your porch, patio, or deck, a Dutch door is a great solution for keeping pets outside and being able to pass food or drinks through the opened top half of the door.

INTERIOR DOORS

Interior doors in a home should be consistent in height, whether a pantry or closet door. Aesthetically it is more pleasing to the eye to look around a room and see all doors at the same height than to move your eye up and down as door heights vary.

There is a direct correlation between the height of the ceiling and the door; the higher the ceiling, the taller the door. A higher ceiling evokes expansiveness. When shorter doors are used, the feeling created is that of a maze. Shorter doors negate that expansiveness feeling. They also imply that whatever is behind this door is unimportant.

When guests use the powder room or coat closet, they have physical contact with the interior of your home by opening and closing the door. Once again, a solid, thick door conjures up a feeling of quality and stability.

Unlike exterior doors, which may all be different, interior doors are generally the same style and material.

SHOWER DOORS

Once you have made your decision on whether you will have a shower or shower/tub combination in each bathroom, you need to determine whether you want a hinged glass door, sliding glass doors, or if you want to use a shower curtain.

There is a direct correlation between the height, weight, and thickness of the shower door and the number of hinges needed, as well as the length of the hinge screws. When selecting shower door hardware, take along the height, weight, and thickness measurements of all of the shower doors in your home.

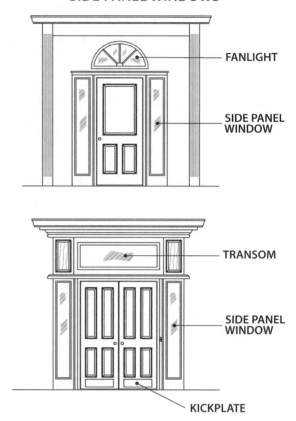

FANLIGHT, TRANSOM, AND SIDE PANEL WINDOWS

FANLIGHT

SIDE PANEL WINDOW

TRANSOM

SIDE PANEL WINDOW

KICKPLATE

FLOOR OPTIONS

There are many different types of floors to use in your home and most homes use more than one type. A home may have a stenciled design on the wood floor of the entry hall, wood planks throughout the living areas, carpet in the bedrooms, and stone in the bathrooms. Each type of floor has many different finishes or applications that can be applied. There are also different levels of quality and price.

When selecting the type of flooring you will use in each room of your home, consider how much traffic this particular floor will receive. The more traffic, the more durable the floor needs to be.

What is the main focal point for this room? You don't want a floor or a finish that will compete with the main focal point. If your interior design is a minimal look, a strong statement by the floor would work well. If your home is filled with art and accessories, a more minimal design on the floor would work better. And keep in mind how your furniture will work with your floor. If you have hand-painted furniture, a stenciled floor may seem too busy.

FORMS TO USE

Ceilings, Doors, Floors, Lighting, Walls, and
    Windows Checklist (page 212)
Individual Room and Closet Fact Sheet(page 81)

WOOD FLOOR GLOSSARY

Distressed: a technique used on wood floors to give an old, worn look. This is achieved by using items such as heavy chains that are beaten against the wood to create nicks, gouges, and other imperfections.

Hand scraped: after floors are installed, a scraping tool is run over the floors either with the grain or against the grain (each creates a different look). You can minimally scrape the floor or use deep scraping for a rougher look.

Parquet floor: hardwood blocks that are glued individually to the subfloor. Examples of patterns include basket weave, diagonal basket weave, brick pattern, single herringbone, and double herringbone.

Saw blade cut: a technique in which the surface of the wood flooring shows the circular motion of the saw used to cut the wood.

Stenciled: designs or borders are stenciled directly onto the wood floor, creating designs through different applications of stain colors or paint.

LIGHTING FIXTURE OPTIONS

Many different lighting fixtures and applications for those fixtures are on the market today. Adequate lighting in the appropriate area is a crucial component of an aesthetically pleasing and functional home. Properly placed light fixtures can add beauty to a room as well as enhance illumination.

Centeredness is an important element of lighting fixtures. All lighting should be centered, either on furniture, on windows, on doors, within a hallway, on a mantel, over an island, and so on for aesthetic purposes. An experienced lighting consultant can help you select the proper lighting fixture, the number of fixtures, and the appropriate location.

FORMS TO USE

Ceilings, Doors, Floors, Lighting, Walls, and
    Windows Checklist (page 212)
Individual Room and Closet Fact Sheet(page 81)

TIP: For light fixtures that are extremely difficult to reach to change a burned-out light bulb, select a light bulb style that you can change with a light bulb extension pole.

LIGHTING FIXTURE GLOSSARY

Halogen strips: a strip of lights that is sold by the foot and can be cut to any length.

Puck lights: approximately the size and shape of a hockey puck, these round light fixtures can be mounted under the upper cabinets, with one puck light per eight to 12 inches of cabinet length.

Rope lights: a strip of lights that resembles a rope. Often used inside a cabinet with a glass cabinet door, underneath an upper cabinet, on top of an upper cabinet, on staircases, or to light the toe kick.

INTERIOR WALL OPTIONS

Interior walls can be made of numerous types of materials, with a wide range of applications and finishes. The most common material is sheetrock, which can be smooth or textured. Other common options include log walls, stone or tile walls, and wallpapered walls. Multiple design elements can be applied to a wall, such as a chair rail and wainscot, a different finish on the lower three or four feet of the wall. You'll see these and other parts of a wall illustrated in Wall Components (below).

FORMS TO USE

Ceilings, Doors, Floors, Lighting, Walls, and
Windows Checklist (page 212)
Individual Room and Closet Fact Sheet(page 81)

INTERIOR WALL GLOSSARY

Beadboard: can be applied to an entire wall, as a wainscot, and to cabinet doors. It has one or more half-round beads milled into the finished surface.

Chair rail: usually installed between 24 and 48 inches from the floor, it is an accent to a room while protecting the walls from scuffs or dents from the backs of chairs.

Faux paint: uses a variety of techniques to apply paint and glaze to a wall. The techniques include sponging, rag rolling, stippling, and dragging.

Dragging: dragging a wide brush through a wet glaze on the wall with the brush bristles slightly bent

Rag rolling: similar to sponging, but you use a bunched up rag and press it against the wall

Sponging: dipping a sponge it in paint, then pressing it against the wall

Stippling: dabbing a brush dipped into paint against the wall with the bristles of the brush slightly bent

Painted design or landscape: a landscape or other scene painted onto the wall.

WALL COMPONENTS

MOLDING
DOOR HEADER
WINDOW HEADER
WINDOW CASING
WINDOW SILL
DOOR CASING
PLINTH BLOCK
CHAIR RAIL
BASEBOARD
WAINSCOT

TYPES OF WINDOWS

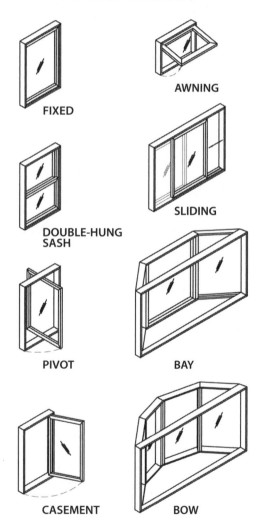

FIXED
AWNING
DOUBLE-HUNG SASH
SLIDING
PIVOT
BAY
CASEMENT
BOW

Skip trowel: a technique using a watered down mixture of joint compound that is applied to a wall or ceiling. The trowel is gently dragged across the mixture that has been applied to the wall, leaving some of the mixture on the wall creating a texture.

Wainscot: applied to the lower portion of a wall, made of wood, stone, tile, or other materials.

WINDOW OPTIONS

The style of the home you have designed will limit the type of windows that will go with that style. However, you will still have decisions to make about the type of windows you can choose. You'll find eight common window types illustrated on page 210.

FORMS TO USE

Ceilings, Doors, Floors, Lighting, Walls, and
   Windows Checklist (page 212)
Individual Room and Closet Fact Sheet(page 81)

WINDOW GLOSSARY

Awning: a rooflike cover extending over or in front of the window.

Bay window: a window or series of windows that form a "bay" and project outward; has at least three sides, each with a window.

Bow window: like a bay window, but with curved walls rather than straight walls; usually five windows.

Casement window: a window with hinges attached so that it opens vertically, like a door.

Double-hung sash window: window panels that open by sliding up and down in vertical grooves, sometimes aided by cords and balanced weights.

Pivot window: opens by pivot points between the sash and frame, usually opening horizontally—allows easier cleaning.

Queen Anne window: has multiple-sized windowpanes, usually on the upper sash, with the lower sash usually one piece of glass.

Tip: Avoid placing windows in areas that will make cleaning them costly and difficult, such as at the top of a vaulted ceiling. As they gather raindrops and dirt, instead of being aesthetically pleasing, the window will always look dirty.

Ceilings, Doors, Floors, Lighting, Walls, and Windows Checklist

Fill out the following checklists for ceilings, doors, floors, lighting, walls, and windows.

Ceilings

Fill in the room name in the left column and then fill in the rest of the information. If all ceilings will be the same height, material, and finish, you can state that and fill in only the rooms with special treatments or windows.

Examples of types of ceilings: cathedral, domed, flat, shed, tray, and vaulted. See Ceiling Shapes (page 206).

Examples of materials: sheetrock, skip trowel technique, log, wood beams, without beams, wood planks, wood planks with beams, brick, and stone/tile.

Examples of types of finish or paint: painted, stained, pickled, painted design or landscape, and wallpaper.

Examples of special treatments applied to the ceiling: distressing the wood or wood beams, glazing, faux paint, stenciling, and wallpaper.

Examples of windows in ceilings: skylight, dormer, glass pitch.

Room	Type of Ceiling	Height	Material	Finish	Special Treatments	Windows	Remarks

Front Doors and Exterior Doors

Circle the shape you want for your front door.

Rectangular   Round arch   Pointed arch

Other _____

Circle the shape you want for your other exterior doors.

Round arch   Pointed arch   Other _____

Will your front door be thicker than the other exterior doors? Explain.

_____

Will your front door be made from a different material than your other exterior doors? _____ If so, explain.

_____

Circle the type finish you want applied to your front door.

Stained   Painted   Faux painted   Other _____

Circle the type finish you want applied to your other exterior doors.

Stained   Painted   Faux painted   Other _____

How many hinges do you want on your front door? (See Door Hinges and Miscellaneous, page 236.) _____

How many hinges do you want on your other exterior doors? (See Door Hinges and Miscellaneous, page 236.) _____

Will your front door have fan lights, a transom, or side windows? (See illustration, page 208.) Explain.

_____

Will any of your other exterior doors have fan lights, a transom, or side windows? (See illustration, page 208.) Explain.

_____

Will your front door have a screen or glass door on the exterior side? _____

Will any of your exterior doors have a screened or glass door on the exterior side? _____

Will there be a wood or stone header over your front door? _____

Will there be a wood or stone header over your other exterior doors? List.

_____

Please fill in all door information on the individual fact sheet for each room that will have an exterior door.

Interior Doors

What are the dimensions (height, width, thickness) of your standard interior door?

_____

What will be the shape of the interior doors? Examples of door shapes: rectangular, round arch, pointed arch. Explain.

_____

Will all interior doors be the same shape? List any that will be a different shape, and what the shape is.

_____

Do you have a preference on the number of hinges you want on your interior doors? (See Door Hinges and Miscellaneous,

page 236.) _____

Interior Doors: Special Features

Fill in the name of any room that will have special interior door features and note those in the appropriate column. (See page 208 for an illustration of a fanlight and transom.)

Examples of types of doors: single doors, double doors, French doors, Dutch doors, double swinging doors, bifold, accordion, pocket, sliding, or other.

Examples of common finishes on a door: stain, paint, faux paint, pickled.

Examples of door headers: wood, stone, brick.

Please fill in all interior door information on the individual fact sheet.

Room	Type of Door	Type of Finish	Fanlight	Transom Light	Side Light	Header Material

Shower Doors

Do you want your shower door oversized or a standard size? _____

Do any of your showers need wheelchair access? Which? _____

If having a steam shower, the shower door needs to go to the top of the door opening. If no steam shower, how high do you

want your shower door? _____

Will shower doors be clear or frosted? _____

Will you want your shower door to swing 90 degrees or 180 degrees? (180 degrees will allow it to swing both into the shower

and open out from the shower.) _____

If having a shower/tub combination, will you use a sliding door, hinged door, or shower curtain? _____

If using a hinged door, how many hinges? _____ (See Door Hinges and Miscellaneous, page 236.)

Please fill in all shower door information on the individual fact sheet for each bathroom with a shower.

Floors

What type of floor material do you want to use in your home: wood, recycled wood, granite, marble, travertine, limestone,

slate, tile, brick, bamboo, cork, glass and metal tiles, leather, linoleum, carpet, concrete, or other? List the types of flooring

material you will use in each room.

_____

_____

_____

_____

Will the wood on any of your floors be stenciled, distressed, saw blade cut, hand scraped, a mixture of wood and stone, or

other? Explain.

_____

_____

Will any of the wood floors be installed with a design pattern such as parquet, herringbone design, basket weave design, or

other? _____

215

If using wood floors, how wide do you want the planks, or do you want a combination of plank sizes? Explain.

_____

_____

If using stone or tile floors, do you want any type of medallion, mosaic, border, or other design? Explain.

_____

If using square pieces of stone or tile, what size square piece do you want to use?

_____

If using brick in this room, what type of brick, size of brick, and pattern do you want?

_____

If using concrete on this floor, do you want patterns scored into the concrete?

_____

_____

If using concrete on this floor, do you want a color in the concrete? Explain.

_____

Please fill in all floor information on the individual fact sheet for each room.

Light Fixtures

Which of the following lighting options will be used in your home and in what room or area of the home will they be located: chandelier, wall sconces, recessed can lights, art lighting, wall light fixtures, ceiling light fixtures, or other? List fixtures and room(s) in which they will be located.

_____

_____

Do you want cove lighting in the ceiling? If so, which room(s)? _____

Do you want special bookcase lighting to illuminate the bookcase? Explain.

_____

Do you want lighting above any of your upper cabinets? Rope, halogen strip, or other?

_____

Do you want lights underneath the upper cabinets? If so, which cabinets and what type: puck lights, rope, halogen strips, fluorescent, or other?

_____

_____

Do you want glass on any cabinet doors requiring lighting inside? If so, which cabinets?

_____

Will you use rope lighting, halogen strips, or puck lights inside your glass-front cabinet door?

_____

_____

Do you want toe kick lighting (lighting in the area between the floor and underneath your lower cabinet door or drawers) in your home? If so, in which areas?

_____

_____

Do you want all upper cabinet lights in a particular room linked to each other (even if the cabinets are separated on different kitchen area walls) and turned on at one light switch, or do you want each section on a separate light switch?

_____

Do you want all lights underneath the upper cabinets to be linked to each other and turned on at one light switch, or do you want to reach under each cabinet section and flip the switch on separately?

_____

Do you want exterior lighting on the house number, along the sidewalk, on the steps, or other?

_____

Circle any of the following light fixtures you will have on the exterior of your home.

Hanging lanterns   Wall-mounted lanterns   Lanterns mounted on a retaining wall

Lanterns mounted on top of a short column   Lamppost   Other _____

Walls

Circle the type of material you want on the walls in your home.

Sheetrock   Wood panels   Skip trowel technique   Log   Other _____

217

Circle any type of application you want on your walls.

Wallpaper   Fabric   Faux paint   Mirror   Landscape-type painted scenery   Other _____

Will the edge where two walls meet be a 90-degree right angle or a soft curved shape?

_____

Will the walls in your home have any of the following: chair rail, crown molding, wood paneling, bead board, baseboard, wainscot, niche in the wall, or other? Explain.

_____

_____

Windows

Do you want many windows or a minimal amount of windows in your home? _____

Which type of the following window(s) do you want to use in your home: double-hung, fixed, sliding, pivot, awning, louver, bay, or other type of window? (See Types of Windows, page 210.)

_____

Will any of the windows have a wood, stone, or other material used for the header? Explain.

_____

Do you want any of the following?

- ❑ Operable windows
- ❑ Window screens
- ❑ Window locks with keys
- ❑ Double pane windows
- ❑ Skylight
- ❑ Removable windows for cleaning
- ❑ Window tinting
- ❑ Other _____

7

Electrical, HVAC, and Plumbing

Three of the most important components of a well-functioning home are electrical, HVAC, and plumbing systems. These three systems bring us the basics: lights, heat/air conditioning, and water. Various options to consider for these essentials will be discussed in this chapter.

ELECTRICAL

For your electrical needs you will need a clean copy of your floor plans and elevation plans, plus a Blank Comment Form for taking notes. Using the Electrical Checklist, make notations regarding your electrical needs on the plans with additional comments on the Blank Comment Form. Label the floor and electrical plan "Electrical Needs." When your architect is ready to produce your electrical plans, this will come in handy during discussions.

OUTLETS

Optimally, your home will have outlets exactly where you need them. To achieve this, identify the items in your home that will need outlets. The Electrical Checklist (page 225) lists the most common items that use an outlet. Check items that you will use, and then check whether it remains plugged in or plugs in and out when used. (An item that plugs in and out when used needs an easily accessible outlet.)

When marking up your clean copy of the floor plans and elevation plans, refer to this checklist to account for every outlet you need.

Some things to consider:

> ◗ A strip of outlets can be mounted under the overhang of the top of a kitchen island, which will give you flexibility when using small appliances.

- Realize that outlets mounted in the baseboard are an additional expense, because of having to cut into the baseboard for each outlet.
- Make floor outlets deep enough so that when items are plugged in, the plug is flush with the floor and does not stick up. Specify if you want a single receptacle outlet in the floor outlet or a double receptacle outlet.

TIP: If you will be hiring an audiovisual consultant, ask if a surge protection will be included with their equipment.

- If you have a piece of furniture with tall legs and a lamp, place the outlet for the lamp just below the table top so that the lamp cord and outlet are not seen, as shown on the right in the illustration on this page. You can see how much more aesthetically pleasing it is to avoid dangling cords.
- Discuss with your architect, interior designer, and builder the pros and cons of placing outlets in bathrooms in the mirror or in the stone splash.
- If your desk will be located away from a wall, consider a floor outlet for plugging in a lamp on your desk. If you run a lamp cord from the desk to the wall, you could trip on it and it is not aesthetically pleasing. You will want this floor outlet connected to a light switch so you can turn it on and off when you enter and exit the room.

TIP: Know your municipal electrical codes, which give guidelines on the distance between outlets on a wall.

POWER SOURCE

Items that will need electric power need to be identified so the electrician will know where to run

CUSTOM PLACEMENT OF OUTLETS

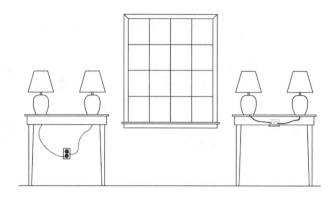

wires. These items usually operate by flipping a light switch, pushing a button, or using a remote control. On the Electrical Checklist (page 225), check items that will need a power source. When marking up the clean copy of the floor plans and elevation plans, refer to this checklist to account for every power source you need.

TIP: Plan for proper lighting to read the labels on the fuse box. Sometimes fuse/breaker boxes are located in closets without enough light to read the labels.

INTERIOR LIGHTING NEEDS

Areas in a home needing illumination that are often overlooked:

- Bookcase, so you can read book titles
- Fuse box, so you can read the fuse box labels
- Linen closet, because any light in the ceiling within the closet does not illuminate lower shelves
- Stereo equipment, so you can read the controls

TIP: When planning the placement of recessed can lights or a chandelier on

your ceiling, consider the distance that the crown molding or cornice over a window will project out from the wall. The distance will affect centering.

EXTERIOR LIGHTING NEEDS

If you will use a landscape architect or an exterior lighting expert, discuss areas around your home that may need illumination with those consultants. If not using a consultant, tell your architect your exterior lighting needs. The Electrical Checklist (page 225) presents a number of potential exterior lighting needs. When marking up the clean copy of the floor plans and elevation plans, refer to this checklist to account for every exterior lighting need.

TIP: If you provide outdoor live music or use a DJ when entertaining, discuss with your builder and electrician where to install outlets for the musicians or DJ.

LIGHT SWITCHES

Analyze the locations of light switches, where you will want three-way, four-way, and five-way light switches, and which outlets should connect to a light switch. If a light switch is in an inconvenient location, you will be reminded of that fact each time you reach for that switch. When you retire for the evening, if you have to walk across the room to reach a light switch, you will be wishing there was a three-way switch at each end of the room. And turning off lamps can be much easier if the lamps are connected to a light switch. Put in time and effort filling in the Electrical Checklist (page 225). You will be glad you did!

FORMS TO USE

Electrical Checklist (page 225)
Electrical Item Shopping Form (page 282)
Individual Room and Closet Fact Sheet (page 81)

ELECTRICAL GLOSSARY

Three-way switch: lets you turn the same light or outlet on from two separate switches.

Four-way switch: lets you turn the same light or outlet on from three separate switches.

Five-way switch: lets you turn the same light or outlet on from four separate switches.

Tip: Using a large font for labeling the fuse box switches will make them easier to read.

Light Switch Placement

At times there will be a trade-off between the function of a light switch location and aesthetics.

The edge of a light switch plate should be a minimum of 2½ inches from the outer edge of the door trim, 3 inches being optimal. This should be consistent on every door. It should be noted on the electrical plans and discussed with your builder. If switch plate covers are mounted on the stud, 16 inches from the door, you will end up with dirty marks on the wall from hands feeling for the light switch.

Make sure no light switches are specified in a wall that has a pocket door behind it, because the pocket door will fill the entire interior wall.

For a group of light switches ganged together, identify what each switch turns on. Spend time determining the most logical sequence of the switches.

Numerous electrical items exist that can add convenience to your lifestyle, add protection to your home, or provide savings, such as a whole-house on-off switch and an integrated home automation system. When marking up the clean copy of the floor plans and elevation plans, refer to the Electrical Checklist (page 225) and add any of these items you want in your home. You will want to add all electrical item decisions you make to the Individual Room and Closet Fact Sheets that you have already started, which are filed in Binder 4.

HVAC

Although many of the choices for HVAC are technical and the size of your home will dictate those needs, you still have important choices to make. From the heating and cooling perspective, decide if you want air conditioning, forced air heat, a heat pump, radiant heated floors, a geothermal system, solar heat, or a combination of these. Experts in the HVAC field can offer recommendations based on your climate and the home you are building.

From an aesthetic and functional perspective, pay attention to the location of air vents, return air vents, and the thermostat—to avoid these being placed where you planned to put furniture, place a rug, or hang art. A furniture plan will help prevent such mistakes. Also consider the location of the outdoor air compressor. Will it be seen by a guest? Will the noise when it is running disturb someone sleeping? Will it be heard while sitting on your porch, patio, or deck? Is it located along a driveway where a car can accidentally run into it?

The location of vents in your home is influenced by the location of your HVAC system. If the system is located in the basement, vents are generally located in the floor or lower wall. If it is located in the attic, the vents are generally located in the ceiling or upper wall.

Note any decisions you make, such as the location of the thermostats and air vents, on the appropriate Individual Room and Closet Fact Sheet and the Miscellaneous Information Checklist, both of which are filed in Binder 4.

FORM TO USE

HVAC Checklist (page 228)

Individual Room and Closet Fact Sheet
   (page 81)

Miscellaneous Information Checklist (page 72)

HVAC GLOSSARY

Desuperheater: a mechanical device that uses the leftover heat from the geothermal system to heat a domestic hot water tank.

Floor register: a vent used to cover the HVAC air source coming out of the floor.

Forced air heat: a common form of heating with natural gas, propane, or electricity. Air is heated and then forced through ducts to various rooms in the home.

Furniture plan: a floor plan showing the placement of furniture to scale.

Heat pump: a mechanical device that moves heat from a cool space into a warm space during the heating season, and moves heat from your cool house into the warm outdoors during the cooling season.

Radiant heat: a method of heating using either water or electricity in pipes that are placed in the floors, walls, ceilings, or other surface.

HVAC VENT AND FILTER PLACEMENT

Ceiling air ducts should not interfere with recessed can lights, pot racks, or chandeliers. Aesthetically, ceiling and floor HVAC vents look more pleasing if they are installed parallel to a wall, not perpendicular. If an HVAC vent is located near a window, it will look better if it is centered on that window whether the vent is located in the floor, ceiling, wall, or baseboard.

In bathrooms, considering locating an HVAC floor vent under the towel bar, which will help dry the towel and in the winter, warm the towel.

You need to be able to easily remove the HVAC filter for changing or cleaning. If they are squished in a closet or a ceiling, access to the filter will be challenging.

Thermostats should be mounted on a wall that will not receive direct sunlight. They should not be placed on a wall where they will interfere with furniture or art placement. In addition, a larger font size will make the thermostat easier to read.

PLUMBING

Discuss with your architect the type of plumbing pipe you will use in your home and the type of water heater you will use. The other plumbing basics, such as sinks, faucets, toilets, showers, and tubs, are addressed in Chapter 5.

TYPE OF PLUMBING PIPE

There are three common choices for plumbing pipes for a home: copper pipes, PEX tube pipes, or PVC.

Copper pipes, which have been around since 1920, have been the pipe of choice for many years. Copper is biostatic, which means it does not allow bacteria to grow inside the pipe. It also resists corrosion. Though it costs more, it has a lengthy warranty.

> TIP: Know your municipal plumbing codes, which give guidelines on the location of exterior house faucets.

PEX is a flexible plumbing tube that has strength and flexibility at temperatures ranging from below freezing to 200 degrees Fahrenheit. It resists corrosion and the scale buildup. It is a cross-linked polyethylene, which makes it more durable under extreme temperatures, and has been used in the U.S. since the 1980s. It can be used with copper and PVC by using special adapters. PEX is a relatively new product in the U.S. and its long-term performance is unknown. (If you live in a cold climate, ask your home insurance agent if PEX rather than copper piping will save on your home insurance.)

PVC (chlorinated polyvinyl chloride) pipe is cheaper than copper, but can be noisy if used vertically in a multistory home. You will hear the water run from one floor to another each time the toilet is flushed or any water runs in the sinks, showers, or tubs. PVC also releases a toxic gas during a fire.

FORMS TO USE
Plumbing Checklist (page 229)
Miscellaneous Information Checklist (page 72)

WATER HEATERS

The number of people living in your home, the number of tubs and showers, and the number of dishwashers and washing machines will determine how many tank or tankless water heaters you will need and the size of each. The layout of your home will determine the location of the water heaters.

Tankless water heater (heat on demand). Tankless water heaters heat water as you need it, instead

Benefits of a Geothermal System

A geothermal system has many benefits. Heat from the earth is renewable and nonpolluting, and geothermal systems last longer than conventional systems because they are protected from harsh outdoor weather. The ground loop has an expected life of more than fifty years and requires no maintenance. The system will give you substantial energy savings. You can have a payback analysis run to determine how long it will take to recoup the cost of the system in energy savings.

Also known as a ground source heat pump, the geothermal system uses the natural heat stored in the earth to heat and cool your home. The constant ground temperature runs between 50 and 57 degrees, depending on your latitude. By using a network of looping tubes filled with water or antifreeze, these tubes collect the earth's heat from underground and run it through the system in your home. When the heated water or antifreeze reaches the heat exchanges, it is converted into warm air. To cool your home, it is reversed simply by flipping a switch. You can use a conventional thermostat or an integrated home automation monitor to set the temperature desired.

of keeping a tank of water hot all the time—which saves money and energy. These have been used in Europe, Asia, and South America for seventy-five years and in the United States since the late 1970s. They have gained popularity in the United States in the last decade. The bigger the gas burner or the bigger the electrical element, the higher the volume of hot water it can supply. Tankless water heaters are about the size of a piece of carry-on luggage. They can be mounted on the exterior of a home in a recessed box or inside the home. You will save the floor space that would have been taken up by a water heater—and you have a never-ending supply of hot water. The disadvantage is that you do not get hot water instantly; cold water must run through the heater until it gets hot. You can add a recirculating pump to the tankless heater for instant hot water at the faucet.

Tank water heater. If you are using a tank water heater, natural gas usually costs less to operate than electric. With a geothermal system, you can add a desuperheater to the system that sends unused heat to heat the water in the water heater tank. Look at Energy Guide labels for yearly operating cost information. Also compare the recovery rate, the number of gallons the water heater can heat in one hour.

What size tank do you need? Two people usually need a 30- to 40-gallon tank; three require a 40-gallon tank; four need a 40- to 50-gallon tank; more than five need a 50- to 80-gallon tank.

A recirculation pump draws hot water from the water heater and simultaneously sends the cooled-off water back to the water heater to be reheated. You will have instant hot water when you turn on the hot water faucet. The recirculation pump can be used on a tank and a tankless water heater. If the water heaters are plumbed in a series, one recirculation pump can operate several water tanks.

FORMS TO USE
Miscellaneous Information Checklist (page 72)

Tip: You may be entitled to a $300 tax credit when purchasing a tankless water heater due to the Energy Tax Incentive Act of 2005. Ask your tax accountant or look it up in your tax software.

Electrical Checklist

Potential Items in Your Home Needing Outlets

For each item that applies below, place a check in the appropriate column to indicate whether the item remains plugged in or is plugged in and out when used.

Item	Remains Plugged In	Plugged In as Needed
Air purifier (portable)		
Appliances		
Appliances (handheld)		
Art or portrait light fixtures that hang above frames		
Christmas decorations		
Clocks on mantel, inside bookcase, on wall, or other		
Clothes steamer		
Computers		
Drill charger		
Dustbuster		
Exercise equipment		
Fans (portable)		
Flashlight charger		
Furniture with interior lighting		
Garage door opener motor		
Hair dryer (plugged in bathroom drawer)		
Humidifier (portable)		
Lamps inside bookcase, in powder room, on tables; floor lamps; etc.		
Office equipment		
Outdoor patio fans (portable)		
Outdoor patio televisions		
Pants press		
Pet feeder, fan, and heater		
Plant lighting (interior)		
Player piano (may need floor outlet)		
Popcorn wagon (may need floor outlet)		
Razor, toothbrush, etc., stored in medicine cabinet		
Screwdriver charger		
Security cameras		
Shoe buffer		
Shop vacuum mounted on a wall		
Stereo equipment		
Surge protectors for audiovisual and office/computer equipment		
Telephone answering machine or cordless phone base		
Televisions including those that pop up out of furniture		
Towel warmers (portable)		
Vacuum cleaner		
Other _____		

Do you want your outlets mounted in the wall or in your baseboard? _____

If in the wall, how high off the finished floor do you want your outlets mounted? _____

Do you want to customize the exact location of some outlets as they relate to the furniture in this room? _____

If so, list the room and describe the location so it can be specified on the electrical plans.

_____

_____

_____

Potential Items in Your Home Needing a Power Source

Check any that apply.
- ❏ Attic areas
- ❏ Bathroom exhaust fan
- ❏ Cabinet lights (above)
- ❏ Cabinet lights (inside)
- ❏ Cabinet lights (underneath)
- ❏ Ceiling fans
- ❏ Doorbell
- ❏ Driveway gates
- ❏ Electric towel heaters (fixed)
- ❏ Exterior steps courtesy lighting
- ❏ Home automation system monitors
- ❏ Gas log light switch starters
- ❏ Gates with release button
- ❏ Invisible fence
- ❏ Kitchen exhaust fan
- ❏ Lawn sprinkler system
- ❏ Motorized retractable television screens
- ❏ Motorized window treatments
- ❏ Outdoor balcony, patio, and porch ceiling fans
- ❏ Pot rack with lights
- ❏ Recessed can lights over headboards
- ❏ Security alarm pads
- ❏ Security cameras
- ❏ Security lights
- ❏ Security systems
- ❏ Thermostats
- ❏ Toe kick heaters
- ❏ Toe kick lights
- ❏ Whole-house vacuum systems
- ❏ Other _____

Potential Exterior Lighting Needs

Check any that apply.
- ❏ Along the driveway
- ❏ Along the sidewalk
- ❏ Basketball goal
- ❏ Corners of the home
- ❏ Entrance to the gate
- ❏ On a flagpole
- ❏ Garage area
- ❏ Grill area
- ❏ House numbers
- ❏ Lampposts
- ❏ Lanterns
- ❏ Shrub lights
- ❏ Steps
- ❏ Trash storage area
- ❏ Tree lights
- ❏ Other _____

Note: Landscape lighting areas are not included in this list.

Potential Items in Your Home Needing a Light Switch to Turn On/Off

Check any that apply.
- ❏ Cabinet lighting (above, underneath, inside)
- ❏ Ceiling fan
- ❏ Ceiling light fixtures
- ❏ Christmas tree
- ❏ Disposal
- ❏ Exterior Christmas lighting
- ❏ Exterior flood lights

Potential Items in Your Home Needing a Light Switch to Turn On/Off (continued)

Check any that apply.

- ❑ Exterior lamppost
- ❑ Exterior lanterns
- ❑ Exterior shrub lights
- ❑ Exterior tree lights
- ❑ Gas logs in fireplace starter
- ❑ Lamps
- ❑ Outlets with lamps plugged into them
- ❑ Reading lights over headboards
- ❑ Recessed can lights
- ❑ Sconces
- ❑ Toe kick heater
- ❑ Toe kick light
- ❑ Wall light fixtures
- ❑ Other _____

Optional Electrical Items

Check any that apply.

- ❑ Three-way switches*
- ❑ Four-way switches*
- ❑ Five-way switches*
- ❑ Dimmer switches*
- ❑ Illuminated light switches*
- ❑ Interior motion sensor light switches*
- ❑ Jamb light switches*
- ❑ Timers on light switches*
- ❑ Whole house surge protector
- ❑ Generator for back-up power
- ❑ Lightning grounding protection system
- ❑ Motion sensors on exterior lights—if so, on which lights? _____
- ❑ Dusk-to-dawn sensors on exterior lights—if so, on which lights? _____
- ❑ Timers on exterior lights—if so, on which lights? _____
- ❑ Other _____

*List specific locations on a Blank Comment Form (page 18).

Will your yard be fenced in with an electronic gate, preventing the meter reader from accessing the meter box? _____

Where would you like your fuse/breaker box located? _____

Do you need a larger font size for labeling the breaker box? _____

Circle the type of light switch you prefer. Toggle   Rocker   Rotary   Push button   Other _____

HVAC Checklist

Which of the following do you want in your home?

- ❑ Air conditioning—if so, one, two, or three units? _____
- ❑ Forced air for heating
- ❑ Heat pump
- ❑ Radiant floor heating—if so, electric or water heated? _____
- ❑ Both forced air and radiant floor heating—if so, explain which room gets what.

   _____

- ❑ Other source of heating _____
- ❑ Radiant heated surfaces (shower floors, shower walls, shower bench, tub deck, other)—list which you will heat.

   _____

- ❑ Humidifier system for entire home
- ❑ Humidifier in select rooms—if so, list rooms. _____
- ❑ Air purifier system
- ❑ Geothermal system
- ❑ Other _____

Do you prefer your HVAC vents to be in the ceiling, walls, floors, baseboard, or a combination of areas? _____

How many HVAC systems will you need? _____

Will you want to use decorative vent covers and return air vent covers or standard ones? What color works best with the location of your vents? Explain.

_____

_____

If you will have two or three systems, what rooms do you want on each system? List.

_____

_____

_____

In what room(s) do you want the thermostat(s) and where in that room will it be located? Explain.

_____

If using radiant heat, where in each room will you want each floor heat control panel located? Explain.

_____

_____

Interior Plumbing

Place a check in each column that applies. For example, a typical bar will have a sink and a faucet; a dog bath area will require a handheld sprayer. Make notes on the next page as needed, such as noting that the bar and garage will have both hot and cold faucets.

Plumbing Checklist

Room	Sink/ Faucet	Tub	Jetted Tub	Toilet	Bidet	Shower- head	Shower Jets	Water Purifier	Hand- held Sprayer	Heated Towel Bar	Steam Shower
Bar											
Bathroom, master											
Bathroom, guest											
Bathroom 1											
Bathroom 2											
Bathroom 3											
Dog bath area											
Garage											
Kitchen											
Laundry room											
Morning kitchen											
Pool house											
Powder room 1											
Powder room 2											
Wine room											
Other_____											

229

Interior Plumbing (continued)

Other notes about these rooms:

_____

_____

_____

_____:

_____:

_____:

Check those that apply:

Other Interior Needs

❏ Aquarium
❏ Ice maker
❏ Water wall
❏ Other _____

Exterior Plumbing

❏ Drinking water fountain
❏ Faucet (back of house)
❏ Faucet (front of house)
❏ Faucet (on garage)
❏ Faucet (other side of house)
❏ Faucet (side of house)
❏ Sink by outdoor grill area
❏ Other _____

Overall Plumbing

❏ Copper and PVC combination
❏ Copper pipes
❏ Geothermal desuperheater
❏ PEX and copper combination
❏ PEX pipes
❏ Recirculation water pump
❏ Tankless water heater
❏ Tank water heater
❏ Other _____

8 Hardware and Stone/Tile

The use of hardware and stone/tile in a home comes with what seems like an endless number of options and applications. Some understanding of these options and applications will help you have an aesthetically pleasing and functional home.

CABINET DOOR AND DRAWER HARDWARE

TAKE A SAMPLE WITH YOU

Various styles of cabinet doors and drawer fronts directly affect the hardware you select, so take a sample of each with you when shopping. Three of the most important concerns are the thickness of the cabinet door, the width of the stile, and the height of the rail. (The stile is the vertical member of the cabinet door on the outer edge of each side; the rail is the horizontal member on the top and bottom edge of the door.)

Cabinet and drawer hardware standard screws are one inch long. Some cabinet doors and drawer fronts require longer screws, which can be specified when you order your cabinet hardware.

The size of the flat surface of a drawer front will determine if it will accommodate two handles or knobs, which are recommended for a drawer more than 24 inches wide. This measurement can be affected by the bevel design or applied molding—which is another reason to take a drawer front sample with you.

MAKE ACCURATE MEASUREMENTS

Knowing the thickness of the cabinet door and drawer front where a knob or pull will be mounted is important—the screws used in mounting the hardware need to be long enough. If you are selecting a European line of hardware and the screw is too short, you may face a challenging and time-consuming job of replacing the short screw. European hardware uses the metric system and the threads inside the hardware piece are metric, as is the screw. If you know you need longer screws when ordering the hardware, specify that on the order.

The width of the stile is an important measurement when selecting cabinet knobs, pulls, and rosettes. If you have a narrow stile with a bulky knob, the knobs on two side-by-side cabinet doors may bump into each other. If you have a large rosette, it might be too wide to fit in the stile. You'll see two common problems with knobs and rosettes illustrated below.

Depending on the placement of your hardware, the height of the rail also factors in when selecting cabinet door hardware. If your preference is to mount the hardware in the upper corner of the door, both the rail and the stile will determine the size of space available in that corner.

The size of the drawer front flat area will determine the size of knobs, drawer pulls, and rosettes that will fit. These are why it is important to take a

sample of your cabinet door and drawer front with you when selecting hardware.

If the holes are pre-cut for cabinet hardware, you will need to know the center-to-center measure on any with two holes.

BATHROOM HARDWARE

The most common pieces of hardware found in a bathroom are towel bars, towel hooks, towel rings, toilet paper holders, cabinet knobs and pulls, and drawer knobs and pulls. Additional hardware options are a wall-mounted soap dish holder for the shower, wall-mounted shower shelves, wall-mounted or counter standing magnifying mirror, heated towel bars, robe hooks, and grab bars. Depending on where you use a glass door or a shower curtain, you may also be selecting door hinges and handles or a curtain rod and brackets.

> **TIP: Allow enough lead time when purchasing your hardware or risk delaying your job. And when selecting cabinet and drawer pulls, keep in mind that they need to be finger friendly.**

When shopping for bath hardware, you need to know the width of the wall where you plan to hang towel bars, heated towel bars, and grab bars; and the height, width, and weight of your glass shower door or the width of the shower/tub for a shower curtain. When measuring for a shower curtain, if you have stone or tile on the wall, measure above the stone or tile where the shower curtain bar will actually be mounted.

FORM TO USE
Individual Bathroom Hardware Checklist
(page 242)

CABINET DOOR RAILS AND STILES

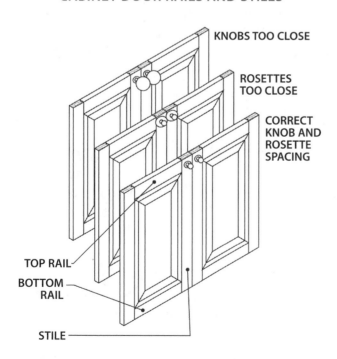

KNOBS TOO CLOSE

ROSETTES TOO CLOSE

CORRECT KNOB AND ROSETTE SPACING

TOP RAIL

BOTTOM RAIL

STILE

BEDROOM CLOSET HARDWARE

Bedroom closets may have large quantities of hardware or relatively few. If you have a bank of drawers or an island with drawers, you can have a half moon cut out of the drawer front or a drawer pull on each drawer front. Hanging clothing may be on open rods or the hanging rods could be located behind several glass doors, each requiring a doorknob or handle. Shoes may be displayed on open shelves requiring no hardware, or stored in a drawer with glass mounted into the front that needs a knob or pull to open the drawer. Alternatively, shoes may be stored on shelves behind glass doors requiring a knob or pull, or stored on pull-out shelves that will need drawer runners.

FORM TO USE

Bedroom Closet Hardware Checklist (page 243)

**Tip: If you are using a wooden
hanging rod in your closet, use a
covering for the rod because hangers
do not glide well over wood.
These coverings are made of glossy
material that slips over the rod
and lets hangers slide smoothly.**

KITCHEN HARDWARE

The kitchen is one of the most hardware-intensive rooms in a home. There are cabinets, drawers, doors, appliance handles, towel hooks, apron hooks, pot holder hooks, magnetic knife holders, and pot racks. Careful planning for all hardware items you will use in your kitchen before going shopping will be very beneficial.

FORM TO USE

Kitchen Hardware Checklist (page 244)

LAUNDRY ROOM HARDWARE

Laundry rooms come in different sizes with different functions that cater to your lifestyle. Your hardware needs will be based on the size of your laundry room and how you use this room. For example, if ironing is an important function in the laundry room, you will want rods or hooks to hang clothes. If your laundry room has an area to wash a dog or boots, you may want a towel bar or hook.

FORM TO USE

Laundry Room Hardware Checklist (page 244)

HARDWARE IN MISCELLANEOUS ROOMS

Rooms other than the bathroom, bedroom closet, kitchen, and laundry room may also require cabinet and drawer hardware. Examples might be drawers in the bar or cabinets in the library. List the hardware for each room separately; make additional copies of the form if you need to list more rooms.

FORM TO USE

Miscellaneous Rooms with Cabinet Hardware Checklist (page 245)

MISCELLANEOUS EXTERIOR AND ARCHITECTURAL HARDWARE

**TIP: Some municipalities require
house numbers on the back of
the house as well on the front if there
is an alley. The size of the house
numbers are often part of the code.**

Besides the basic doorknobs and cabinet door and drawer hardware, you'll want to consider exterior hardware such as shutter hardware, decorative garage door hardware, mailboxes, house numbers, and weather vanes. Additionally, there is architectural hardware such as finials, conductor heads or leader boxes on gutters, chimney caps, and louvers.

FORM TO USE

Exterior and Architectural Hardware Checklist (page 246)

TIP: Identity theft can occur when people steal from mailboxes. When shopping for a mailbox, consider one that can be locked. Make sure it has the approval of the U.S. Postal Department and your Homeowner Association.

DOOR HARDWARE

You have at least five different types of doorstops and six different types of dead bolts to choose between, as shown in Doorstop Options (above, right) and Door Bolt Options (page 235). Selecting the correct door hardware can be complicated, but these illustrations and the checklist will help you choose the correct door hardware.

Measure the size and location of all existing holes in the door. This includes the opening for the mortise lock, which should include the depth of the hole as well as the height and width. (See Mortise Locks, page 235.) Measure from the center of one hole to the center of the other. This could be from doorknob hole to the dead bolt hole or any other holes in the door. If the hardware you want does not fit the existing holes, new holes can be cut. The old holes can be filled and covered by paint or stain, but stain does not quite hide the location of old holes. You can more thoroughly cover old holes with large decorative plates that fit under the doorknob or lever, or use finger plates (a flat protective covering to protect against finger marks).

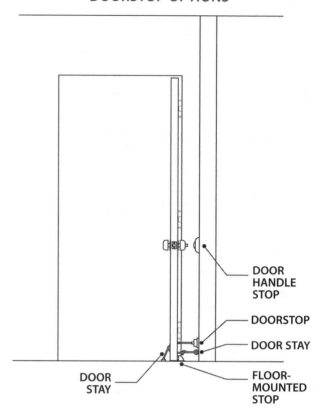

DOORSTOP OPTIONS

DOOR HANDLE STOP

DOORSTOP

DOOR STAY

DOOR STAY

FLOOR-MOUNTED STOP

FORM TO USE

Door Hardware Checklist (page 247)

TIP: Round doorknobs may be too difficult to grip and operate for a person with arthritis or other conditions— lever handles may be the best option. However, avoid them if you have toddlers or young children around, because they can easily open the doors.

DOOR HARDWARE GLOSSARY

Dummy door: a door with a doorknob that does not turn or have any type of locking mechanism, usually a closet door. The door uses a ball catcher to keep it closed, and the knob is used as a grip to open the door.

DOOR BOLT OPTIONS

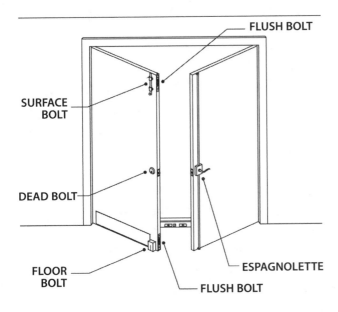

MORTISE LOCKS

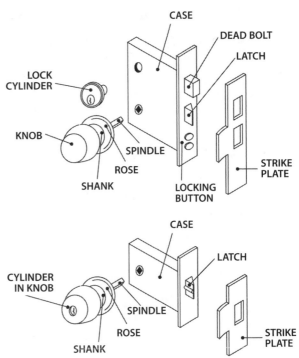

Passage door: usually a hallway door you would pass through, hence the name passage; it does not lock.

Privacy door: a door that can be locked from inside the room, usually a bedroom, bathroom, or powder room.

FACTS ABOUT DOORS

The quality of your door hardware should at least match the quality of your door.

Generally, all interior privacy, dummy, and passage doors are the same thickness. Front doors and other exterior doors are often thicker than interior doors.

Ball bearing hinges are stronger and work well with heavier doors, making the door glide open and close more smoothly. It is not uncommon to use a ball bearing hinge on a heavier exterior door and another type of hinge on interior doors.

If your front door is nine feet or taller, adding a decorative surface bolt to the top and bottom of the door will help prevent it from warping due to the sun and other elements.

Standard baseboard doorstops are three inches

long, so any towel bar located behind a door should not extend out from the wall more than three inches, or the door will bump into the towel bar.

The height of the threshold will affect which doorstop will work.

Know codes in your municipality regarding door locks before selecting hardware.

Avoid using a doorknob with a push button lock if you are using a door handle doorstop because it will lock each time the button hits the doorstop.

If you are on a tight budget, spend more money on a nicer entry set and less money on other exterior door hardware. However, the keyways must be compatible if you want all doors keyed alike.

KNUCKLE BUSTERS

If you will be installing plantation shutters on a door with glass, take into account that the frame of the shutter may affect the placement of your doorknob. It also may create a "knuckle buster" problem.

When the door stile is narrow and you select a round knob, especially an oversized one, your knuckles, may strike the doorjamb when turning the knob and you may "bust" your knuckles. Raised door panels and plantation shutters can also contribute to busted knuckles.

KEYING LOCKS

Make a list of all doors that will use keys. Note which doors will be keyed the same and which need to be keyed differently.

During installation, you will want all of your doors keys to be inserted the same way, with the teeth of the keys either upward or downward.

Give your builder and hardware salesperson a list of any locks that need to be keyed alike.

DOOR HINGES AND MISCELLANEOUS

Door hinges will have either a square corner or a rounded corner, so it is important to know the shape if you are replacing an existing hinge and if the doors are precut for hinges. Wherever possible, take a photograph and measurement of the hinge area and take it with you when selecting door hardware. Other information you'll need:

Right or left? Handing of the door is identified as left or right, as illustrated below. From the outside of the door while facing the door, whatever side the hinges are mounted is the handing of the door. If the hinges are on the left, the handing is left. If the hinges are mounted on the right, the handing is right. The handing of the door is important if you use a lever handle or if you are using a mortise lock set.

Distance from floor. For doorstops, you will need to know the distance from your floor to the bottom of the door to determine the height of your floor mounted doorstop: the higher the door threshold, the higher the doorstop.

Backset measurement. This is the distance from the center of the hole cut for a doorknob (or lever or dead bolt) to the outer edge of the door. The

HANDING OF THE DOOR

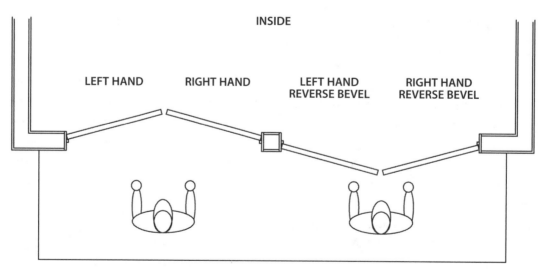

INSIDE

LEFT HAND   RIGHT HAND   LEFT HAND REVERSE BEVEL   RIGHT HAND REVERSE BEVEL

OUTSIDE

center of the hole is located in the part of the door called the lock stile.

Weight. Heavier doors may require a mortise lock, extra hinges, and possibly a ball bearing hinge to ensure stability. Also, the length of the screws will ensure stability. Ask your hardware expert about the requirements for your doors.

STONE AND TILE

This section will familiarize you with some of the decisions that need to be made regarding stone and tile. If you selected another product such as brick, concrete, Corian, laminate, synthetic concrete, synthetic stone, or stainless, the information in this chapter will still be of great assistance.

Once you have decided where you want to use stone and tile, you will need to select the individual pieces of stone and tile you would like to use for each application. Following that decision, you will need to become familiar with the various options regarding stone and tile.

Later, in Chapter 12, you will complete the Entire-Home Stone/Tile Selections form (page 331), which will ask for details about the stone and where and how it will be used. You'll file the following forms in Binder 4.

FORMS TO USE

Interior Applications for Stone/Tile (Excluding Bathrooms) Checklist (page 249)

Bathroom Applications for Stone/Tile Checklist (page 251)

Exterior Applications for Stone/Tile Checklist (page 252)

Stone/Tile Cuts Checklist (page 253)

POLISHED, HONED, OR TUMBLED

The most common finish on stone is polished, a smooth glossy finish that is reflective. It brings out the colors and natural finish in a piece of stone. However, if not wiped properly, you can see streaks in the reflection.

A honed finish is not fully polished. The stone is sanded down to a smooth but dull finish. It does not enhance the colors, but presents a muted look. A honed piece of granite in the kitchen can be easier to clean than polished, because polished granite streaks. There is a charge per foot to hone the stone. Not all stones look good honed, so ask for samples of polished versus honed to compare.

Tumbled stone has imperfections such as nicks in the stone and chips in the sides of each piece. If polished stone can be compared to a sanded and polished floor, then tumbled stone can be compared to a distressed and hand-scraped floor. Tumbled stone is an excellent material to use on the floor in a bathroom or shower. However, not all pieces of stone or tile can be tumbled. Generally, you cannot tumble pieces greater than a 12-inch square, and some stone suppliers limit it to a 6-inch square.

SIZES AND SHAPES

The variety is endless. The most common sizes of stone and tile pieces are 4-inch, 6-inch, and 12-inch squares. However, you can go smaller or larger, depending on the stone and design you select. Mosaic designs can use tiny pieces and be custom made or can be prenetted into 12-inch sheets.

ACCENT PIECES

Accent pieces come in an array of sizes, shapes, colors, and textures. They do not have to be stone; they can be pieces of glass, acrylic, metal, or other materials. Examples of accent pieces are borders, medallions, and mosaic designs applied to floors, walls, and backsplashes. Another type of accent is a stone cap: this fabricated piece of stone is glued onto the flat edge of a stone feature. Decorative caps can

Basic Stone Facts

The most common size of a piece of granite slab is 116 inches (9 feet 8 inches) long by 72 inches (6 feet) wide. If your kitchen island is longer or wider than this, you will need to use two pieces of granite slab. You will need to decide where you want the seams and where you want your sinks in relation to those seams. Kitchen Counter Stone Cut Options (below) shows the different ways of having corners meet, at a diagonal or flat, and different options for positioning your sinks.

In bathrooms, you'll want to place tiles so that the showerhead, faucets, and handles can be centered on the tiles or on grout lines (see illustration, page 239, top). If the tub deck is made of stone, you will need to have some cuts made in the stone in order to cover the area. Almost always, a piece of stone slab is not large enough to cover the entire deck. Three different places to cut the stone are shown in Bathtub Stone Cut Options (page 239, bottom).

KITCHEN COUNTER STONE CUT OPTIONS

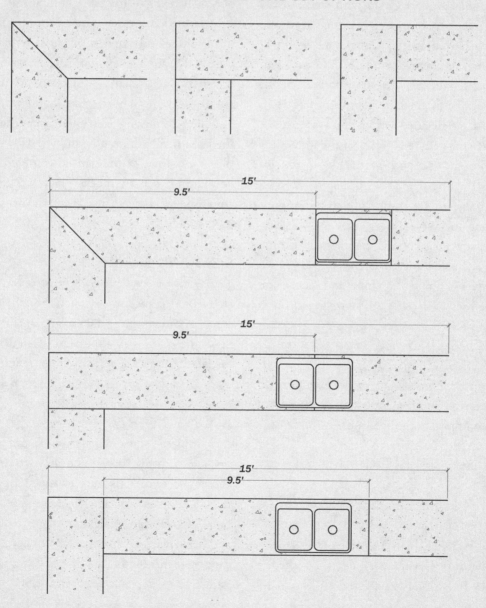

TILE INSTALLATION FOR SHOWER FIXTURE PLACEMENT

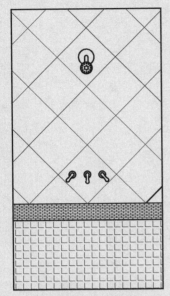
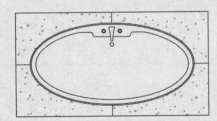

TILE IS PLACED SO THAT FIXTURES CAN BE CENTERED ON TILES.

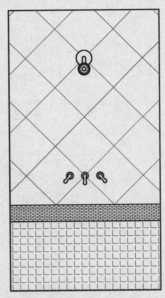
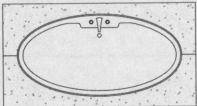

TILE IS PLACED SO THAT FIXTURES CAN BE CENTERED ON GROUT LINES.

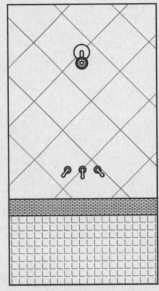
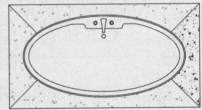

IMPROPER TILE PLACEMENT WILL NOT ALLOW CENTERING OF FIXTURES.

BATHTUB STONE CUT OPTIONS

Tub skirt. If installing a jetted tub, with a tub skirt made of stone slabs, the tub skirt will need to be able to be removed for maintenance and repair on the jetted motors under the tub. Depending on the location of the tub, sometimes the access to the motors can be through a wall in the closet, or the ceiling below.

Multiple sinks. With double or triple sinks, do not allow the counter stone to run between the sinks. When you move your running faucet from sink to sink, water will run all over the counter and often will soak the front of you. Instead, either use a self-rimming sink or an under-mounted sink with the divider between the sinks lower than the counter. (Refer back to Kitchen Sink Divider Pitfall, page 116).

Custom tile splash. For a custom-painted tile splash in your kitchen, order early, as it requires a long lead time.

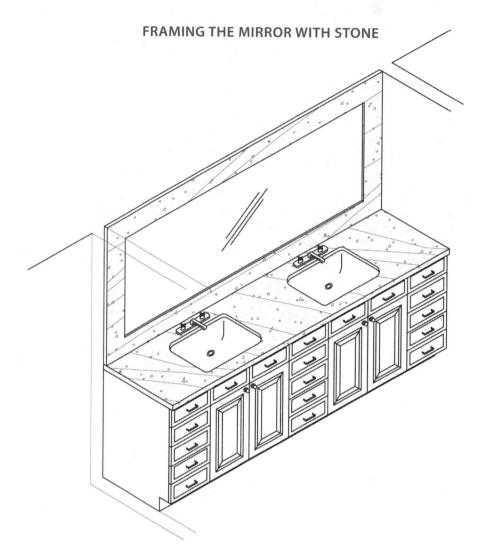

appear on top of stone pieces such as backsplashes, chair rails, and baseboards.

DESIGN PATTERN

The patterns in which you can apply stone are limitless. You can mix granite with marble, stone with wood, or square pieces with hexagonal pieces. You can do a herringbone pattern, a basket weave, or a diamond pattern. The size and shape of the room will greatly affect the design pattern, as you want all edges of the room to end up with the same design.

EDGE

The edge is generally referred to as the edge of the counter or the edge of a shelf. The design choices vary, as does the actual thickness of the edge. The natural design pattern within the slab will influence the type of edge that will look the best. A larger patterned design such as a swirl can look odd when the edge is applied, because the swirl will not continue with the applied piece of stone edge—which leaves too much contrast. A slab with a tiny design or a consistent design of small flecks works well with any edge. Your stone fabricator can advise you and even create a sample. The decorative edge is not cut into the slab counter or shelf, but is a separate piece that is adhered to it.

GROUT

Grout is made of water, cement or epoxy, and sand, which hardens after application. It is used to adhere tile and stone pieces to surfaces. It comes in different colors. The tile pieces can be installed with a thin line of grout showing or can be spaced further apart with a more prominent line of grout.

WORKING WITH YOUR STONE FABRICATOR

Cuts for faucets, sprayers, soap pumps, and hot water dispensers along the back of a counter between the backsplash and sink need to be far enough out from the backsplash or wall so that you can fit the side of your hand between the sink faucet fixture and the backsplash for cleaning. (Refer back to Faucet/Backsplash Relationship, page 94.) This includes bathroom, kitchen, laundry, and powder room sinks. To gain space may involve moving the placement of the sink forward. The depth of a counter has a standard dimension, and deviations may affect the fit of appliances under the counter. Explain to your stone fabricator what you are trying to achieve.

Work with your fabricator regarding the location of any slab cuts in your counters. You will want the counter cuts to line up with tile or slab pieces in the backsplash.

If you will have outlets in any of the stone/tile splash on a counter, talk to your fabricator regarding the splash height. Is it tall enough to be cut for a horizontally installed outlet?

Ask your stone fabricator to use a leftover piece of slab from the bar or the kitchen to create a cutting board for you. You can add rubber feet to the bottom.

Discuss with your fabricator framing the wall in front of your bathroom counter, using a four-, six-, or eight-inch piece of slab that serves as the backsplash, then goes up the walls on both sides and across the ceiling. Within this framed area will be your mirror, as you can see in Framing the Mirror with Stone (page 240). The framed mirror can even extend out to the side walls.

Individual Bathroom Hardware Checklist

Homeowner _____ Date _____

Check any items that you will use in the bathroom named above and indicate the quantity and specifications.

Bathroom name _____

- ❑ Bath towel bar: Quantity _____ Length _____
- ❑ Bath towel hooks : Quantity _____
- ❑ Hand towel bars : Quantity _____ Length _____
- ❑ Hand towel hooks : Quantity _____
- ❑ Hand towel rings : Quantity _____
- ❑ Heated towel bar: Wall space dimensions _____ Water heated or electric? _____
- ❑ Towel-warming drawer: Dimensions _____
- ❑ Toilet paper holder
- ❑ Wall-mounted soap dish holder : Quantity _____
- ❑ Wall-mounted shower shelf: Quantity _____ Corner mounted or other? _____
- ❑ Washcloth hook : Quantity _____
- ❑ Grab bars in shower : Quantity _____ Length of each bar _____
- ❑ Grab bars in the bathtub : Quantity _____ Length of each bar _____
- ❑ Robe hooks : Quantity _____
- ❑ Magnifying mirror: Wall-mounted or counter standing? _____ Lighted or not? _____
- ❑ Shower curtain rod and brackets: Length _____
- ❑ Shower door hinges: Quantity _____ Specifications of door _____
- ❑ Shower door handle
- ❑ Cabinet doorknobs or pulls: Quantity _____ Stile width _____ Rail height _____
- ❑ Drawer pulls: Quantity _____
- ❑ Self-closing drawer runners: Quantity _____ Length of runner _____

Is there any additional bathroom hardware needed? _____

What is the budget for bathroom hardware? _____

Comments:

_____

_____

_____

_____

_____

Bedroom Closet Hardware Checklist

Homeowner _____ Date _____

Check any that apply to the bedroom closet hardware. Fill in the name of the bedroom closet that is represented, and copy more forms as needed.

Name of bedroom closet _____

- ❑ Cabinet doorknobs or pulls: Quantity _____ Stile width _____ Rail height _____
- ❑ Drawer pulls: Quantity _____
- ❑ Self-closing drawer runners: Quantity _____ Length of runner _____
- ❑ Hanging rods: Quantity in feet _____ Number of brackets _____ Length _____
  Adjustable rods? _____ Wood, metal, or plastic? _____ Shape of rod _____
- ❑ Pull-out rods: Quantity _____ Depth of rods _____
- ❑ Hooks for gently worn clothes: Quantity _____
- ❑ Behind the door hooks: Quantity _____

Approximate number of neckties _____

Options or guidelines for mounting tie racks or other tie storage _____

Are there any additional bedroom closets needed? _____

What is the budget allocated for this bedroom closet hardware? _____

Name of bedroom closet _____

- ❑ Cabinet doorknobs or pulls: Quantity _____ Stile width _____ Rail height _____
- ❑ Drawer pulls: Quantity _____
- ❑ Self-closing drawer runners: Quantity _____ Length of runner _____
- ❑ Hanging rods: Quantity in feet _____ Number of brackets _____ Length _____
  Adjustable rods? _____ Wood, metal, or plastic? _____ Shape of rod _____
- ❑ Pull-out rods: Quantity _____ Depth of rods _____
- ❑ Hooks for gently worn clothes: Quantity _____
- ❑ Behind the door hooks: Quantity _____

Approximate number of neckties _____

Options or guidelines for mounting tie racks or other tie storage _____

Are there any additional bedroom closets needed? _____

What is the budget allocated for this bedroom closet hardware? _____

Kitchen Hardware Checklist

Homeowner _____ Date _____

Check any that apply to your kitchen hardware.

- ❑ Cabinet doorknobs or pulls: Quantity _____ Stile width _____ Rail height _____
- ❑ Drawer pulls: Quantity _____
- ❑ Self-closing drawer runners: Quantity _____ Length of runner _____
- ❑ Other drawer runners: Quantity _____ Length of runner _____
- ❑ Appliance handles: List _____
- ❑ Hooks for aprons: Quantity _____
- ❑ Pot holder hooks: Quantity _____
- ❑ Dish towel bars, hooks, or rings: Quantity_____
- ❑ Pot rack specifications _____
- ❑ Wall-mounted magnetic knife holder specifications _____

Will you use a dish towel bar, dish towel hook, or a dish towel ring? _____ If bar, length? _____

Is there any additional kitchen hardware? _____

What is the budget allocated for kitchen hardware? _____

Laundry Room Hardware Checklist

Homeowner _____ Date _____

Check any that apply to your laundry room hardware.

- ❑ Cabinet doorknobs or pulls: Quantity _____ Stile width _____ Rail height _____
- ❑ Drawer pulls: Quantity _____
- ❑ Self-closing drawer runners: Quantity _____ Length of runner _____
- ❑ Pull-out rods: Quantity _____ Depth of rods _____

Is there any additional laundry room hardware? _____

What is the budget allocated for the laundry room hardware? _____

Miscellaneous Rooms with Cabinet Hardware Checklist

Homeowner _____ Date _____

Fill in the name of the room, such as the bar or library, that will need cabinet hardware. Check any that apply to the room you have filled in. If you have additional rooms requiring hardware, photocopy the form.

Room _____

❑ Cabinet doorknobs or pulls: Quantity _____ Stile width _____ Rail height _____
❑ Drawer pulls: Quantity _____
❑ Self-closing drawer runners: Quantity _____ Length of runner _____

Room _____

❑ Cabinet doorknobs or pulls: Quantity _____ Stile width _____ Rail height _____
❑ Drawer pulls: Quantity _____
❑ Self-closing drawer runners: Quantity _____ Length of runner _____

Room _____

❑ Cabinet doorknobs or pulls: Quantity _____ Stile width _____ Rail height _____
❑ Drawer pulls: Quantity _____
❑ Self-closing drawer runners: Quantity _____ Length of runner _____

Room _____

❑ Cabinet doorknobs or pulls: Quantity _____ Stile width _____ Rail height _____
❑ Drawer pulls: Quantity _____
❑ Self-closing drawer runners: Quantity _____ Length of runner _____

Room _____

❑ Cabinet doorknobs or pulls: Quantity _____ Stile width _____ Rail height _____
❑ Drawer pulls: Quantity _____
❑ Self-closing drawer runners: Quantity _____ Length of runner _____

Room _____

❑ Cabinet doorknobs or pulls: Quantity _____ Stile width _____ Rail height _____
❑ Drawer pulls: Quantity _____
❑ Self-closing drawer runners: Quantity _____ Length of runner _____

Exterior and Architectural Hardware Checklist

Homeowner _____ Date _____

Check the potential miscellaneous exterior and architectural hardware you may want for your home. Take this list with you when you go hardware shopping.

Exterior Hardware

❑ Shutter hardware: Quantity _____ Specifications _____

❑ Garage door decorative hardware: Quantity _____ Specifications _____

❑ Mailbox: Specifications _____ Location _____

❑ Mail drop: Specifications _____ Location _____

❑ Weather vane: Specifications _____ Location _____

❑ Address plate: Specifications _____ Location _____

What other hardware do you need? _____

What is the budget allocated for exterior hardware? _____

Architectural Hardware

❑ Finial: Quantity _____ Specifications _____

❑ Conductor heads/leader box for gutters: Quantity _____
Specifications _____

❑ Chimney caps: Specifications _____

❑ Other _____

Comments:

_____
_____
_____
_____
_____

Door Hardware Checklist

Homeowner _____ Date _____

Check the door hardware you want, and fill in quantities needed throughout your home. Take this list with you when you go hardware shopping.

- ❑ Privacy doorknobs: Quantity for the entire home _____
- ❑ Passage doorknob:s Quantity for the entire home _____
- ❑ Dummy doorknobs: Quantity for the entire home _____
- ❑ Pinhole doorknobs: Quantity for the entire home _____
- ❑ Doorstops: Quantity for the entire home _____ Note if more than one style is being used and locations. (See Doorstop Options, page 234.) _____
- ❑ Pocket door handles and locks: Quantity for the entire home _____
- ❑ Dead bolt locks: Quantity for the entire home keyed on one side _____ keyed on both sides _____
- ❑ Code-activated door lock

List doors receiving dead bolt locks on one side or both sides. Note if interior door or exterior door.

_____

_____

_____

Any additional locking systems to be used on any doors? Explain.

_____

_____

- ❑ Door knockers: Quantity for the entire home _____
- ❑ Doorbells: Quantity for the entire home _____
- ❑ Doorbell escutcheons: Quantity for the entire home _____
- ❑ Finger plates: Quantity for the entire home _____ Length and width specifications _____
- ❑ Kickplates: Quantity for the entire home _____ Length and width specifications _____

What are the pertinent specifications for the entry set(s)?

Backset measurement _____

Center-to-center measurement _____

Mortise lock measurement _____

Door height and weight _____

Door thickness _____

Door rails, widths, and heights _____

Door stiles widths, and heights _____

Handing of the door _____

What are the pertinent measurements for all other exterior doors?

Backset measurement _____

Center-to-center measurement _____

Mortise lock measurement _____

Door height and weight _____

Door thickness _____

Door rails, widths and heights _____

Door stiles widths and heights _____

Handing of the door _____

What are the quantities of hinges for interior doors? _____

What are the quantities of hinges for the front door? _____

What are the quantities of hinges for other exterior doors? _____

What are the quantities and measurements for thresholds? List for each door.

_____

_____

Will all exterior doors be keyed alike? Explain.

_____

Do you have any interior doors that need to be keyed alike? Explain.

_____

Any additional door hardware?

_____

_____

What is the budget allocated for door hardware? _____

Interior Applications for Stone/Tile (Excluding Bathrooms) Checklist

Homeowner _____ Date _____

For each area where you want to use stone and/or tile, place a check in the appropriate column to indicate whether you will use a stone slab, or stone or tile pieces. For applications with an asterisk, list all rooms in the home receiving that application in the far right column. If using stone or tile on your floors, see Entire-Home Floor Selections (page 320).

Application	Stone Slab	Stone or Tile Pieces	Which Rooms
Bar backsplash			
Bar counter			
Bar floor			
Bar open shelf			
Built-in desk top			
Butler's pantry backsplash			
Butler's pantry counter			
Butler's pantry floor			
Cap along the top of a backsplash			
Chair rail*			
Closet counter*			
Closet island counter*			
Closet shelves*			
Cutting board			
Door header*			
Door threshold*			
Door trim*			
Door trim plinth block*			
Entry foyer baseboard			
Entry foyer floor			
Fireplace hearth*			
Fireplace mantel*			
Fireplace surround*			

*For these items, list the rooms involved.

Application	Stone Slab	Stone or Tile Pieces	Which Rooms
Kitchen backsplash			
Kitchen counter			
Kitchen floor			
Kitchen island counter			
Kitchen peninsula counter			
Laundry room backsplash			
Laundry room counter			
Laundry room island counter			
Laundry room floor			
Laundry room hose-off area			
Laundry room washer/dryer shelf			
Morning kitchen backsplash			
Morning kitchen counter			
Morning kitchen floor			
Powder room baseboard*			
Powder room floor*			
Powder room vanity backsplash*			
Powder room vanity counter*			
Stair riser			
Stair step			
Wainscot			
Walls			
Window header			
Windowsills			
Window trim			
Other _____			

*For these items, list the rooms involved.

Bathroom Applications for Stone/Tile Checklist

Homeowner _____ Date _____

Make one copy of this checklist per bathroom. Fill in the name of the bathroom on each copy. For each area in your bathroom where you want to use stone and/or tile, place a check in the appropriate column to indicate whether you will use a stone slab, or stone or tile pieces. If using stone or tile on your floors, see Entire-Home Floor Selections (page 320).

Bathroom Name _____

Application	Stone Slab	Stone or Tile Pieces
Bathroom baseboard		
Bathroom floors		
Bathroom towel shelves		
Bathroom vanity backsplash		
Bathroom vanity counters		
Cap along the top of a backsplash		
Shower bench		
Shower bench skirt		
Shower floors		
Shower shelf		
Shower walls		
Tub deck		
Tub deck backsplash		
Tub skirt		
Tub step and riser		

Exterior Applications for Stone/Tile Checklist

Homeowner _____ Date _____

Check the exterior areas where you want to use stone and/or tile.

- ❑ Balcony floors
- ❑ Balcony wainscot
- ❑ Cap on hand rail
- ❑ Chimney cap
- ❑ Door header
- ❑ Door thresholds
- ❑ Door trim
- ❑ Exterior entry floors
- ❑ Fire pit
- ❑ Fireplace hearth
- ❑ Fireplace surround
- ❑ Grill area counter
- ❑ Patio floors
- ❑ Patio tabletop
- ❑ Pedestal or base
- ❑ Planter
- ❑ Porch floors
- ❑ Stair risers
- ❑ Stair steps
- ❑ Window header
- ❑ Windowsills
- ❑ Window trim
- ❑ Other _____

Comments:

_____

_____

_____

_____

_____

Stone/Tile Cuts Checklist

Homeowner _____ Date _____

The left column lists common items that require a cut into stone or tile to install them. For each item in your home that will need a cut into stone or tile, list the room(s) and check the appropriate column to indicate whether you need a cut into a slab or into a piece. An example of a cut into slab is a cut into a slab counter for a soap dispenser. An example of a cut into a piece is a shower with 12-inch square stone or tile pieces on the wall; cuts will be made into those pieces for the showerhead and faucet.

Item	Room or Rooms	Cut into Slab	Cut into Piece	Remarks
Disposal on/off button				
Electric outlets				
Faucets				
Handheld sprayer				
Holes in a desk for computer, lamp, telephone cords				
Holes in a vanity counter to throw trash				
Hot water dispenser				
Kitchen faucet spray nozzle				
Light switches				
Shower fittings (see Tile Installation for Shower Fixture Placement, page 239)				
Soap dispenser				
Steam heads				
Trash hole				
Tub decks (see Bathtub Stone Cut Options, page 239)				
Other _____				

9 Special Considerations

Whether you are a parent or grandparent, there are many things to consider for your home to make life with children or grandchildren more enjoyable, safer, and better organized. You'll also want to plan for display, storage, and electrical requirements for Christmas, and if you have an older person in your household or want to plan for your own advancing years, you can do many things to make your home senior-friendly. To keep your home quiet and serene, you'll also want to consider ways to minimize noise.

In terms of home protection, you have many options, from security systems to safe rooms to fire escape plans. Plan carefully to meet your needs.

Finally, consider going "green" in your home design—using special guidelines to make an energy efficient home that minimizes harmful effects on the environment.

INFANTS AND TODDLERS

Infants and toddlers require lots of equipment. Designate a closet to store this equipment while the children are young, knowing that once they have outgrown it, the closet will have another use. Examples of equipment you might store are a swing, infant seat, walker, portable bathtub, tub chair, and so on. Closet shelves should be deep enough and tall enough for this equipment, so take measurements.

Outlets should be accessible for cameras and sound monitors, night-lights, sound machines, heated diaper wipes, and so on. A handheld sprayer is extremely helpful when bathing infants and toddlers.

Sliding shower doors on tubs makes bathing a baby more difficult. The rail cuts into your abdomen when you're leaning over the side of the tub, and access to the tub is limited because half of the tub is blocked by the sliding doors. A shower curtain or glass door that swings open works better.

If you have toddlers, plan for gates on both interior and exterior stairways. Consider having a decorative gate made out of the same material, whether iron, wood, glass or other. Make sure it meets safety code specifications so your child's head cannot get stuck between rails. Discuss with a craftsman how to remove the gate without aesthetic consequences once you no longer need it. A porch with steps to the yard also may need a gate. These gates are also useful for containing pets.

Bolt chests of drawers into the wall so that children cannot tip over the chests if they open them and climb into the drawers. Another possibility is built-in drawers and shelves in a closet. Make sure all built-ins, including entertainment centers, are bolted to the wall in case a toddler or child climbs on them. This will prevent the built-in from falling on top of the child.

A toy drawer comes in handy in the kitchen area.

Toddlers can easily reach up and open doors with lever handles. However, lever handles are easier to operate than knobs if you have an arthritic condition. A solution is to add a second lock. Discuss options with your hardware salesperson.

Toddlers can turn plumbing fixtures with lever handles on and off. If you have a tub with lever handles, your toddler will be able to turn on the tub water. A knob-type handle is the best alternative.

CHILDREN OF ALL AGES

There are many steps you can take to make your home safer and more enjoyable for all children.

Books are an important part of child development. Placing appealing books within reach of toddlers and young children may encourage them to read; keep this in mind when you are planning built-in book shelves.

Put locks on medicine cabinets or store all medicines in a closet with a lock to keep your children safe.

Store all cleaning supplies in a closet or cabinet that can be locked.

If you have a two- or three-story home, do not use lever window locks that young children can open.

Plan a storage area that locks for guns or other weapons, liquor or wine, cleaning products, or other items that could cause harm to a child.

Request childproof locks on cabinet doors and drawers.

If particular rooms in your home will be off-limits to your children, plan for a door or doors to that room so the room can be closed off.

Lockers or cubbyholes in a mudroom or garage door entry room are a great tool to teach your children to be organized. Before going to bed, children can store their backpacks, coats, gloves, hats, signed parental forms, musical instruments, school sports equipment, sports, band, and cheerleader or other uniforms they need to take to school, and during the summer they can store their sports equipment, uniforms, camp items, and art class supplies. They can store their shoes in the locker or cubbyhole as well. In the morning, lunches can be placed in the locker.

If you plan to have a mini-refrigerator in your kitchen to store snacks or beverages for your children, do not locate it in the kitchen work triangle or you will have little feet underneath you when preparing meals.

When designing your kitchen, designate a lower cabinet or drawer for snacks for your children, well away from the kitchen work triangle.

Plan a successful study environment for children, whether in the child's bedroom or another area. Allow adequate space for a computer and books. Many experts advise against computers in children's bedrooms because of the lack of supervision. Some parents have a computer study room with multiple computer stations for several family members. Others like a desk in the kitchen area so they can watch and help the child study while they are preparing dinner. Provide adequate light.

Decide if you need climate-controlled storage areas for storing baby equipment and clothing you are not using. Discuss these needs with your architect.

Consider adjustable hanging rods in closets that can be adjusted as your child grows.

If storing riding toys, tricycles, and bicycles in the garage, designate an area away from the vehicles so they do not get scratched or dented.

If you live in a tornado-prone area, consider designating a closet to be structurally reinforced near your children's bedrooms for them to gather for safety. Also see Safe Room (page 125).

Consider every type of security for all water areas, whether you have a pool, pond, hot tub, or waterfall. Ask about any additional safety measures, such as an alarm that will go off if a child falls into the pool.

When selecting door hardware, discuss options such as pinhole locks on interior doors in case a child gets locked into a room

Make a fire escape plan.

In addition to a regular tub faucet, consider a faucet halfway up the wall in the bathtub for young children to stand under when having their hair washed.

> TIP: Some people prefer their light
> switches lower than the standard
> 48 inches in height from the subfloor.
> If you have toddlers in your home, leave
> the light switches at the standard height.
> If lowered, it can be an invitation for
> toddlers to play with the switch,
> turning the light on and off repeatedly.

NOISE CHECKLIST

You have finally moved into your dream home. You are exhausted from the moving experience. Finally, you can crawl into your bed. All is quiet as you think of how much you have accomplished and how proud you feel. All of a sudden you hear your children, who have decided to watch a movie in the media room. Your master bedroom wall is opposite the television wall in the media room—and the movie is keeping you awake. Or you can hear the motor in the mini-refrigerator in your morning kitchen or master bathroom kicking on and off all night. Or someone decides to get a late-night snack and you can hear the stairs squeak as they walk down them. Believe me, noise can carry!

As you design your home with the architect, pay attention to what is on the other side of all bedroom walls, especially the headboard wall. Take note of what is above or below all bedrooms. Discuss with your architect and builder what preventive measures can be taken to avoid noise problems. These may include acoustical wall products, sound membrane on the floor, fabric in the ceiling to prevent noise transfer, floor floaters, silent joists, soundboards, and fiberglass insulation. Check any of the boxes on the Things That Make Noise Checklist (page 264) that concern you. Note the soundproofing options on that form that you can discuss with your architect and builder.

CHRISTMAS DECORATIONS

Plan ahead for your home's Christmas decorations. Not only will you save money, but you'll be able to eliminate extension cords draped around the home and yard. Review the Exterior and Interior Christmas Lights and Decorations Checklist (page 262), and file it in Binder 4. Discuss any items you check with your architect, interior designer, and builder. If you own or plan to purchase decorations that need structural support, include those plans in your discussions.

Consider a light switch tucked away in the coat closet that operates the outlets that would be used for exterior Christmas lights, so you won't have to go outside to turn the lights off and on. If you prefer to use a timer, discuss this with your builder and electrician.

A freestanding Santa Claus or other decoration that speaks or moves will need an outlet, which could be located inside or outside.

Ask your builder to incorporate aesthetically placed hardware to mount any wreaths, swags, or garlands that you plan to hang on a door, window, or other part of the home. Don't forget to inform your builder if any of these need an outlet.

If you know where your Christmas tree will be placed, have the outlet you will use to plug in your tree lights on a switch, so you do not have to straddle presents to plug and unplug it.

SENIOR NEEDS

Whether you are building your last home or have an elderly relative who will eventually live with you, it is imperative that you plan for a senior lifestyle when designing your home. Long-range planning can save you time, money, and a whole lot of hassles. Consider the following tips.

APPLIANCES

- Use touch controls on appliances instead of knobs.
- Install a platform under your dishwasher to raise it.
- Purchase a pedestal stand with your washers and dryers or have a platform built to raise them.

BACKING

- Install backing (lumber installed between wall studs to give additional support) in the shower walls for installation of grab bars.
- Install backing on both sides of the staircase for installation of hand rails on both sides.

CLOSET

- Plan for all closet storage to be reachable without a ladder.

DOORS

- Specify flush thresholds at all doors to accommodate a wheelchair or persons who have trouble lifting their feet when walking.
- Use gate release buttons.
- Specify wider doorways to accommodate a wheelchai; they should be a minimum of 32 inches wide.
- Use lever handles for doors instead of knobs.

ELECTRICAL

- Lower light switches to 48 inches from the finished floor instead of 54 inches.
- Use illuminated light switches.
- Install courtesy lights for the steps on the stairway.
- Make any outlet that will be used for a space heater dedicated so it will not trip the fuse box.

FLOOR LEVELS

- Stick to a one-level house unless you will install an elevator.
- Have at least one entrance to your home at ground level, with no steps to maneuver.
- If needed, plan for a ramp for wheelchair access to your home.

PLUMBING

- Use lever handles or a motion trigger faucet, not knobs, to turn on faucets.
- Use a one-lever control faucet that operates both hot water and cold water.
- Specify comfort-height toilet seats that make getting up easier.
- Specify a nonscalding showerhead.

- Install a handheld sprayer for the shower that will allow someone to sit in the shower and bathe.

MISCELLANEOUS

- Throughout the home, install nonslip surfaces, especially in the bathroom and shower.
- Plan for handrails on both sides of the stairway; add backing in the wall for the second handrail.
- Plan for adequate lighting throughout the home.
- Use large lettering and adequate lighting for reading thermostats, security pads, integrated home automation monitors, stereo and television components, fuse box lettering on labels, and titles on books in the bookcase.
- Specify lower counter heights.
- Have all hallways a minimum 36 inches wide.
- Separate HVAC zones if you tend to use only a few rooms in your home.
- Plan for the addition of a ramp.

PROTECTING YOUR HOME AND FAMILY

The first step in safety and security is to make a list of what you want to protect. Do you have any rooms or closets that need extra protection, such as a silver closet, gun room, master closet, fur storage closet, or other? Do you need protection from hurricanes, tornados, or earthquakes?

Electric protections you may consider include a whole-house surge protector to protect your household equipment from power surges and a generator that will kick on when there is a power failure to keep your home functioning. You may also want a lightning grounding protection system to protect against lightning strikes.

Next, determine your budget. Home security systems come in many forms and a wide range of costs. You can buy a system with no monthly fee that sets off an alarm if someone opens a door or breaks in, or one with a monthly service fee that calls the police for you when someone enters without turning off your security system.

At the top of the range is a high-end system that includes custom sensors and detectors, with sophisticated systems that will monitor changes in humidity and temperature levels, monitor a pool and send an alarm if a child falls in, and monitor gases and send an alarm if poisonous gases are detected.

TIP: A basic security system is better than no security system.

TYPES OF PROTECTION

Protection comes in many forms.

Alarms/sensors. You probably already have a carbon monoxide alarm and smoke alarm. Other useful alarms and sensors are a door opening sensor, driveway alarm, fence line sensor, fire alarm, glass break sensor, medical alarm, panic alarm, propane gas, radon, screen sensor, swimming pool alarm, and other water source sensors. You can also install a fixed temperature alarm to protect pipes from breaking if your heating system goes out, a hot tub alarm to alert you to prevent freezing, a wine cellar sensor for temperature and humidity changes, and a sprinkler system in case of a fire in your home.

Motion detectors. You can place motion detectors in areas where an intruder would have to travel to get around the home, such as hallways, staircases, around doors, and an office with a computer.

Cameras. A camera will let you see who is on the other side of the door and will let you know who has come by your home and when. For a vacation home, you can pull up the camera view on your computer and check weather conditions or the condition of your home. You can also have a camera take a snapshot of anyone who comes within the camera sensor range and have it e-mailed to you. This would allow you to see that your children have made it home from school, a housekeeper has shown up, and so on.

Lighting. You can choose from exterior motion sensor lights, exterior security lights, and interior fire alarm lights.

Safe room and fire-protected room. A safe room and fire-protected room buy time for the police to respond and for the fire department to arrive. If valuables are kept in a fire-protected room, it will extend the time before fire would reach inside the room. (See Safe Room, page 125.)

Options for entry. Decide on what type of system you want for entering and exiting your home. Options include keys, fingerprint system, eye print system, code punch system, proximity card in wallet, key fob, and a swipe card mixed with a code. Though technology is advancing with fingerprinting and eye scanning, in some environments, there are glitches, and a scanning process is necessary for any new person added to the system.

> Tip: For added security for your bedroom door, install locks at the top, the bottom, and in the middle of the door.

SEVEN COMMON SAFETY MISTAKES TO AVOID

1. Use a hardwired system when wiring your home instead of wireless security. The only reason to use wireless is if the house is already built. Wireless requires replacing batteries and requires more maintenance.
2. For added protection, add a commercial cellular security phone. If your phone lines are cut, the cellular phone will automatically call the security company.
3. Your alarm should have a siren that alerts the intruder as well as you that the alarm system has been triggered. The sound of the alarm going off usually causes an intruder to flee the premises.
4. Discuss with your architect and life safety consultant options for a fire escape. Make sure you are comfortable with these options, especially if children are in the home.
5. Never install the security box (which holds the security wiring) outside the secured area where it can be disarmed without an alarm going off.
6. A silent alarm should only be used in a specific situation by trained people. You want to avoid an intruder, not sneak up on one.
7. Poisonous gas protection is as important as home intruder protection. At the minimum, have carbon dioxide, natural gas, and propane gas detectors.

> Tip: Duel technology motion detectors sense both density and heat. Previous systems were infrared, which only sensed heat.

GOING GREEN

Designing a "green" home is not only positive for the environment, but positive to your pocketbook in the long term. Most people think this means conserving water and electric power and using environmentally friendly building materials. It does, but more is involved.

The best and most authoritative resource for a green home is the U.S. Green Building Council, which has developed The LEED for Homes Rating System for green buildings (www.usgbc.org/).

There are many factors involved in a green home.

Innovation and design. The architect, mechanical engineer, civil engineer, landscape designer, and others trained in green building meet periodically to review the process and goals of the project. The designers promote durability and high performance of building components and systems through design, material selection, and construction practices.

Location and linkages. Your house location should avoid environmentally sensitive sites and farmland, be built within half a mile of existing water and sewer lines, be close to public transit and community resources, and have access to public green spaces.

Sustainable sites. Your home site should have erosion controls and minimize disturbing the land; landscaping should involve no invasive plants, limit turf, and use drought-tolerant plants. Trees should be planted to shade the home. You should use environmentally friendly insect and pest control—and meet home density per acre standards.

Water efficiency. Rainwater should be collected for reuse, and the irrigation system should be designed by a licensed and certified professional. Your home should use high efficiency fixtures for toilets, showers, and faucets.

Energy and atmosphere. Your home should meet the standards of an Energy Star home. This means it will have improved hot water distribution and pipe insulation; the refrigerant will minimize ozone depletion and global warming contributions; insulation, air infiltration, and ducts will be tested and inspected; windows will meet or exceed Energy Star specifications, with at least three Energy Star light fixtures, along with energy-efficient fixtures and controls; all appliances will be from an approved list; and the house will have a renewable electric generation system.

Materials and resources. Overall waste for framing should be limited to 10 percent, using advanced framing techniques or structurally insulated panels. The home should use tropical woods from an environmentally preferred products list and manage wastes so that 25 to 100 percent less waste is sent to the landfill.

Indoor environmental quality. Your home should use combustion venting: space heating and DHW equipment with closed/power-exhaust and a high-performance fireplace. Other considerations may be a moisture control system, a dedicated outdoor air system with heat recovery, third party testing of outdoor air flow rate, bathroom exhaust fans with timers and automatic controls, and special filters in the air supply. Ducts should be sealed during construction; the house should have permanent walk-off mats or shoe storage, or a central vacuum system. It should be radon resistant, with no air handling or return ducts in the garage, tightly sealed surfaces between the garage and home, and an exhaust fan in the garage (or a detached garage or no garage).

Some municipalities require a homeowner to use a green point system. The home must meet a set number of points to obtain a use and occupancy certificate. More and more municipalities are including green standards in their building codes department; Aspen, Colorado, for instance, takes a very aggressive approach.

One green approach involves the selection of materials for your home. Green items include bamboo or cork flooring; a tankless water heater; a hot water recirculation pump; a geothermal heating and cooling system; solar panels to capture sunlight to convert to energy; environmentally friendly building materials including paint, caulk, sealers, stains, and formaldehyde-free plywood; green-designated plumbing fixtures, appliances, and fireplaces; and recycle bins.

You'll want to start early in the process to plan a green home, including selecting an architect and designer who are experienced in building green. This can involve more work and planning, and in some cases more expense, but the rewards can be big.

Exterior and Interior Christmas Lights and Decorations Checklist

Homeowner _____ Date _____

Exterior

Check those that apply and discuss them with your architect, interior designer, and builder.

1. Driveway and yard

Will you have any of the following?
- ❏ Christmas lights on your driveway gate or sidewalk gate.
- ❏ Christmas lights along your driveway
- ❏ Christmas lights around your mailbox
- ❏ Lights on a lamppost(s) in your yard
- ❏ Freestanding Christmas trees in the yard that will need lights
- ❏ Lights in any of the trees
- ❏ Lights in bushes around your home

2. Front entry to house

Will you have any of the following?
- ❏ Lights on any columns
- ❏ Lights on any stair railings
- ❏ Lights around the front door
- ❏ Lights around lanterns
- ❏ Lights in a trellis

3. Windows

Will you have any of the following?
- ❏ Lighted garlands or swags around windows
- ❏ Lighted wreaths hanging in each window

4. Porch or balcony lights

Will you have any of the following?
- ❏ Lights on any balcony railings
- ❏ Lights on porches
- ❏ Christmas tree on your porch
- ❏ Christmas tree on your balcony

5. Porte cochere

Will you have any of the following?
- ❏ Lighted swags
- ❏ Lighted wreaths
- ❏ Lights on your porte cochere
- ❏ Other _____

6. Roof

Will you need any of the following?
- ❏ An outlet in soffit, attic, or on the roof for roof decorations
- ❏ An outlet near the chimney for chimney decorations

7. Backyard lighting

Will you need outlets in the backyard for any of the following?
- ❏ Christmas trees
- ❏ Freestanding Christmas decorations
- ❏ Lights in any bushes
- ❏ Lights on a boat house
- ❏ Light on the back porch
- ❏ Lights on any columns

8. Garage

Will you have any of the following?
- ❏ Lighting on the garage door
- ❏ Lighting or decorations on the garage roof
- ❏ Lighting in the garage windows

9. Other

Will you have any of the following?
- ❏ Architectural elements on the exterior of your home that will have Christmas lights attached
- ❏ Spotlights in the yard to light up the front door or other areas of your home

Interior

Check those that apply and discuss them with your architect, interior designer, and builder.

1. Windows

Will you have any of the following?

- ❏ A candle in each window
- ❏ A lighted wreath on the interior windows
- ❏ A lighted wreath on the exterior windows

2. Mantel

Will you have any of the following?

- ❏ A lighted garland on the mantel
- ❏ A lighted garland above any doorways

3. Stairway

Will you have the following?

- ❏ A lighted garland on the stairway railing. (Outlet needs to be aesthetically placed.)

4. Christmas tree

Will you have any of the following?

- ❏ A single Christmas tree
- ❏ A group of several Christmas trees
- ❏ Christmas trees in more than one room

5. Exposed beams

Will you have the following?

- ❏ Christmas lights wrapped around your exposed beams. (An outlet can be placed into a carved out area of the beam. You will want a light switch for these outlets.)

6. Above cabinets

Will you have any of the following?

- ❏ Christmas lights above your kitchen cabinets
- ❏ Christmas lights above your bar cabinets

7. Bookcases

Will you have any of the following?

- ❏ Christmas lights above your library bookcase
- ❏ Any Christmas items on your bookcase that require a plug to operate
- ❏ Any lighted swags or garlands on your bookcase

Things That Make Noise Checklist

Homeowner _____ Date _____

Check the items you want to address with your architect and builder: discuss their location and options to reduce noise.

Appliances
- ❑ Dishwasher drawers
- ❑ Dishwashers
- ❑ Exhaust fans/hoods
- ❑ Freezers with ice makers
- ❑ Ice makers
- ❑ Washers and dryers

Bathroom
- ❑ Exhaust fan
- ❑ Faucets running
- ❑ Hair dryers
- ❑ Shower
- ❑ Toilet flushing

Doorbell
- ❑ Ringer

Exterior
- ❑ Driveway in relation to bedrooms
- ❑ HVAC compressor
- ❑ Street in relation to house and bedrooms

Exercise room
- ❑ Cardio-machines
- ❑ Televisions and stereo

Floor and stair steps
- ❑ Location of stair steps
- ❑ Silent joists

Water heater furnace
- ❑ Gas igniting

Garage door
- ❑ Opening and closing

HVAC system
- ❑ Exterior compressor
- ❑ Interior system

Office equipment
- ❑ Fax machine
- ❑ Printer

Plumbing
- ❑ Pipe insulation
- ❑ Type pipe used

Security
- ❑ Alarm siren
- ❑ Alarm that beeps each time an exterior door is opened
- ❑ Driveway alarm
- ❑ Operation of the alarm security pad, whether turning the alarm on or off

Miscellaneous
- ❑ Sump pump
- ❑ Television and stereo speakers

Rooms That Make Noise
- ❑ Bathrooms
- ❑ Kitchen
- ❑ Laundry room
- ❑ Media room
- ❑ Playroom
- ❑ Water closets

Soundproof Options
- ❑ Acoustical wall products
- ❑ Ceiling fabric
- ❑ Fiberglass batting for sound insulation
- ❑ Floor membrane
- ❑ Silent floor joists
- ❑ Soundboard on specific walls
- ❑ Window insulation

- ❑ Other _____

Reviewing Architectural
Plans

Reviewing architectural plans can be daunting if you do not know what the symbols mean or know what to look for. Each plan should have a legend explaining each symbol. You'll find a list of the basic symbols on page 359.

Although it is the intent of every architect to listen to the needs, wants, and desires of his or her client, it is not uncommon that a need, want, or desire that you have communicated to the architect is not shown on the plans. Why? It could be as simple as the architect having been distracted before putting your request on the plans. Or the architect could have communicated the request to the staff and it was overlooked. It is not a perfect world. It's up to you to check and recheck your plans.

Step 1. Request two sets of floor plans, electrical plans, elevation plans, HVAC plans, and plumbing plans from your architect. Use one plan to mark on and keep one plan as a clean copy.

Step 2. Answer the questions on the Floor Plan Review Checklist (page 267), Electrical Plan Review Checklist (page 270), Elevation Plan Review Checklist (page 273), HVAC Plan Review Checklist (page 276), and the Plumbing Plan Review Checklist (page 277). Items for which you checked "no" are issues you need to discuss with your architect. Use the Blank Comment Form (page 18) to write down your comments.

Step 3. Once you have reviewed the plans, set up a meeting with your architect. Take your set of marked-up plans, the checklists, your comment sheets, and your architect meeting note forms. Agree on a date that your architect will have revisions ready based on changes made from the discussions.

Step 4. When you receive the revisions, keep repeating Steps 1, 2, and 3 until you are satisfied with the plans. Go through your checklist, and write the letter R next to the check box to indicate those items that have been resolved.

Later in the design process, the architect will provide the elevation plans, which are plans that show the walls, including doorways, cabinets, bookcases, windows, and so on as if you are facing them. Use Steps 1, 2, and 3 when reviewing the elevation plans.

ELECTRICAL PLANS: DO AN IMAGINARY WALK-THROUGH

When reviewing your electrical plans, imagine the following scenarios. As you visualize these scenes, ask yourself these questions: Are the light switches in the most efficient and convenient location? Are the correct ones ganged together? Are lamps connected to light switches? Note any problems and suggestions for improvements on the Blank Comment Form.

> **Tip: Make sure the doorbell ringer is not located on a wall that is the focal point of that room, and that it will not interfere with art or mirrors being hung on a wall. Consider the location in relationship to hearing it from your bathroom, kitchen, or other room where you will spend a great deal of time.**

Scenario 1. You have pulled into your garage at night and your house is dark. You get out of your car and enter your home from the garage. Imagine reaching for the light switches as you move through your home. Are the light switches shown on the plans in a convenient and logical place?

Scenario 2. You enter your home through your front door at night and your house is dark. Imagine walking in the door reaching for a light switch. As you proceed through your home, imagine reaching for the light switch in other rooms. Are the light switches shown on the electrical plan in convenient and logical places?

Scenario 3. You have been visiting your neighbor and it's dark as you enter your home through the back door. Repeat the previous scenario, starting from the back door. Are light switches in convenient and logical places?

Scenario 4. You are up before the sun and going from your bedroom to the kitchen. As you turn on lights on the way to the kitchen, are the light switches in convenient and logical places? Do you have to turn on a lamp and wish it was connected to a light switch?

Scenario 5. It is morning and you like to have certain lights, chandeliers, sconces, or lamps illuminated all day long. Imagine the path you take to turn on all of these. If you had three-way, four-way, or five-way switches and lamps connected to light switches, would it be easier?

Scenario 6. You are in your kitchen and headed to your bedroom to retire for the evening. Imagine the path you take to turn out all the lights that are usually turned on inside and outside your home. Is there an easier way so you don't have to take so many steps?

> **Tip: It is imperative that you keep a list of each change you request on any plans so that you can check the request against the revised plans.**

Floor Plan Review Checklist

Homeowner _____ Date _____

Look carefully at your floor plan and answer the questions below. Skip any question that does not apply to your home. For any questions that you answer "no," use a copy of the Blank Comment Form (page 18) to record your remarks to discuss with your architect.

YES   NO

Basic Information

❑   ❑   Are all rooms requested shown? (Compare the list of rooms you submitted to your architect with the rooms shown.)

❑   ❑   Are the rooms shown on the correct level?

❑   ❑   Are the dimensions of each room correct?

❑   ❑   Are the closets shown on the correct level? (Compare the list of closets you submitted to your architect with the closets shown.)

❑   ❑   Are all closets requested shown?

❑   ❑   Are the dimensions of each closet what you requested?

❑   ❑   Are the dimensions for all showers what you requested?

❑   ❑   Is the width of hallways what you requested?

❑   ❑   If you have a pair of windows in any room, is there room on each side to hang curtains?

Appliances

❑   ❑   Is every appliance you requested in the correct location?

❑   ❑   If you requested two dishwashers or two microwaves, are both shown?

❑   ❑   Do you approve of the location of your refrigerator?

❑   ❑   Will you be able to open the refrigerator doors 180 degrees to remove shelves and drawers, or is there a wall in the way that will prevent the door from opening wide?

Attic Access

❑   ❑   Does the floor plan show access to the attic in the location(s) requested?

❑   ❑   Is the opening to the attic wide enough for your needs?

Bar

❑   ❑   Is the shape of the bar what you requested?

Bathroom

❑   ❑   Is there a convenient place in the bathroom or closet to place a trash can, scale, and/or laundry basket?

Bedroom

❑   ❑   Is the width of the stairway what you requested?

❑   ❑   If you wanted two staircases, are both shown?

❑   ❑   Will the size and number of beds you plan to use fit on the bedroom wall?

❑   ❑   Do the locations of the windows on the headboard wall work with the locations of the headboard and the bedside tables? (See Bedroom Window Placement Pitfall, and Headboard Overlapping Windows Pitfall, page 101.)

YES   NO

Bedroom (continued)

❏   ❏   Imagine lying in bed with your partner; if one of you prefers to sleep on the side of the bed closest to the bathroom, are you satisfied with the side of the bed that is closest to the bathroom?

❏   ❏   If someone in bed in any of the bedrooms is prone to middle-of-the-night visits to the bathroom, will it be easy to go from the bed to the bathroom in the dark?

❏   ❏   If one partner uses the bathroom during the night and turns on the light, will the person still in bed be clear from having the bathroom light shine directly in his or her face?

❏   ❏   Paying attention to the path of a vehicle on your driveway, are all bedrooms safe from noise and headlights?

❏   ❏   Will any of the bedrooms be affected by street traffic noise?

❏   ❏   Are all staircases located away from headboard walls, preventing someone sleeping from being disturbed by foot-steps?

❏   ❏   Are all beds far enough away from the bathroom shower or toilet so when in use a person still in bed is not disturbed?

❏   ❏   Are all bedrooms safe from the noise of a laundry room?

❏   ❏   Are all bedrooms safe from the noise of the media room, playroom, or televisions in any other room?

❏   ❏   As you compare one level of your home to another level, are you in agreement with the rooms that are located above and below each other?

Built-ins

❏   ❏   Are all built-ins you requested (cabinets, entertainment center, islands, desks, and so on) shown?

❏   ❏   Do you like the sizes and shapes of all islands (kitchen, laundry, closet)?

Door

❏   ❏   Is the proper type door shown on the plans; single, double, pocket, sliding, barn door, swinging door, and so on?

❏   ❏   Are all door sizes correct?

❏   ❏   Is the direction of all door swings and the side the doors are hinged correct? (Pay close attention to what is on both sides of the door.)

❏   ❏   Will all doors located in the same area clear each other when opened at the same time?

❏   ❏   Will all doors clear furniture when opened?

❏   ❏   Do the floor plans indicate all exterior doors that you requested?

❏   ❏   Is the size and type of all exterior doors correct?

Driveway and Porte Cochere

❏   ❏   Does the distance you have to walk to unload groceries work for you?

❏   ❏   Is there adequate parking for occupant and visitor vehicles?

❏   ❏   Is the porte cochere requested shown?

❏   ❏   Does the logistics of the driveway and porte cochere work if you have several visitors with cars?

Fireplaces

❏   ❏   Are all fireplaces requested shown?

❏   ❏   Is the hearth size and shape correct?

YES   NO

Furniture

YES	NO	
❑	❑	Are wall measurements the correct dimensions for furniture to fit?
❑	❑	Are the dumbwaiter, elevator, and laundry chute shown and correctly located?
❑	❑	Are all balconies requested shown on the plans?
❑	❑	Are the window sizes and locations correct?
❑	❑	Are the specifications for the windows you selected correct?
❑	❑	Will persons sitting at the breakfast table or counter be clear of morning sunlight shining directly in their face?
❑	❑	Will all furniture be clear of direct sunlight fading fabric or bleaching wood on furniture?
❑	❑	Will all televisions, bathroom toiletries on a tray, food in the pantry, bottles in a bar, and so on be clear of direct sunlight through a window or skylight?
❑	❑	Are you happy with the view in and out of each window?

Garage

YES	NO	
❑	❑	Is the garage the correct size?
❑	❑	Will the garage hold all vehicles and equipment you want to store in your garage?
❑	❑	Are closets, counters, and shelves requested shown?

Sight Lines

YES	NO	
❑	❑	Are all sight lines you see standing in each doorway or sitting in a room looking out windows or through doorways acceptable?
❑	❑	Are you satisfied if you look down a hallway or through a doorway and see a partial door or partial window instead of the entire door or window?
❑	❑	Does the swing of the door and the location of the powder room toilet prevent you from seeing the toilet if the door is left open?
❑	❑	Is the line of sight a visitor sees when first entering your home clear of a powder room door left open and a visible toilet?
❑	❑	Are all toilets out of the line of sight if curtains are open, lights are turned on in any bathroom, and a visitor looks through the window?
❑	❑	If you look down a hallway, is what you see at each end acceptable? (Avoid seeing a partial door or window at either end.)
❑	❑	If you look through a doorway into the kitchen, are you satisfied with the part of the kitchen that you will see first?
❑	❑	Will any framing members interfere with centering the fold-down stairs in the hallway?

Electrical Plan Review Checklist

Homeowner _____ Date _____

Look carefully at your electrical plan and answer the questions below. Skip any question that does not apply to your home. For any questions that you answer "no," use a copy of the Blank Comment Form (page 18) to record your remarks to discuss with your architect.

YES   NO

Outlets

❑ ❑ Are all outlets requested shown in the proper location?

❑ ❑ Are all floor outlets requested shown in the proper location?

❑ ❑ If you want the floor outlet connected to a light switch, is that shown? (If you have one, involve your interior designer in floor outlet placement.)

❑ ❑ Is there an outlet or power source shown for jetted tubs, steam showers, heated towel bars, exhaust fans, ceiling light heaters, and motorized window treatments?

❑ ❑ Are outlets connected to light switches shown correctly?

❑ ❑ Are four-receptacle outlets you requested shown in the correct locations?

❑ ❑ Is the placement of outlets, light switches, and telephone jacks around headboards, correct? (See Headboard Wall, page 100.)

❑ ❑ Is the outlet easily accessible to plug in your laptop while sitting in bed? (It is best to have an outlet below the top of the bedside table and between the headboard and bedside table so you can plug in a laptop computer to use while in bed without moving the bedside table to reach the outlet. (See Headboard Wall, page 100.)

❑ ❑ Are the outlets shown in the correct location for illuminating houseplants?

Light Switches

❑ ❑ Are all light switches in the correct location? (Note all door swings and make sure no switches are located behind a door.)

❑ ❑ Are the three-way, four-way, and five-way light switches you requested shown in the correct location?

❑ ❑ Are the correct light switches ganged together?

❑ ❑ Are the ganged light switches in the correct order?

❑ ❑ Are the dimmers on the light switches you requested noted?

❑ ❑ Are the illuminated light switches you requested noted?

Light Fixtures

❑ ❑ Are the chandeliers you requested shown in the correct locations? (See Chandelier Placement Pitfall, page 105.)

❑ ❑ Are the sconce locations you requested shown in the correct locations?

❑ ❑ Are the lighted toe kicks you requested shown in the correct locations?

Appliances

❑ ❑ Are outlets shown in the correct locations for all appliances?

Cabinet Lighting

❑ ❑ Are lights under all of the upper cabinets you requested shown correctly?

❑ ❑ Are lights above all of the upper cabinets you request shown correctly?

❑ ❑ Are lights you requested inside any cabinets shown correctly?

YES   NO

Ceiling Fan

❏   ❏   Are all ceiling fans shown?

❏   ❏   Are the ceiling fans with lights attached noted?

❏   ❏   Are the correct manufacturers, models, and colors of ceiling fans specified?

Computer Wiring Connectors

❏   ❏   Are all locations for computer wiring connectors correctly shown?

Doorbell

❏   ❏   Are the doorbell ring button(s) shown correctly?

❏   ❏   Are the doorbell ringer box(es) shown correctly?

Dumbwaiter and Elevator

❏   ❏   Is there a notation for electric power for the dumbwaiter?

❏   ❏   Is there a notation for electric power for the elevator?

Interior Jamb Switches, Motion Switches

❏   ❏   Are the jamb switches you requested on the correct doors?

❏   ❏   Are the motion detector switches on lights shown correctly?

Office Equipment

❏   ❏   Are the outlets for your office equipment (printers, fax machines, hard drives, computer monitors, routers, etc.) shown correctly?

Stereo Equipment

❏   ❏   Are the outlets for stereo equipment shown in the correct locations?

❏   ❏   If using a surge protector strip for your stereo equipment, is that noted?

Telephone

❏   ❏   Are telephone jacks requested shown correctly?

❏   ❏   Are outlets shown next to the telephone jacks that will have a cordless telephone base?

Television

❏   ❏   Are outlets and cable or dish wiring for all televisions shown correctly? (Don't forget under-cabinet flip-down televisions and any televisions that will be in pop-up furniture at the foot of a bed or other locations. There should be an outlet next to all cable or dish connectors.)

Attic

❏   ❏   Are outlets you requested shown correctly?

❏   ❏   Are the lighting fixtures you requested shown correctly?

❏   ❏   Is there adequate lighting in the attic?

YES   NO

Bathroom

❑   ❑   Are outlets requested in medicine cabinets shown?

❑   ❑   Are outlets requested for hair dryers in drawers shown?

❑   ❑   Is there a notation for either electric wiring or an outlet for a wall-mounted lighted magnifying mirror?

❑   ❑   Is there a notation for electric wiring for a heated towel bar?

❑   ❑   Is there a notation for electric wiring for a towel-warming drawer?

❑   ❑   Is there a notation for electric wiring for a jetted tub?

❑   ❑   Is there a notation for electric wiring for a ceiling light heater?

Exterior

❑   ❑   Are all exterior lighting fixtures requested shown?

❑   ❑   Are the ones designated for natural gas specified?

❑   ❑   Are the motion sensors, dusk-to-dawn sensors, or timers you requested shown?

❑   ❑   Are exterior outlets requested for Christmas decorations shown correctly?

❑   ❑   Are exterior outlets connected to an interior light switch, such as those used for Christmas decorations, shown correctly?

❑   ❑   Is any exterior lighting requested to illuminate your home or shrubs shown? (This may be on a landscape plan.)

❑   ❑   Is your flat-screen television or ceiling fan shown in your covered patio area?

❑   ❑   Is the cable or dish connector shown?

❑   ❑   Is the telephone jack you requested on your covered porch or patio shown?

❑   ❑   Is the location of the fuse box(es) acceptable?

❑   ❑   Is the location of the electric meter for the meter reader acceptable?

Garage

❑   ❑   Are all outlets requested for charging equipment shown correctly?

❑   ❑   Are the outlets used for battery tenders shown correctly?

❑   ❑   Are the outlets used for hand tools shown correctly?

❑   ❑   Is the outlet for the garage door motor noted?

❑   ❑   Is the lighting shown for the interior garage acceptable?

❑   ❑   Are the light switch locations shown correctly?

❑   ❑   Are the correct light fixtures shown?

❑   ❑   Is the location of the light switches acceptable?

Interior Christmas

❑   ❑   Are outlets requested for Christmas lighting (tree, mantel, exposed beams, candles in windows, staircase railing) shown correctly?

Elevation Plan Review Checklist

Homeowner _____ Date _____

Look carefully at your elevation plan and answer the questions below. Skip any question that does not apply to your home. For any questions that you answer "no," use a copy of the Blank Comment Form (page 18) to record your remarks to discuss with your architect.

YES NO

Appliances
- ☐ ☐ Are all appliances requested shown?
- ☐ ☐ Are the appliances shown in the correct location?
- ☐ ☐ Are the correct manufacturers, model numbers, colors, and so on specified?
- ☐ ☐ Are the sizes shown correct?

Bathrooms
- ☐ ☐ Are the vanities in the bathrooms the right dimensions, including height?
- ☐ ☐ Is the configuration of the vanities correct? (the number of drawers, cabinets, kneeholes)
- ☐ ☐ Are the fixed mirror sizes and locations correct?
- ☐ ☐ Is the border around the mirror shown?
- ☐ ☐ Is the tub deck shown correctly?

Built-ins
- ☐ ☐ Are all built-ins requested shown?
- ☐ ☐ Are the dimensions and configuration of the built-ins correct?
- ☐ ☐ Is the distance between the counter and upper cabinets correct?
- ☐ ☐ If you want upper cabinets to go to the ceiling, is this shown correctly?
- ☐ ☐ Are the correct number of shelves noted in the correct locations?
- ☐ ☐ Are adjustable shelves noted?
- ☐ ☐ Is the custom-made medicine cabinet noted?
- ☐ ☐ Is the built-in ironing board noted?
- ☐ ☐ Is the built-in ironing board installed for both a right-handed and left-handed person?
- ☐ ☐ Is the height of all toe kicks correct?

Doors
- ☐ ☐ Do the elevations show the correct door shapes (rectangular, arched, cathedral, other)?
- ☐ ☐ Are the heights and widths of the doors shown correctly?
- ☐ ☐ Are specific headers shown if requested?
- ☐ ☐ Is the door trim the correct design and width?
- ☐ ☐ Is the direction of all door swings correct?
- ☐ ☐ Is the header shown above the door correct?

Electrical
- ☐ ☐ Are outlets shown in the correct location: walls or baseboard?
- ☐ ☐ Are the outlets on the wall above the vanities shown in the correct locations?
- ☐ ☐ Are light switch plates shown in the correct locations?

YES   NO

Electrical (continued)

❑   ❑   Are the security touch pads shown in the correct locations?

❑   ❑   Are the integrated home automation monitors shown in the correct locations?

❑   ❑   Are telephone jacks shown in the correct locations?

❑   ❑   Are computer wiring connectors shown in the correct locations?

❑   ❑   Are the doorbell boxes shown in the correct locations?

❑   ❑   Are the television cables or dish connections shown in the correct locations?

❑   ❑   Are the individual speaker volume controls shown in the correct rooms and in the correct locations?

Fireplaces

❑   ❑   Are all fireplaces you requested shown?

❑   ❑   Are the fireplaces the correct size?

❑   ❑   Are the hearths on the correct fireplaces and are they the correct sizes?

❑   ❑   Are the mantels shown on the correct fireplaces and the correct heights?

❑   ❑   Is the gas key shown in the correct location?

Garage

❑   ❑   Are windows you requested shown correctly?

❑   ❑   Are counters and cabinets you requested shown correctly?

❑   ❑   Is the number of vehicles you requested shown correctly?

❑   ❑   Is there room for the non-automobile vehicles you requested?

Kitchen Cabinets

❑   ❑   Is the configuration of upper and lower cabinets correct?

❑   ❑   Is the height of the counter correct?

❑   ❑   Is the distance between the counter and the bottom of the upper cabinet correct?

❑   ❑   Is the island configuration correct?

❑   ❑   Is the height and size of the island correct?

Plumbing

❑   ❑   Is the pot filler faucet you requested shown?

❑   ❑   Is the pot filler faucet mounted on the wall high enough to swing over your pot?

❑   ❑   If applicable, is the faucet to the free-standing tub correctly placed and noted?

Staircases

❑   ❑   Are the widths of the staircases correct?

❑   ❑   Are the heights of the risers correct?

❑   ❑   Are the railings and spindles correct?

YES   NO

Walls

- ❑ ❑ Are the wall dimensions correct where existing furniture will be placed?
- ❑ ❑ Are the wall dimensions correct where art, portraits, or decorative mirror will hang?
- ❑ ❑ Is the crown molding correct?
- ❑ ❑ Is the height of the baseboard correct?

Windows

- ❑ ❑ Will you be able to reach all windows for cleaning with just a ladder?
- ❑ ❑ Are the dimensions of the windows correct?
- ❑ ❑ Are the shapes of the windows correct?
- ❑ ❑ Is the trim on the windows noted correctly?

Miscellaneous

- ❑ ❑ Is the dumbwaiter shown?
- ❑ ❑ Is the elevator shown?

HVAC Plan Review Checklist

Homeowner _____ Date _____

Look carefully at your HVAC plan and consider the locations of HVAC vents, thermostats, the air compressor, and return air vents. Skip any question that does not apply to your home. For any questions that you answer "no," use a copy of the Blank Comment form (page 18) to record your remarks to discuss with your architect.

YES   NO

Vents

❑   ❑   Identify the location of the HVAC vent in each room. Are the vents aesthetically placed?

❑   ❑   Are the vents shown in the wall, floor, baseboard, ceiling, or a mixture, as you requested? (Whether vents are in the ceiling or upper wall or in the floor, in the baseboard, or in the lower wall is determined by the location of the HVAC system.)

❑   ❑   Are the vents centered on a wall, window, door, or other area?

❑   ❑   Are the vents positioned so they will not interfere with curtains, furniture, art, or rugs?

❑   ❑   Will the air blow directly on people when seated or in bed?

❑   ❑   Will the location of the return air vent be an eyesore?

Thermostats

❑   ❑   Are these aesthetically placed?

❑   ❑   Will direct sunlight shine on the thermostat?

❑   ❑   Are they located on a wall that would interfere with art, furniture, or a mirror?

❑   ❑   If you requested a programmable thermostat, is that noted?

Return Air Vent

❑   ❑   Is the location of the return air vent aesthetically pleasing?

❑   ❑   Is the return air vent centered on a wall?

❑   ❑   Is the location of the return air vent clear of curtains, furniture, art, or mirrors?

Exterior Air Compressor

❑   ❑   Is the location of exterior air compressor accessible for the repairman?

❑   ❑   Will the noise created when running disturb anyone in nearby rooms?

❑   ❑   Is the compressor out of harm's way if located along a driveway?

HVAC System

❑   ❑   Is the location of HVAC system accessible for a repairman?

❑   ❑   Is the HVAC system the proper size in relation to the size of the house?

❑   ❑   Are there an appropriate number of HVAC or radiant heat zones?

❑   ❑   Are the correct rooms connected to the correct radiant heat thermostats?

❑   ❑   Is access to the HVAC filter convenient?

❑   ❑   Do any rooms require extra HVAC vents? If so, are those shown?

Geothermal System

❑   ❑   If installing a geothermal system, is that noted?

Plumbing Plan Review Checklist

Homeowner _____ Date _____

Look carefully at your plumbing plan and answer the questions below. Skip any question that does not apply to your home. For any questions that you answer "no," use a copy of the Blank Comment form (page 18) to record your remarks to discuss with your architect.

YES   NO

Sinks and Faucets

❑   ❑   Are all sinks requested shown?
❑   ❑   If you have selected the sinks, are the correct manufacturers, model numbers, colors or finishes, and so on specified?
❑   ❑   Are soap dispensers noted in the correct location?
❑   ❑   Is the hot water dispenser you requested by the correct sink?
❑   ❑   Are all water purifiers noted?

Tubs and Showers

❑   ❑   Are all tubs requested shown?
❑   ❑   Are tub/shower combinations shown in the correct bathrooms?
❑   ❑   Are the directions the tub are positioned correct?
❑   ❑   Are all showers requested shown in the correct bathrooms?
❑   ❑   If you have already selected tub fixtures, shower fixtures, and accessories that will be installed, are the correct manufacturers, model numbers, colors or finishes, and so on specified?
❑   ❑   Are the showerheads shown in the correct locations?
❑   ❑   If having multiple showerheads, is that noted?
❑   ❑   Does the spray from the showerhead clear the shower bench?
❑   ❑   Does the spray from the showerhead clear the shower door?
❑   ❑   Does the spray from the showerhead clear the soap dish?
❑   ❑   Is the specification listed for the height of the showerhead correct?
❑   ❑   If you want shower jets, are they noted on the plans?
❑   ❑   If you requested a handheld shower, is that correctly located?
❑   ❑   Are all steam showers requested shown?
❑   ❑   If you requested two steam heads, is that noted?
❑   ❑   Are heated towel bars shown in the correct location? (Heated towel bars should be within reach of the shower or tub.)

Toilets

❑   ❑   Are all toilets requested shown?
❑   ❑   Are the manufacturers, model numbers, and colors specified correctly?
❑   ❑   If a quiet-close toilet lid was requested, is that specified?
❑   ❑   If a comfort-height toilet seat was requested, is that specified?
❑   ❑   If a padded toilet seat was requested, is that specified?

YES   NO

Appliances
❏   ❏   Is the water source for all appliances (ice makers, freezers with ice makers, dishwasher, dishwasher drawers, coffeemakers, washing machines, refrigerators with water dispensers, and so on) shown correctly?

Water Heater
❏   ❏   Are all water heaters requested shown?
❏   ❏   Are the specifications for the manufacturers, model numbers, sizes, gas, or electric correct?
❏   ❏   If using a tankless water heater, is that noted on the plans?
❏   ❏   Are you happy with the locations of the water heater(s)?

Exterior Faucets
❏   ❏   Are all exterior faucets requested shown?
❏   ❏   Are the exterior faucet locations aesthetically pleasing?
❏   ❏   Are faucets located on every porch, patio, and balcony for hosing off and watering plants? (Consider the aesthetics of the location as well as the function.)
❏   ❏   Is there a faucet near the gazebo, pool area, and grilling area?
❏   ❏   If you want a hot and cold water faucet in the garage, is that specified?
❏   ❏   Will the hot and cold water faucet in the garage be clear of vehicle doors?
❏   ❏   If a drinking faucet was requested, is it shown?

Natural Gas
❏   ❏   Are all items needing natural gas noted? (These may include HVAC, water heaters, fireplaces, fire pits, grills, stove top, ovens, outdoor lanterns, outdoor fireplaces, pool heater, hot tub, and so on.)
❏   ❏   Is the key to operate the gas on a fireplace aesthetically placed?
❏   ❏   If you requested that the gas key be inside the bookcase located next to the fireplace, is that noted?
❏   ❏   If you requested the gas key to be on the wall behind the curtain return, is that noted?

Miscellaneous
❏   ❏   If you will have an aquarium needing water, is that noted?
❏   ❏   If any interior water fountains or water walls are requested, are they shown?
❏   ❏   If any exterior water fountains, waterfalls, and so on are requested, are they shown? (These may be on a landscape plan or consultant's plan.)
❏   ❏   If any exterior sinks are requested, are they shown?
❏   ❏   Are all exterior plumbing needs for pools, hot tubs, waterfalls, ponds, or other items noted? (These may need to be on landscape plans and not architectural plans. Ask your architect.)
❏   ❏   Are the number and location of the water shutoff valves acceptable?
❏   ❏   Is the water meter in an acceptable location for the water meter reader?
❏   ❏   Is the gas meter in an acceptable location for the gas meter reader?

For radiant heat, see HVAC Plan Review Checklist (page 276).

11

Shopping Forms

You'll use the forms in this chapter when you go shopping for various components for your home. The forms serve two purposes: to record information needed before you go shopping and to record the selections you have made. Although not every single item a homeowner needs to shop for is listed, these forms represent the most common purchases. Meet with your architect and builder to gather the facts you need before you go shopping. Where applicable, review the completed hardware checklists in Binder 9 (Individual Bathroom, Bedroom Closet, Kitchen, Laundry Room, Miscellaneous Rooms with Cabinet Hardware, Exterior and Architectural, and Door) before you meet with your architect and builder.

Some of the forms will need multiple copies; this will be indicated in the instructions on the form. Once you begin filling in the information on these forms, file them in Binder 9.

Appliance Shopping Form

Date _____

Homeowner _____ Contact number_____

Make multiple copies of this form. Fill in as many copies as you need to list all the appliances in your home.

Room _____ Type of appliance _____

Manufacturer _____ Model number _____

Will your appliance fronts be stainless, a color, or have a wood panel front? _____

If colored, what color? _____ If wood front, will it be stained or painted? _____

Will the appliance front match the cabinets? ❑ Yes ❑ No Dimensions _____

Handle to open door on the left or right side? _____ Availability _____

Cost _____ Lead time _____

Other specifications _____

Budget allocated for appliances _____

❑ Check if you are attaching a specifications printout for any of these appliances.

Room _____ Type of appliance _____

Manufacturer _____ Model number _____

Will your appliance fronts be stainless, a color, or have a wood panel front? _____

If colored, what color? _____ If wood front, will it be stained or painted? _____

Will the appliance front match the cabinets? ❑ Yes ❑ No Dimensions _____

Handle to open door on the left or right side? _____ Availability _____

Cost _____ Lead time _____

Other specifications _____

Budget allocated for appliances _____

❑ Check if you are attaching a specifications printout for any of these appliances.

Ceiling Fan Shopping Form

Date _____

Homeowner _____ Contact number_____

Make multiple copies of this form. Fill in as many copies as you need to list all the ceiling fans in your home.

Room _____ Is this room inside or outside? _____

Manufacturer _____ Model number _____

Color/finish _____ Remote control ❑ Yes ❑ No   Lights on fan ❑ Yes ❑ No

3- or 4-way switch _____ Number of fan blades _____ Drop-down extension distance _____

Diameter of fan dimension _____ Fan budget _____ Cost _____

Lead time _____ Availability _____

Budget allocated for ceiling fans _____

❑ Check if you are attaching a specifications printout for this model.

Room _____ Is this room inside or outside? _____

Manufacturer _____ Model number _____

Color/finish _____ Remote control ❑ Yes ❑ No   Lights on fan ❑ Yes ❑ No

3- or 4-way switch _____ Number of fan blades _____ Drop-down extension distance _____

Diameter of fan dimension _____ Fan budget _____ Cost _____

Lead time _____ Availability _____

Budget allocated for ceiling fans _____

❑ Check if you are attaching a specifications printout for this model.

Electrical Item Shopping Form

Date _____

Homeowner _____ Contact number_____

Fill in this form for the electrical items needed in your home.

Light Switches

Single pole light switches Quantity _____ Manufacturer_____

Model number _____ Color _____ Cost _____

Lead time _____ Dimmer ❑ Yes ❑ No   Illuminated switch ❑ Yes ❑ No

Double pole light switches Quantity _____ Manufacturer_____

Model number _____ Color _____ Cost _____

Lead time _____ Dimmer ❑ Yes ❑ No   Illuminated switch ❑ Yes ❑ No

Single pole light switches Quantity _____ Manufacturer_____

Model number _____ Color _____ Cost _____

Lead time _____ Dimmer ❑ Yes ❑ No   Illuminated switch ❑ Yes ❑ No

Three-way light switches Quantity _____ Manufacturer_____

Model number _____ Color _____ Cost _____

Lead time _____ Dimmer ❑ Yes ❑ No   Illuminated switch ❑ Yes ❑ No

Four-way light switches Quantity _____ Manufacturer_____

Model number _____ Color _____ Cost _____

Lead time _____ Dimmer ❑ Yes ❑ No   Illuminated switch ❑ Yes ❑ No

Jamb switches Quantity _____ Manufacturer _____ Model number _____

Color _____ Cost _____ Lead time _____

Interior motion detector switches Quantity _____ Manufacturer _____ Model number _____

Color _____ Cost _____ Lead time _____

List doors and door locations that will receive jamb switches.

_____

Exterior motion detector switches Quantity _____ Manufacturer _____ Model number _____

Color _____ Cost _____ Lead time _____

List doors and door locations that will receive jamb switches.

_____

Exterior dusk-to-dawn light sensors Quantity _____ Manufacturer _____ Model number _____

Color _____ Cost _____ Lead time _____

List locations for dusk-to-dawn sensors.

_____

Dual receptacle outlets Quantity _____ Manufacturer _____ Model number _____

Color _____ Cost _____ Lead time _____

GCFI ❑ Yes ❑ No   Connected to light switch? ❑ Yes ❑ No

Four-receptacle outlets Quantity _____ Manufacturer _____ Model number _____

Color _____ Cost _____ Lead time _____

GCFI ❑ Yes ❑ No   Connected to light switch? ❑ Yes ❑ No

List rooms that will receive four-receptacle outlets.

_____

Floor outlets/single receptacle Quantity _____ Manufacturer _____ Model number _____

Color _____ Cost _____ Lead time _____

Single or dual receptacle? _____   GCFI ❑ Yes ❑ No   Connected to light switch? ❑ Yes ❑ No

List rooms that will receive single receptacle floor outlets.

_____

Floor outlets/dual receptacle Quantity _____ Manufacturer _____ Model number _____

Color _____ Cost _____ Lead time _____

Single or dual receptacle? _____ GCFI ❑ Yes ❑ No   Connected to light switch? ❑ Yes ❑ No

List rooms that will receive dual receptacle floor outlets.

_____

Telephone jacks Quantity _____ Manufacturer _____ Model number _____

Color _____ Cost _____ Lead time _____

Face plates for light switches

Fill in the number needed for each type.

Single light switch plate covers _____ Double light switch plate covers _____ 3-gang light switch plate covers _____

4-gang light switch plate covers _____ 5-gang light switch plate covers _____

Manufacturer _____ Model number _____ Color _____

Cost _____ Lead time _____

Face plates for outlets

Fill in the number needed for each type.

Dual receptacle outlet plate covers _____ Quad receptacle plate covers _____ Floor outlet plate covers _____

Other _____ Cable and telephone combination outlet plate covers _____

Manufacturer _____ Model number _____ Color _____

Cost _____ Lead time _____

Face plates for telephone jacks Quantity _____ Manufacturer _____ Model number _____

Color _____ Cost _____ Lead time _____

Budget allocated for light switches _____

Budget allocated for outlets _____

Bathroom Hardware Shopping Form

Date _____

Homeowner _____ Contact number_____

Make a copy of this form for each bathroom in your home. Fill out a separate form for each bathroom.

Which bathroom? _____

Bath towel bars Quantity _____ Manufacturer_____

Model number _____ Color/finish _____

Maximum length _____ Cost _____ Lead time _____

Availability _____

Bath towel hooks Quantity _____ Manufacturer_____

Model number _____ Color/finish _____

Maximum length _____ Cost _____ Lead time _____

Availability _____

Hand towel bars Quantity _____ Manufacturer_____

Model number _____ Color/finish _____

Maximum length _____ Cost _____ Lead time _____

Availability _____

Hand towel hooks Quantity _____ Manufacturer_____

Model number _____ Color/finish _____

Maximum length _____ Cost _____ Lead time _____

Availability _____

Hand towel rings Quantity _____ Manufacturer_____

Model number _____ Color/finish _____

Maximum length _____ Cost _____ Lead time _____

Availability _____

Towel-warming bars Quantity _____ Manufacturer_____

Model number _____ Color/finish _____

Electric or hot water _____ Dimensions _____

Cost _____ Lead time _____

Availability _____

Towel-warming drawer Quantity _____ Manufacturer_____

Model number _____ Color/finish _____

Maximum length _____ Cost _____ Lead time _____

Availability _____

Wall-mounted soap dish Quantity _____ Manufacturer_____

Model number _____ Color/finish _____

Maximum length _____ Cost _____ Lead time _____

Availability _____

Wall-mounted shower shelves Quantity _____ Manufacturer_____

Model number _____ Color/finish _____

Maximum length _____ Cost _____ Lead time _____

Availability _____

Washcloth hooks for shower Quantity _____ Manufacturer_____

Model number _____ Color/finish _____

Maximum length _____ Cost _____ Lead time _____

Availability _____

Shower grab bars Quantity _____ Manufacturer_____

Model number _____ Color/finish _____

Length _____ Cost _____ Lead time _____

Availability _____

Robe hooks Quantity _____ Manufacturer _____

Model number _____ Color/finish _____

Maximum length _____ Cost _____ Lead time _____

Availability _____

Magnifying mirrors Quantity _____ Manufacturer _____

Model number _____ Color/finish _____

Maximum length _____ Cost _____ Lead time _____

Availability _____ (Circle) Wall-mounted or freestanding   Light or no light

Shower curtain rod Quantity _____ Manufacturer _____

Model number _____ Color/finish _____

Maximum length _____ Cost _____ Lead time _____

Availability _____

Shower door hinges Quantity _____ Manufacturer _____

Model number _____ Color/finish _____

Maximum length _____ Cost _____ Lead time _____

Availability _____

Shower door handles Quantity _____ Manufacturer _____

Model number _____ Color/finish _____

Maximum length _____ Cost _____ Lead time _____

Availability _____

Cabinet pulls Quantity _____ Manufacturer _____

Model number _____ Color/finish _____

Maximum length _____ Cost _____ Lead time _____

Availability _____

Drawer pulls Quantity _____ Manufacturer _____

Model number/Size _____ Width of stile/height of rail _____

Finish _____ Cost _____ Lead time _____

Availability _____

Self-closing drawer runners Quantity _____ Manufacturer _____

Model number _____ Finish _____

Cost _____ Lengths _____ Lead time _____

Availability _____

Other bathroom hardware

_____

_____

_____

Budget allocated for bathroom hardware _____

❑ Check if you are attaching a specifications printout for any of these models.

Bedroom Closet Hardware Shopping Form

Date _____

Homeowner _____ Contact number_____

Make a copy of this form for each bedroom closet in your home. Fill out a separate form for each bedroom closet.

Which closet? _____

Cabinet pulls Quantity _____ Manufacturer_____

Model number/Size _____ Width of stile/height of rail _____

Maximum length _____ Cost _____ Lead time _____

Availability _____

Drawer pulls Quantity _____ Manufacturer_____

Model number/Size _____ Width of stile/height of rail _____

Maximum length _____ Cost _____ Lead time _____

Availability _____

Self-closing drawer runners Quantity _____ Manufacturer_____

Model number _____ Color/finish _____

Maximum length _____ Cost _____ Lead time _____

Availability _____

Clothing hanging rods and brackets Quantity _____ Manufacturer_____

Model number _____ Color/finish _____

Maximum length _____ Cost _____ Lead time _____

Availability _____

Telescoping pull-out rod Quantity _____ Manufacturer_____

Model number _____ Color/finish _____

Maximum length _____ Cost _____ Lead time _____

Availability _____

Clothes hooks Quantity _____ Manufacturer_____

Model number _____ Color/finish _____

Maximum length _____ Cost _____ Lead time _____

Availability _____

Behind door hooks Quantity _____ Manufacturer_____

Model number _____ Color/finish _____

Maximum length _____ Cost _____ Lead time _____

Availability _____

Towel bars, hooks, or rings for ties Quantity _____ Manufacturer_____

Model number _____ Color/finish _____

Maximum length _____ Cost _____ Lead time _____

Availability _____

Tie racks Quantity _____ Manufacturer_____

Model number _____ Color/finish _____

Maximum length _____ Cost _____ Lead time _____

Availability _____

Other hardware for closet

_____

_____

Budget allocated for bedroom closets _____

❑ Check if you are attaching a specifications printout for any of these models.

Kitchen Hardware Shopping Form

Date _____

Homeowner _____ Contact number_____

If you will have more than one kitchen in your home, make a copy of this form for each kitchen. Fill out a separate form for each kitchen.

Which kitchen (if you will have more than one)? _____

Cabinet pulls Quantity _____ Manufacturer_____

Model number/size _____ Color/finish _____

Maximum length _____ Cost _____ Lead time _____

Availability _____

If more than one size cabinet pull, note the sizes and number of each size.

Drawer pulls Quantity _____ Manufacturer_____

Model number/size _____ Color/finish _____

Maximum length _____ Cost _____ Lead time _____

Availability _____

If more than one size drawer pull, note the sizes and number of each size.

Self-closing drawer runners Quantity _____ Manufacturer_____

Model number _____ Color/finish _____

Maximum length _____ Cost _____ Lead time _____

Availability _____

If you will have more than one size self-closing drawer runner, note the sizes and the quantity of each size.

Hooks for aprons Quantity _____ Manufacturer_____

Model number _____ Color/finish _____

Maximum length _____ Cost _____ Lead time _____

Availability _____

Hooks for pot holders Quantity _____ Manufacturer_____

Model number _____ Color/finish _____

Maximum length _____ Cost _____ Lead time _____

Availability _____

Dish towel bars, hooks or rings Quantity _____ Manufacturer_____

Model number/size _____ Color/finish _____

Maximum length _____ Cost _____ Lead time _____

Availability _____

Pot racks Quantity _____ Manufacturer_____

Model number/size _____ Color/finish _____

Maximum length _____ Cost _____ Lead time _____

Availability _____

Magnetic knife holder Quantity _____ Manufacturer_____

Model number/size _____ Color/finish _____

Maximum length _____ Cost _____ Lead time _____

Availability _____

Other kitchen hardware

_____

_____

Budget allocated for kitchen hardware _____

❏ Check if you are attaching a specifications printout for any of these models.

Laundry Room Hardware Shopping Form

Date _____

Homeowner _____ Contact number_____

If you will have more than one laundry room, copy and fill out this form for each one.

Which laundry room (if you will have more than one)? _____

Cabinet pulls Quantity _____ Manufacturer_____

Model number/size _____ Color/finish _____

Maximum length _____ Cost _____ Lead time _____

Availability _____

Drawer pulls Quantity _____ Manufacturer_____

Model number/size _____ Color/finish _____

Maximum length _____ Cost _____ Lead time _____

Availability _____

Self-closing drawer runners Quantity _____ Manufacturer_____

Model number/size _____ Color/finish _____

Maximum length _____ Cost _____ Lead time _____

Availability _____

Telescope hanging rods Quantity _____ Manufacturer_____

Model number/size _____ Color/finish _____

Maximum length _____ Cost _____ Lead time _____

Availability _____

Clothes hooks Quantity _____ Manufacturer_____

Model number/size _____ Color/finish _____

Maximum length _____ Cost _____ Lead time _____

Availability _____

Behind door hooks Quantity _____ Manufacturer_____

Model number _____ Color/finish _____

Maximum length _____ Cost _____ Lead time _____

Availability _____

Towel bars, hooks, or rings Quantity _____ Manufacturer_____

Model number _____ Color/finish _____

Maximum length _____ Cost _____ Lead time _____

Availability _____

Hanging rods Quantity _____ Manufacturer_____

Model number _____ Color/finish _____

Maximum length _____ Cost _____ Lead time _____

Availability _____

Other hardware for laundry room

_____

_____

Budget allocated for laundry room hardware _____

❏ Check if you are attaching a specifications printout for any of these models.

Miscellaneous Rooms with Cabinet Hardware Shopping Form

Date _____

Homeowner _____ Contact number_____

Make a copy of this form for each room in your home that requires cabinet hardware (bar, library, playroom, and so on). Fill out a separate form for each room.

Room _____

Cabinet pulls Quantity _____ Manufacturer_____

Model number/size _____ Color/finish _____

Maximum length _____ Cost _____ Lead time _____

Availability _____

Drawer pulls Quantity _____ Manufacturer_____

Model number/size _____ Color/finish _____

Maximum length _____ Cost _____ Lead time _____

Availability _____

Self-closing drawer runners Quantity _____ Manufacturer_____

Model number/size _____ Color/finish _____

Maximum length _____ Cost _____ Lead time _____

Availability _____

Other cabinet hardware

_____

_____

Budget allocated for miscellaneous rooms hardware _____

295

Door Hardware Shopping Form

Date _____

Homeowner _____ Contact number_____

Fill in this form for the door hardware in your home.

Privacy doorknobs Quantity _____ Manufacturer_____

Model number _____ Finish _____

Maximum length _____ Cost _____ Lead time _____

Availability _____

List rooms that will receive privacy knobs.

_____

_____

Dummy doorknobs Quantity _____ Manufacturer_____

Model number _____ Finish _____

Maximum length _____ Cost _____ Lead time _____

Availability _____

List rooms that will receive dummy doorknobs.

_____

_____

Passage doorknobs Quantity _____ Manufacturer_____

Model number _____ Finish _____

Maximum length _____ Cost _____ Lead time _____

Availability _____

List rooms that will receive passage doorknobs.

_____

_____

Entry sets Quantity _____ Manufacturer_____

Model number _____ Finish _____ Mortise set ❑ Yes ❑ No

Backset Measure _____ Cost _____ Lead time _____

Availability _____

Exterior door sets Quantity _____ Manufacturer_____

Model number _____ Finish _____ Mortise set ❑ Yes ❑ No

Backset Measure _____ Cost _____ Lead time _____

Availability _____

Dead bolts (keyed both sides) Quantity _____ Manufacturer_____

Model number _____ Finish _____

Cost _____ Lead time _____ Availability _____

List doors receiving _____

Dead bolts (keyed one side, lever or other) Quantity _____ Manufacturer_____

Model number _____ Finish _____

Cost _____ Lead time _____ Availability _____

List doors receiving _____

Pinhole lock on interior doors Quantity _____ Manufacturer_____

Model number _____ Finish _____

Cost _____ Lead time _____ Availability _____

Other type of locks Quantity _____ Manufacturer_____

Model number _____ Finish _____

Cost _____ Lead time _____ Availability _____

Doorstops Quantity _____ Manufacturer_____

Model number _____ Finish _____

Cost _____ Lead time _____ Availability _____

If you will use different styles of doorstops, fill in the door, the room in which the door is located, and other pertinent information listed above on a Blank Comment Form (page 18) and attach it. (See Doorstop Options, page 234.)

Hinges Quantity _____ Manufacturer_____

Model number _____ Finish _____

Cost _____ Lead time _____ Availability _____

Square or rounded corners _____

Door knockers Quantity _____ Manufacturer_____

Model number _____ Finish _____

Cost _____ Lead time _____ Availability _____

Doorbell escutcheons Quantity _____ Manufacturer_____

Model number _____ Finish _____

Cost _____ Lead time _____ Availability _____

Door kickplates Quantity _____ Manufacturer_____

Model number _____ Finish _____

Cost _____ Lead time _____ Availability _____

Finger push plates Quantity _____ Manufacturer_____

Model number _____ Finish _____

Cost _____ Lead time _____ Availability _____

Pocket door handles and lock Quantity _____ Manufacturer_____

Model number _____ Finish _____

Cost _____ Lead time _____ Availability _____

Other door hardware

_____

_____

Budget allocated for door hardware _____

❑ Check if you are attaching a specifications printout for any of these models.

Exterior Hardware Shopping Form

Date _____

Homeowner _____ Contact number_____

Check any that you have selected for your home.

❏ **Shutter hardware** Quantity _____ Manufacturer_____

Model number _____ Finish _____

Cost _____ Lead time _____ Availability _____

❏ **Garage door hardware** Quantity _____ Manufacturer_____

Model number _____ Finish _____

Cost _____ Lead time _____ Availability _____

❏ **Mailbox** Quantity _____ Manufacturer_____

Model number _____ Finish _____

Cost _____ Lead time _____ Availability _____

❏ **Mail Drop** Quantity _____ Manufacturer_____

Model number _____ Finish _____

Cost _____ Lead time _____ Availability _____

❏ **Weathervane** Quantity _____ Manufacturer_____

Model number _____ Finish _____

Cost _____ Lead time _____ Availability _____

❏ **Address plate** Quantity _____ Manufacturer_____

Model number _____ Finish _____

Cost _____ Lead time _____ Availability _____

❏ **Finials** Quantity _____ Manufacturer_____

Model number _____ Finish _____

Cost _____ Lead time _____ Availability _____

❑ **Boot scraper** Manufacturer_____

Model number _____ Finish _____

Cost _____ Lead time _____ Availability _____

❑ **Sundial** Manufacturer_____

Model number _____ Finish _____

Cost _____ Lead time _____ Availability _____

❑ **Other** Manufacturer_____

Model number _____ Finish _____

Cost _____ Lead time _____ Availability _____

Budget allocated for exterior hardware? _____

❑ Check if you are attaching a specifications printout for any of these models.

Gas Log Fireplace Shopping Form

Date _____

Homeowner _____ Contact number_____

Make a copy of this form for each gas log fireplace in your home. Fill in a separate form for each gas log fireplace.

Room _____

Manufacturer _____ Model number _____

Vented or ventless _____ Remote control starter ❑ Yes ❑ No

Dimensions of your fireplace _____ Hood ❑ Yes ❑ No

Size of fireplace _____ Style of log _____

Finish/color _____Cost _____

Glass door or fixed glass front _____

Cost _____ Lead time _____ Availability _____

Remarks _____

Budget allocated for gas log fireplace _____

❑ Check if you are attaching a specifications printout.

12

Entire-Home Selection Forms

The forms in this chapter will be extremely helpful to your whole team, especially your builder. Devote enough time to make sure the information is accurate. These forms represent your final selections.

Copy any of these forms that apply to items you will be selecting for your home and keep the blank forms in Binder 1. When you begin filling in these forms, file them in Binder 11. Upon completion of a form, make copies for each of your team members and file your final copy in Binder 11. If you receive an order form, specification forms, or other useful material, file it along with the form in Binder 11. Be sure to date the form each time you make a change.

The Entire-Home Selection forms do not represent every item you will select for your home. The number of selections and the options for some selections are too numerous to create a form for each. The checklists, shopping forms, and selection forms are extremely useful tools, however, to use when selecting items for your home.

Here are the Entire-Home Selections forms you will fill out.

Entire-Home Appliance Selections (page 306). form provides a comprehensive list of appliances that you might use in your home. Fill in the room location, manufacturer, model number, color/finish, handle on left or right, and check if you have a specification sheet on this appliance. You will find some appliances duplicated on the form in case you want more than one.

Entire-Home Built-in Selections (page 309). This lists the parts of the home most likely to have built-ins. Check the boxes for the built-ins you want, and on the lines below, note the room in which the built-in will be located. Add comments; if you need more comment space, make a copy of the Blank Comment Form (page 18).

Entire-Home Ceiling Fan Selections (page 312). On this form you'll find the most common rooms in which ceiling fans are located. Beside each room where you want a ceiling fan, fill in the manufacturer's name, model number, and color/finish; indicate whether you want a fan only, lights on the fan, or a remote control; and check if you have a specification sheet on this fan.

Entire-Home Computer Wiring Selections (page 313). This lists the rooms most commonly wired for computers; describe the approximate location in the room where you want connectors, outlets, and telephone jacks.

Entire-Home Door Hardware Selections (page 314). On this form, indicate which doors will have a privacy doorknob, passage doorknob, or dummy doorknob, and fill in the total number of each for that room. Note if any of the doors in that room will have an additional lock, such as a dead bolt, and what type doorstop the door will use. Refer back to Doorstop Options (page 234) and Door Bolt Options (page 235). Exterior doors can be different, so there is another space for exterior doors. If you need more space, attach a Blank Comment Form (page 18) with your comments to this form.

Entire-Home Exterior Component Selections (page 317). For each exterior component outside your home, such as columns or gutters, fill in the material you will use, the manufacturer, model number, color or finish, and any remarks. In the remarks column, fill in comments such as the size and pattern of a roof piece or the size and pattern of a paver.

Entire-Home Fireplace Selections (page 318). The most common rooms where homeowners want a fireplace are listed. For each room that will have a fireplace, indicate if you want a raised hearth and a mantel, and if you want a gas log fireplace or a wood-burning fireplace. For gas log fireplaces, indicate each option you want.

Entire-Home Fixed Mirror Selections (page 319). Fill in the name of any room that will have a fixed mirror, along with the desired location within the room. Fill in the approximate dimensions of the area, and indicate whether you will require cuts into the mirror for items such as light switches, outlets, and lighting fixtures. If you want a beveled mirror, any etching on the mirror, or other special design, fill in that information, along with any other instructions.

Entire-Home Floor Selections (page 320). A variety of choices are provided here for floors and basic applications to those floors. Put a check next to the rooms that you will have in your home, and fill in the type of floor for that particular room and any application that you want.

Entire-Home Exterior Paint Color Selections (page 323). The form lists the basic areas outside a home that are painted. Fill in information regarding the paint color, paint finish, and special instructions.

Entire-Home Interior Paint Color Selections (page 324). The form lists the basic areas in a home that are painted, including the ceiling and trim. Fill this form out for each room in your home, and fill in information regarding the paint color, paint finish, and special instructions.

Entire-Home Plumbing Selections (Excluding Bathrooms) (page 325). Here you'll find details regarding the general plumbing components of your home, such as the pipes and water heater, as well as the plumbing features for each room (bathrooms and powder rooms have a separate form). Fill in the manufacturer, model number, color or finish, and any other detail regarding the plumbing fixture you have selected for your home.

Individual Bathroom and Powder Room Plumbing Selections (page 327). The most common plumbing fixtures in a bathroom are listed. Make as many copies of this form as you will have bathrooms and powder rooms in your home, and fill in the name of the bathroom or powder room this form represents. For the items you will want in your home, fill in the manufacturer, model number, color/finish, and any other pertinent information.

Entire-Home Security Alarm and Integrated Home Automation Monitor System Selections (page 328). The form lists the rooms most likely to have a security alarm pad or a home automation monitor. Put a check next to the rooms where you want a pad or a monitor. Write in if you will use a security alarm pad, or if your security system will be part of the home automation monitor. Fill in the approximate location for the pad or monitor in the room and closet.

Entire-Home Stereo Equipment Selections (page 329). Record what stereo equipment you will have and in what room(s) that equipment will be located.

Entire-Home Stereo Speaker Selections (page 330). The rooms that commonly have stereo speakers are listed. For the rooms in which you want speakers, indicate whether you want them mounted in the wall or ceiling. Also indicate if you want an individual speaker volume control in that room and if that room will have surround sound.

Entire-Home Stone/Tile Selections (page 331). List any rooms in your home that will have stone or tile, and indicate what the stone or tile will be used for: countertop, floor, shower floor, shower wall, tub deck, chair rail, and so on. Then supply information about the material.

Entire-Home Telephone Jack Selections (page 333). For each room that needs a telephone jack, fill in the exact location in the room and desired telephone jack options.

Entire-Home Television Selections (page 334). For those rooms that will have a television, fill in the information on the form.

After filling in the Entire-Home Selections forms, record these selections on the appropriate Individual Room and Closet Fact Sheet you filed in Binder 4. Every fact about a particular room or closet should be found on that particular room or closet fact sheet. Remember to date all fact sheets, forms, and checklists each time you add or delete information, and return it to the appropriate binder.

Entire-Home Appliance Selections

Fill out the following table for appliances in your home (the appliances most commonly purchased in multiples are listed twice).

Appliance	Room Location	Manufacturer	Model Number	Color/Finish	Handle Left or Right	Gas or Electric	Specifications Sheet Provided
Advantium oven							
Coffemaker (built-in)							
Convection oven							
Cooktop							
Daiquiri machine							
Deep fryer							
Dishwasher							
Dishwasher							
Dishwasher drawer							
Dishwasher drawer							
Disposal*							
Disposal*							
Dryer							
Dryer							
Exhaust hood							

*Note by the disposal if you will use a light switch, push button, or batch system activated at the drain to turn on your disposal.

Appliance	Room Location	Manufacturer	Model Number	Color/Finish	Handle Left or Right	Gas or Electric	Specifications Sheet Provided
Freezer							
Freezer							
Hot water dispenser							
Ice maker							
Margarita machine							
Microwave							
Microwave							
Oven							
Oven							
Oven/microwave combination							
Popcorn wagon							
Range							
Refrigerator							
Refrigerator							
Refrigerator drawer							

(Entire-Home Appliance Selections, continued)

Appliance	Room Location	Manufacturer	Model Number	Color/Finish	Handle Left or Right	Gas or Electric	Specifications Sheet Provided
Refrigerator drawer							
Refrigerator/freezer combination							
Stackable washer/dryer							
Trash compactor							
Trash compactor							
Warming drawer							
Warming drawer							
Washing machine							
Washing machine							
Wine chiller							
Other _____							
Other _____							

Submission date _____ Homeowner signature _____

Homeowner contact number _____

Entire-Home Built-in Selections

Check the built-ins you want in your home. Next to the built-in, write the room in which it will be located. In the blank lines, write specific instructions. If necessary, use the Blank Comment Form (page 18) and attach to this form. Do not forget to include built-ins in the attic and garage.

For bedroom closet built-ins, use the Bedroom Closet Checklist (page 144). For kitchen cabinets, use the Kitchen Cabinet Layout Checklist (171).

❑ Banquette

_____

_____

❑ Bath vanity

_____

_____

❑ Bookcases

_____

_____

❑ Bunk beds

_____

_____

❑ Cabinets above the toilet

_____

_____

❑ Cabinets in bar

_____

_____

❑ Cabinets in butler's pantry

_____

_____

❑ Cabinets in laundry

_____

_____

❑ Cabinets in pantry

_____

_____

❑ Credenza

_____

_____

❑ Cubbyholes

_____

_____

❑ Desk

_____

_____

❑ Entertainment center

_____

_____

❑ Fishing pole racks

_____

_____

❑ Gift wrap center

_____

_____

❑ Gun racks

_____

_____

❑ Ironing board

_____

_____

❑ Island

_____

_____

❑ Lockers

_____
_____

❑ Peninsula

_____
_____

❑ Photo gallery shelves

_____
_____

❑ Seated makeup area

_____
_____

❑ Window seats

_____
_____

❑ Wine racks

_____
_____

❑ Other

_____
_____
_____
_____
_____
_____
_____

Submission date _____ Homeowner signature _____

Homeowner contact number _____

Entire-Home Ceiling Fan Selections

For any rooms that will have ceiling fans, fill in the information and check the appropriate columns.

Room	Manufacturer	Model Number	Color/Finish	Fan Only	Lights on Fan	Remote Control
Bedroom, master						
Bedroom, guest						
Bedroom 1						
Bedroom 2						
Bedroom 3						
Covered patio						
Den/family room						
Garage						
Kitchen						
Laundry Room						
Porch						
Other _____						

☐ Check here if you have additional pages to attach to the ceiling fan list.

Submission date _____ Homeowner signature _____

Homeowner contact number _____

▶ File in Binder 11:
Final Selections

Entire-Home Computer Wiring Selections

For any rooms that will have computer wiring, fill in the information and check the appropriate columns.

Room	Connector Location	Outlet by Connector	Telephone Jack by Connector	Telephone Jack/ Connector Combined
Bedroom, master				
Bedroom, guest				
Bedroom 1				
Bedroom 2				
Bedroom 3				
Bedroom 4				
Den/family room				
Office, hers				
Office, his				
Kitchen				
Library				
Other _____				

Submission date _____ Homeowner signature _____

Homeowner contact number _____

Entire-Home Door Hardware Selections

For all rooms in your home, fill in the door information and check the appropriate columns.

Room	Number of Doors/ Hinges	Privacy	Passage	Dummy	Additional Lock	Type of Doorstop	Color/Finish	Interior or Exterior Door	Remarks
Bar									
Bathroom, master									
Bathroom, guest									
Bathroom 1									
Bathroom 2									
Bathroom 3									
Bedroom, master									
Bedroom, guest									
Bedroom 1									
Bedroom 2									
Bedroom 3									
Bedroom 4									
Bedroom closet, master, hers									
Bedroom closet, master, his									
Bedroom closet, master, joint									

(Entire-Home Door Hardware Selections, continued)

Room	Number of Doors/ Hinges	Privacy	Passage	Dummy	Additional Lock	Type of Doorstop	Color/Finish	Interior or Exterior Door	Remarks
Bedroom closet, guest									
Bedroom 1 closet									
Bedroom 2 closet									
Bedroom 3 closet									
Bedroom 4 closet									
Breakfast room									
Butler's pantry									
Control room									
Dining room									
Entry foyer									
Exercise room									
Family room									
Kitchen									
Kitchen pantry									
Laundry room									

(Entire-Home Door Hardware Selections, continued)

Room	Number of Doors/ Hinges	Privacy	Passage	Dummy	Additional Lock	Type of Doorstop	Color/Finish	Interior or Exterior Door	Remarks
Library									
Living room/ great room									
Mechanical room									
Media room									
Mudroom									
Nursery									
Office									
Playroom									
Pool house									
Porch									
Wine room									
Other_____									

Submission date _____ Homeowner signature _____

Homeowner contact number _____

Entire-Home Exterior Component Selections

Fill in the information for the exterior components you will use in your home. Remarks could include the size of roof pieces, thickness, and pattern, or the size, thickness, and pattern of any pavers.

Exterior Component	Material	Manufacturer	Model Number	Color/Finish	Remarks
Columns					
Decorative architectural elements					
Decorative iron					
Dormers					
Driveway material					
Exterior walls					
Fencing					
Finials					
Flashing					
Foundation					
Garage door					
Gutters					
HVAC system					
Iron railing					
Lanterns					
Patio material					
Porch					
Porch railing					
Roof					
Shutters					
Sidewalk material					
Weather vane					
Windows					

Submission date _____ Homeowner signature _____

Homeowner contact number _____

Entire-Home Fireplace Selections

For all rooms that will have fireplaces, check the appropriate columns and fill in the information.

Room	Raised Hearth	Mantel	Gas Log or Wood Burning?	GAS LOG ONLY Vented or Ventless?	GAS LOG ONLY Manual or Remote Control?	GAS LOG ONLY Light Switch to Start
Bedroom, master						
Bedroom, guest						
Den/family room						
Exterior patio						
Library						
Living room/ great room						
Playroom/ game room						
Other _____						
Other _____						

If you will have a hearth, what material would you like to use? _____

What size hearth do you want: height, depth, and width?_____

If you want a mantel, will you provide one, have the builder purchase one, or have it custom built?

Explain. _____

If you will have a mantel, will you want a shelf on the mantel? _____ From what type of material do you prefer your mantel

to be made? _____

Wood burning

Do you want an ash pit under the fireplace for ashes to drop so they can be removed from the exterior of your home? _____

Do you want special wood storage inside your home, in your garage, or outside your home? _____

❑ Check if you have additional pages to add to the fireplace list.

Submission date _____ Homeowner signature _____

Homeowner contact number _____

Entire-Home Fixed Mirror Selections

Fill in the information for all fixed mirrors you want in your home. Examples of special instructions include any etching, floor-to-ceiling mirrors, three-paneled mirror with two panels on hinges, beveled or other type of edge design, cuts in the mirror for outlets or light switches, doors that will have mirror panels, and so on.

Room	Location of Mirror	Dimensions	Cuts into Mirror	Special Design Instructions

Submission date _____ Homeowner signature _____

Homeowner contact number _____

Entire-Home Floor Selections

For all rooms in your home, fill in the floor information and check the appropriate columns.

Room	Square Footage	Budget	Wood	Carpet	Carpet Pad	Carpet Pad Thickness	Stone/ Tile	Brick	Concrete	Other	Shoe Mold	Special Treatment/Design Pattern/Finish	Manufacturer/ Model Number/Color	Remarks
Balcony														
Bar														
Bathroom, master														
Bathroom, guest														
Bathroom 1														
Bathroom 2														
Bathroom 3														
Bedroom, master														
Bedroom, guest														
Bedroom 1														
Bedroom 2														
Bedroom 3														
Bedroom 4														
Bedroom closet, master, hers														

Room	Square Foot-age	Budget	Wood	Carpet	Carpet Pad	Carpet Pad Thick-ness	Stone/ Tile	Brick	Con-crete	Other	Shoe Mold	Special Treat-ment/Design Pattern/Finish	Manufacturer/ Model Num-ber/Color	Remarks
Bedroom closet, master, his														
Bedroom closet, master, joint														
Bedroom closet, guest														
Bedroom 1 closet														
Bedroom 2 closet														
Bedroom 3 closet														
Bedroom 4 closet														
Breakfast room														
Butler's pantry														
Control room														
Dining room														
Entry foyer														
Exercise room														
Family room														

Room	Square Foot- age	Budget	Wood	Carpet	Carpet Pad	Carpet Pad Thick- ness	Stone/ Tile	Brick	Con- crete	Other	Shoe Mold	Special Treat- ment/Design Pattern/Finish	Manufacturer/ Model Num- ber/Color	Remarks
Kitchen														
Kitchen pantry														
Laundry room														
Living room/ great room														
Mechanical room														
Mudroom														
Nursery														
Office														
Patio														
Playroom														
Pool house														
Porches														
Wine room														

Submission date _____   Homeowner signature _____

Homeowner contact number _____

Entire-Home Exterior Paint Color Selections

Fill in the paint information for any of the items listed below. Some items may not require paint.

Item	Color	Paint Finish*	Paint/Stain Manufacturer	Special Instructions
Balcony ceilings				
Brick				
Built-in planters				
Columns				
Door, back				
Door, front				
Doorjamb, back door				
Doorjamb, front door				
Doorjamb, other doors				
Doors, other				
Dormers				
Downspouts				
Exterior walls				
Garage door				
Garage door trim				
Garage floor				
Gutters				
Pedestal or sculpture base				
Porch ceiling				
Porch floor				
Railing				
Screen door				
Shutter				
Soffit				
Step riser				
Stucco				
Windows				
Windows trim				
Wood siding				
Wood trim				

*Paint finish may be satin, flat, semigloss, eggshell, or other.

Submission date _____ Homeowner signature _____

Homeowner contact number _____

Entire-Home Interior Paint Color Selection

Make a copy of this form for each room in your home. Fill in the paint information for each room on a separate form.

Room _____

Item	Color/Stain	Manufacturer	Paint Finish*	Specialty/Faux Paint	Special Instructions
Ceiling					
Walls					
Trim**					
Other ____					

*Paint finish may be flat, satin, semigloss, gloss, eggshell, or other.

**Trim commonly includes crown, beams, baseboard, chair rail, door trim and jamb, window casing, and shoe mold.

Submission date _____   Homeowner signature _____

Homeowner contact number _____

Entire-Home Plumbing Selections (Excluding Bathrooms)

Will you use copper, PEX tubing, or PVC for your pipes? _____

Will you use a tank or tankless water heater? _____

Will you use a recirculating pump on your water heater? _____

Will you use a desuperheater to heat your tank? _____

Fill in the information below for all plumbing fixtures you want (excluding those in the bathrooms and powder rooms, which have a separate form on page 327). In the bottom rows, under Other Rooms/Fixtures add any rooms and plumbing fixtures not listed above, such as craft room/sink.

Fixture	Manufacturer	Model Number	Color	Remarks
Desuperheater				
Recirculating pump				
Tankless water heater				
Tank water heater				
Bar				
Sink faucet				
Wine sink				
Wine sink faucet				
Garage				
Sink				
Sink faucet				
Kitchen				
Commercial sprayer				
Hot water dispenser				

Fixture	Manufacturer	Model Number	Color	Remarks
Second sink				
Second sink faucet				
Sink				
Sink faucet				
Soap pump				
Sprayer				
Laundry Room				
Sink				
Sink faucet				
Sink sprayer				
Soap pump				
Sprayer in tiled area				
Other Rooms/Fixtures				

Submission date _____ Homeowner signature _____

Homeowner contact number _____

Individual Bathroom and Powder Room Plumbing Selections

Make a copy of this form for each bathroom and powder room in your home. Write in the name of the bathroom or powder room. Once each page is filled out, attach to the Entire-Home Plumbing Selections (Excluding Bathrooms) form (page 325).

Bathroom or Powder Room Name _____

Fixture	Manufacturer	Model Number	Color/Finish	Other
Bidet				
Handheld shower sprayer				
Handheld sprayer in tub				
Jetted tub				
Showerhead				
Shower only				
Shower wall jets				
Sink				
Sink faucet				
Steam shower				
Toilet				
Tub				
Tub faucet				
Tub/shower combination				
Urinal				
Other _____				

Submission date _____ Homeowner signature _____

Homeowner contact number _____

327

Entire-Home Security Alarm and Integrated
Home Automation Monitor System Selections

For each room, note if you want an alarm pad or an integrated home automation monitor and describe the location within the room.

❏ Bedroom, master

_____

_____

❏ Closet

_____

_____

❏ Den/family room

_____

_____

❏ Entry foyer

_____

_____

❏ Kitchen

_____

_____

❏ Laundry room

_____

_____

❏ Mudroom

_____

_____

❏ Check if you have additional pages to add to the alarm or home monitor list.

Submission date _____ Homeowner signature _____

Homeowner contact number _____

328

Entire-Home Stereo Equipment Selections

For all rooms that will have stereo equipment, check the appropriate columns. Create a list of other equipment on a separate page and number each piece of equipment on that page. Under the heading Other Equipment below, write in the number that corresponds with the numbered equipment on the separate page.

Room	DVD Player	VCR Player	CD Player	Cassette Player	Turn-table	Receiver	Second Receiver	Speaker	Volume Control Box	Satellite Radio	MP3 Accessories	Other Equip-ment
Bedroom, master												
Bedroom, guest												
Bedroom 1												
Bedroom 2												
Bedroom 3												
Bedroom 4												
Den/ family room												
Library												
Other _____												

❑ Check if you have additional pages to add to the stereo equipment list.

If you currently own any stereo equipment you will use in this home, list each piece, provide the dimensions, and note which room you want this equipment placed in.

_____

_____

Submission date _____ Homeowner signature _____

Homeowner contact number _____

Entire-Home Stereo Speaker Selections

For all rooms that wil have stereo speakers, check the appropriate columns.

Room	Wall-Mounted	Ceiling-Mounted	Individual Volume Control	Surround Sound
Bar area				
Bathroom, master				
Bedroom, master				
Bedroom, guest				
Bedroom 1				
Bedroom 2				
Bedroom 3				
Bedroom 4				
Breakfast room				
Den/family room				
Dining room				
Entry foyer				
Exterior patio				
Kitchen				
Laundry room				
Library				
Living room/great room				
Porch				
Other _____				

❑ Check if you have additional pages to add to the stereo speaker list.

Submission date _____ Homeowner signature _____

Homeowner contact number _____

Entire-Home Stone/Tile Selections

In the left column, write the names of the rooms that will have stone or tile, and indicate what the stone or tile will be used for (countertop, floor, tub deck, etc.). Then fill in the information about the material. When filling in this form, refer to Stone and Tile (page 237) in Chapter 8.

☐ Check if you would like to pick your own slabs.

☐ Check if you want to meet with the stone/tile installer and lay out the boxes of stone or tile pieces so that you can discard any pieces that do not match.

Room/Usage	Mat-erial	Color	Stone Thick-ness	Edge Thick-ness	Edge Design	Slab or Tile Pieces	Tile Size Piece	Honed or Pol-ished	Grout Color	Grout Width	Accent Pieces	Cuts in Stone	Special Design Pattern	Remarks

Room/Usage	Mat-erial	Color	Stone Thick-ness	Edge Thick-ness	Edge Design	Slab or Tile Pieces	Tile Size Piece	Honed or Pol-ished	Grout Color	Grout Width	Accent Pieces	Cuts in Stone	Special Design Pattern	Remarks

Submission date _____

Homeowner signature _____

Homeowner contact number _____

Entire-Home Telephone Jack Selections

For all rooms that will have telephone jacks, fill in the information and check the appropriate columns.

Room	Location in Room	Wall or Desk Mount	Number of Lines	Connector/Jack Com-bination	Separate Connector, Separate Jack
Bathroom, master					
Bedroom, guest					
Bedroom, master (her side)					
Bedroom, master (his side)					
Bedroom 1					
Bedroom 2					
Bedroom 3					
Bedroom 4					
Den/family room					
Kitchen					
Library					
Office, hers					
Office, his					
Other _____					

☐ Check if you have additional pages to add to the telephone jack list.

Submission date _____ Homeowner signature _____

Homeowner contact number _____

333

Entire-Home Television Selections

For all rooms that will have televisions, check the appropriate columns.

Room	Sur-round Sound	DVD Player	VCR	DVD/VCR	VCR Copier	Cable Box	Dish Box	Number of Tele-visions	Wall-Mount-ed	In Book-case	In Ar-moire	Pop Up from Furni-ture	Free-stand-ing	On Top of Furni-ture	Other
Bathroom, master															
Bedroom, master															
Bedroom, guest															
Bedroom 1															
Bedroom 2															
Bedroom 3															
Bedroom 4															
Den/family room															
Kitchen															
Laundry room															
Library															
Office															
Other															
Other															

❑ Check if you have additional pages to add to the television list.

Submission date _____ Homeowner signature _____

Homeowner contact number _____

13

Building Basics

Although this book focuses on the design aspects of building a home, this chapter will touch on some of the basic information homeowners need to know as they embark on the building process. These include the budget, the timetable, framing, backing, construction protection, and other miscellaneous items.

The Builder Discussion Form (page 345) lists 40 different items related to designing and building your home. Use the blank lines after each item to record questions and concerns to discuss with your builder. Once you begin filling in this form, file it in Binder 12: Builder Discussions.

BUILDER'S BUDGET

You should be familiar with the items most commonly found in a builder's budget. The Builder's Budget Glossary following this list offers select definitions (page 337). Common budget categories include:

General costs
  Cleanup
  Construction protection
  Construction soft costs
  Contingencies
  Job site equipment
  Permits and tap fees
  Preconstruction design and engineering
  Utilities for construction
Site work
  Demolitions, if applicable

Drains
Driveway
Excavations
Landscape
Retaining walls
Utilities underground
Concrete
  Concrete test
  Flatwork
  Foundation
  Lightweight concrete
  Miscellaneous concrete (random uses of
    concrete, such as firewood area and a
    dog pen)
  Waterproofing
Masonry
  CMU foundations
  Exterior stucco/plaster, brick
  Fireplace masonry
  Flagstone and pavers
  Stone veneer
Metals
  Ornamental metalwork
  Structural steel
Woods
  Framing
  Framing material
  Trim carpentry
  Trim carpentry materials
Insulation/roof/gutter
  Deck/roof waterproofing
  Foundation waterproofing
  Gutter/downspouts
  Insulation
  Roofing
Doors/windows/glass
  Door hardware
  Exterior custom door
  Garage doors
  Glass and glazing

Interior specialty door
Finishes
  Drywall
  Floors
  Paint, stain, lacquer
  Tiles and slabs
Specialties
  Bath access
  Fireplaces and fire pits
  Other specialties
  Pest control
Equipment
  Appliances
  Vacuum system
Cabinetry
  Cabinets
  Built-in closets
  Specialty rooms (e.g., library, wine room)
Special construction
  Boat dock, shoreline construction
  Hot tubs/swimming pools
Elevators
  Dumbwaiters
  Elevators
Mechanical
  Alternative power
  Fire suppression system
  HVAC
  Hydronic heat
  Plumbing
Electrical/low voltage
  Audio/video
  Electrical
  Lighting fixtures
  Low voltage
Construction company charges
  Construction fee
  Overhead and administration
  Site supervision and general labor
  Warranty reserve

BUILDER'S BUDGET GLOSSARY

CMU foundations: acronym for concrete masonry unit; cinder block.

Concrete test: a test done at the job site on the concrete that is ready to be poured, to test the strength of the concrete. Concrete strength differs depending on the mix, which is spelled out by a structural engineer. Make sure the specified standard of concrete is delivered.

Construction fee: percentage of job costs or flat fee paid to builder.

Construction protection: protection from scratches, dents, and nicks of building materials, appliances, glass, and so forth that have been installed in your home.

Construction soft costs: anything that is not related to a permanent part of the project; includes architecture, building and other permits, consultants, soil test, survey tests, structural engineer reports, permits, inspections, and so on.

Contingencies: Money set aside for unknowns, including the punch list. (The punch list is a list of items that are missing, defective, poorly installed, and so forth, and need to be fixed by the contractor before the walk-through.)

Flatwork: concrete used on flat surfaces such as floors, basements, sidewalks, driveway, and patios.

Hydronic heat (radiant heat): transfers heated water through tubing in floors, walls, and ceilings so that the heated water will radiate heat throughout the home.

Lightweight concrete: a lighter strength concrete, such as concrete over the radiant heated water tubes used in a radiant heated floor.

Miscellaneous concrete: random uses of concrete, such as an area to stack wood and a dog pen.

Tap fee: fee charged for hooking up utilities to be used on the construction site, generally water or sewer.

Warranty reserve: funds to cover a one-year warranty on the home (for things such as defective windows, closets that won't close, and so on).

THE BUILDING PROCESS

Ask your builder for a timetable. It will be a checkpoint as to whether the job is moving along on time, and will give you an idea of when certain selections must be made so that the builder can order the materials. Following is a construction sequence, a timetable without the time elements given. The time of year, the availability of subcontractors, and other factors will greatly influence a construction timetable. The sequence could change depending on how much of the job has been specified for cabinets, timber, doors, floors, windows, and so on, and if the builder can place those orders.

A typical sequence a builder goes through to build a home with a slab foundation, stucco and natural stone siding, and wood shake roofing includes the following steps. (Consult the Glossary at the end of the book for definitions of any unfamiliar terms.)

1. Stake land for excavation.
2. Apply for building permit.
3. Order any items with long lead time, such as an elevator and slide set of doors.
4. Order windows.
5. Order timber package (rustic beams and so on).
6. Order cabinets, per cabinet drawings.
7. Order interior doors and trim.
8. Order trusses.
9. Remove trees and vegetation.
10. Stake land for footings.
11. Dig trenches for footings.
12. Build forms for footings.
13. Request that the municipality perform a footing inspection.
14. Order geotechnology soil tests.

15. Perform concrete tests.
16. Pour concrete into the footings built to contain the concrete for the foundation.
17. Build forms for walls.
18. Request that the municipality conduct a wall inspection.
19. Pour concrete into the foundation walls.
20. Remove foundation forms.
21. Apply waterproofing on the paved walls and retaining walls.
22. Request that the municipality perform a foundation inspection.
23. Backfill excavated area. (Be cautious if walls are over eight feet tall.)
24. Dig and install water line.
25. Dig and install sewer line.
26. Dig and install MEPS underground (mechanical, electrical, plumbing pipes, and wires).
27. Apply pest control to the slab.
28. Add prep material to slabs (vapor barrier, gravel).
29. Request that the municipality conduct a slab inspection.
30. Pour concrete into slabs.
31. Frame lower-level walls.
32. Frame main-level floor.
33. Order fireplaces.
34. Frame main-level walls.
35. Install trusses.
36. Install roof sheathing.
37. Apply black felt to roof to dry in the area below the roof.
38. Apply stucco or stone veneer to the chimney.
39. Install windows and exterior doors.
40. Install siding and timbers.
41. Install shingles.
42. Create a framing punch list (walls plumb, doors fit, windows fit, and so on).
43. Order exterior lights.
44. Order door hardware.
45. Order appliances.
46. Order bath hardware.
47. Order plumbing fixtures.
48. Install electric boxes and cans for lights for homeowner inspection.
49. Perform HVAC and natural gas rough-in by installing the duct work and gas pipes.
50. Install fireplace units.
51. Request that the municipality inspect the HVAC and gas.
52. Apply interior stone veneer.
53. Perform plumbing rough-in by installing all plumbing pipes needed in the home.
54. Request that the municipality conduct a plumbing inspection.
55. Perform electrical rough-in by running all electrical wire through studs and framing members.
56. Perform security rough-in by running all wiring needed for security.
57. Request that the municipality perform an electrical inspection.
58. Install porch ceiling.
59. Request that the municipality conduct a framing inspection.
60. Apply stucco.
61. Install exterior stone.
62. Install decorative slabs (stain concrete for patios, and so on).
63. Apply exterior paint.
64. Install gutters and downspouts.
65. Install sleeves.
66. Install landscaping.
67. Install insulation.
68. Request that the municipality perform an insulation inspection.
69. Stock drywall.
70. Hang drywall.
71. Apply tape and texture to drywall.

72. Clean up after drywall applied.

73. Prime walls and ceilings.

74. Measure and order handrails for stairs, balconies, porches, and so on.

75. Install tile flooring.

76. Install shower tile.

77. Measure and order shower glass.

78. Install cabinets, interior doors, and trim.

79. Install hardwood floor.

80. Make template for granite countertops.

81. Install granite countertops.

82. Install pavers (driveway).

83. Perform electrical trim-out by installing outlets, switches, light fixtures, face places, and so on.

84. Do HVAC trim-out by installing vents, thermostat, and so on to make system operable.

85. Do plumbing trim-out by installing plumbing fixtures and making all plumbing operable.

86. Request that the municipality conduct MEPS final inspections (mechanical, electrical, plumbing).

87. Install shower doors and mirrors.

88. Install bath hardware.

89. Install baseboard at hardwood floor.

90. Stain and lacquer wood trim and baseboard.

91. Apply interior paint.

92. Apply final faux paint.

93. Install carpet.

94. Clean up construction site inside and out.

95. Construction team walk-through.

96. Request that the municipality issue a Certificate of Occupancy.

97. Create punch list to resolve before homeowner walk-through.

98. Do final cleanup.

99. Owner walk-through and owner punch list created.

100. Complete punch list.

FRAMING

Framing occurs after the foundation is set and involves installing lumber or steel for the structural support of the home. The main framing components of the home are the walls, doors, windows, floors, and roof. These are built with framing members such as studs, joists, rafters, and trusses. Location of these framing members can affect the interior design and function of your home. Identify all framing concerns using the following list as a guide and discuss these with your builder. Also give

Construction Tips

- Treat the land for termites before putting in the foundation.
- Absolutely do not cut corners when it comes to your foundation.
- The quality and cost of concrete differs. A test should be done on the concrete in a cement mixer before it is poured to make sure you are getting the quality you wanted.
- Aluminum studs are more expensive than wood studs. Check with your insurance agent to calculate potential savings when using aluminum studs.
- Once the slab foundation is poured, make sure no standing water touches the foundation.
- Never use anything but pencil to write on unpainted sheetrock walls. During construction it is not unusual for notes to be written on the sheetrock. Markers and ink pens require extra coats of paint to cover.
- Sewer pipes that are not tightened properly can leak sewer gases, and the smell will eventually seep into the residence.
- The sprinkler system pipes located in the ceiling interfere with the preferred location of recessed can lights or a chandelier. These locations should be discussed before framing and roughing-in of plumbing.

your builder a complete electrical plan, which will allow him to consider items such as recessed can lights and chandeliers in framing decisions.

Your final electrical plan must be submitted before framing begins so that the framer knows which light fixtures need to be centered in a room, in a hallway, on a mantel, over a sink, over an island, and so on, and where the fold-down staircase is located, so the framer can make adjustments to framing plans. Review the following areas with your builder and framer:

Attic. Fold-down staircase will be centered in a hallway.

Chandeliers and pendant light fixtures. All hanging light fixtures need to line up on the center of the dining room table, center of a room, center of an island, center of a kitchen sink, center of a table, or other location. Identify the location of these and make sure the floor or ceiling joists will not interfere with centering any of these.

Door. The door frame area should be reinforced around the jamb. The door most used should also have additional framing along the wall, especially if that door is self-closing.

Floors. The weight of such items as a piano, gun safe or other safe, commercial stove, and exercise and weight equipment may need reinforcement.

HVAC. Vents should be centered on a window, door, or other element for symmetry. Return air vents should be centered on a wall or in a hallway. The return air vent will be placed between two studs. With your builder, identify where it is shown on the HVAC plans.

Recessed can lights. These need to line up in the center of a hallway, on a mantel, on bookcases, on the center of an island or table. Make sure the floor or ceiling joists will not interfere with centering these.

Retractable movie screen. Floor and ceiling joists need to run parallel, not perpendicular, so the screen can be retracted into the ceiling.

Safe room. Additional framing is needed in the ceiling, floors, walls, and door frame.

ADDITIONAL BACKING

Ask your builder to install backing, frame lumber installed between wall studs to give additional support for drywall or interior items such as a handrail bracket, cabinets, or a towel bar. Items are screwed and mounted into solid wood rather than drywall so that art, mirrors, portraits, towel bars, and coat hooks will have wood to grip into, not just sheetrock. Items to consider for backing include the following.

Audio/stereo equipment
   Ceiling-mounted projectors
   Ceiling-mounted screens
   Wall-mounted speakers
   Wall-mounted televisions
Bathroom
   Bathroom art
   Bathroom mirror, if decorative hanging type
   Ceiling fans
   Grab bars
   Magnifying mirror if mounted on the wall
   Medicine cabinet
   Shower curtain bar
   Shower door
   Television if mounted on the wall
   Toilet paper holder
   Towel bars, rings, and hooks
   Towel warmer
   Wall above toilet for cabinets
Decorative hanging pieces
   Art
   Mirrors
   Portraits
   Sculpture
   Wall-mounted corner cupboard or other
      wall-mounted furniture

Garage
   Garage door motor
   Walls where tools will be mounted
Hardware
   Clothes hooks or robe hooks
   Wall-mounted coat rack
Kitchen
   Pot rack
   Six-burner range
Lighting
   Chandeliers
   Sconces
   Wall fixtures
Mantels
Staircase
   Hand rails
Window treatments
   Cornice
   Curtain rod
   Decorative curtain tie backs

PROTECTION

Going the extra mile to protect your house as it is being built will prevent headaches and time delays at the end. Review the construction protection list with your builder and come to an agreement on what will be done. Monitor the situation throughout the building process and tell the builder when protective materials are torn, removed, or forgotten. Many items that show up on the punch list could have been prevented with proper protection during construction. There are a number of things to watch out for on your site.

Counters need to be covered if the surface will scratch or stain, and the edges need protection from being chipped. Pay special attention to porous stone such as shell stone.

Fireplaces need to be covered to keep anyone from burning things in them. You don't want to find cigarette butts inside the fireplace. When your builder paints the walls or sands the floors, the interior of your fireplace needs protection.

Floors made of marble, granite, tile, or other surfaces that can be scratched need to be protected. Light-colored grout needs to be protected from dirt and staining.

Glass windows and doors need protection from scratches.

HVAC ducts need protection from being bent or crushed and protection from construction debris and dust. Your builder should cover all HVAC vent holes and air return holes during construction. When the vent covers are installed, your builder should cover them with filters so that dust does not get into the vents when the floors are sanded. Your builder should make sure workers will not be able to operate the HVAC system during construction.

Your builder should also prevent workers from pouring unfriendly liquids down the sink, causing stains or clogging the drain. In addition, sinks need to be protected from being scratched.

Toilet holes need to be covered before the toilet's installation, so that materials that may clog the pipes do not fall down the hole. This will also prevent the hole from being damaged. Once the toilet is installed, the builder should close and tape down the lid so that it is not used.

Once tubs are installed, your builder should place a piece of plywood or other wood over them. You do not want them scratched or stained; you also don't want liquid poured down the drain that might cause a clog.

Damage caused by improper protection can include stopped-up toilets; excrement left in toilets; liquids poured down shower, tub, and sink drains, causing stains; stained tubs and sinks; scratched and stained sinks; chips in counter edges; scratched marble floors; chips or cracks in the corners of mirrors; scratched windows; dented and scratched appliance doors; windows that will not lock due to being jammed open; and gouges in wood floors that will not sand out.

PHOTOS AND VIDEOS

Take photos and make videos periodically during construction. Make sure you write on each photo what the photo represents. It is especially important to take photos and make videos just before sheetrock is installed. If there is a Freon leak inside a wall or a water leak, these photos will help pinpoint the location of the problem. If you decide you want an opening through the wall in the future, the photo will let you see what wires, pipes, duct work, and so on lie behind the wall. You cannot count on the architectural plans to show you the location, because during a job builders may need to deviate from the plans.

Note on each photo what room and what wall in that room you are photographing. If possible, measure distances from the corners of the room to the location of the pipes or wires and write those measurements on the studs so that they will show up on the photo or video. Don't forget to take photos of the ceiling. You might want to add a recessed can light or a pendant light and it is helpful to know whether there is duct work in the way.

TREES AND EXCESS DIRT

Discuss with your builder which trees you want removed and a foolproof system for tagging them. Also discuss fertilizing those that remain and installing a system to water the roots. The size and shape of the lot and the proposed building envelope on the lot will determine if any trees, landscape boulders, or other materials need to be placed in the backyard before breaking ground begins. Ask your builder what will be done with excess dirt and make sure you are in agreement with the builder's plan.

TIP: If installing a lawn sprinkler system, ask for a cost analysis to install a second water meter for the sprinkler system only. This water use will not be billed the sewer fee, but you will have to pay for the meter.

DELAYS

To break ground on a new home construction project, you need to dot many i's and cross many t's. No matter how organized and prepared you may be, some delays are out of your control. However, often delays occur that could have been prevented. The more organized you are, the more timely you are in doing your homework and following through, the fewer delays you will incur.

TEN MOST COMMON CAUSES FOR DELAYS IN BREAKING GROUND

Based on my experience and from surveying people I know in the industry, here are the top ten things that can delay your groundbreaking.

Warranty Reserve

Ask your builder for a one-year warranty on your home. This does not include appliances, HVAC systems, the roof, and other things you buy for the home. (You can purchase a policy from companies such as American Home Shield to cover home appliances, HVAC, garage door openers, and other things in your home that may break down.)

Within the first year after building the home, there will be things that don't work properly. A door may not close without sticking, a hinge may be defective, a cabinet door might sag, or a faucet may leak. If you have a one-year warranty, your builder will repair these without charge if it is within that first year period.

When the builder creates a budget for a home, there will be a warranty reserve, the cost for covering those one-year warranty issues.

1. Waiting on final numbers from the builder to put into the contract
2. Contract with builder hung up with attorney
3. Final architectural plan delayed
4. Homeowner not making timely decisions
5. Homeowner Association being slow or not giving approval
6. Permits from the municipalities not obtained
7. Soil and other tests not done
8. Weather preventing site work
9. Marketplace is booming—waiting for subcontractors
10. Construction loan delayed

9. Homeowner being unavailable to answer questions that arise during construction
10. Delays in receiving the municipal inspector's final approvals

Even after the ground has been broken, you may still experience delays. Regularly visit your site and phone the builder if there is no work going on.

TEN MOST COMMON CAUSES OF DELAYS IN COMPLETING YOUR HOME ON TIME

Here are what I and my industry experts have found are the top ten things that will delay your home completion.

1. Weather
2. Architect or engineer made errors in plans—what is shown cannot be built
3. Marketplace is booming—time waiting for subcontractors exceeds expectations
4. Builder not placing orders in a timely manner
5. Problems with materials—manufacturer delay in shipping materials, wrong materials shipped, damaged materials shipped, or an incomplete order shipped
6. Homeowner not meeting selection deadlines set by the builder
7. Products selected by the homeowner being discontinued or back-ordered
8. Homeowner making too many change orders

GOING OVER BUDGET

A common complaint heard from people building a home is that it took three times as long to build and cost three times more than anticipated. Though some of the delays and increased costs are out of your control, a prudent and organized homeowner can keep the project in line.

TWELVE REASONS THE HOME EXCEEDS THE BUDGET

1. Inaccurate topography. Either no topography is done or a flown topography (taken from a helicopter or airplane) is submitted, which only shows the land from an aerial photo. Topography shot by a surveyor on the ground is more accurate than flown topography. If building on a steep lot, inaccurate topography can affect the cost of concrete and retaining walls by tens of thousands of dollars. Even a piece of land that appears to be flat may have a topography variance of five feet.

2. Emotional decisions. Emotions can cause rational thinking to go out the door. Even the most astute financial planner can be affected by the emotional aspect of designing and building a dream home and lose sight of the financial aspect. Homeowners often feel this is the only chance to obtain certain items in their home. These emotions can lead to decisions that are not in their budget.

3. Upgrading architectural specifications. When building a home, the mentality of most people is to "go grand." They want everything they have ever dreamed of in a home. They have the feeling that this is the home they will live in for the rest of their lives and think if they don't say yes to certain things, they will never be able to have them in their home. Homeowners will ignore their architect's specifications, which were based on the original budget supplied by the homeowner, and request upgrades. Unfortunately, these upgrades do not always fit the budget.

4. Inaccurate predetermined budget. The budgets for appliances, plumbing fixtures, lighting fixtures, hardware, roofing, and so on should be set with the homeowner's input. Problems occur when an architect or builder sets these budgets without input from the homeowner. The architect or builder, without truly knowing the homeowner's taste level and quality expectations, may create a budget that reflects moderately priced items—while the homeowner wants upscale items. It is not until the time comes to select these items that a homeowner truly understands the level of quality the budget represents.

5. Ignoring your budget. A homeowner begins selecting appliances, plumbing fixtures, lighting fixtures, hardware, roofing, and so on without knowing their cost. The products the homeowner feels he or she cannot live without end up being more expensive than allowed in the budget.

6. Hurry-up mentality. Construction is underway and the clock is ticking. The homeowner is paying to live in one place and at the same time paying for the land and the construction loan. This causes a hurry-up mentality, which can translate into decisions based on product availability instead of cost. To get products delivered quickly, the homeowner ends up paying charges for expedited shipping that were not part of the budget.

7. Change orders. The homeowner makes changes throughout the construction process, which

are not only costly, but can also delay the project. The homeowner hears about the latest and greatest product that just hit the market and must have it. This product was not in the budget and will not be available for several weeks. Both the budget and timetable have just been blown.

8. Too many decision makers. The homeowner allows the architect, interior designer, and their consultants to make change orders with the builder without the homeowner's approval. This is a sure way to blow your budget.

9. Delayed completion. Some builders charge a monthly supervision fee. These fees can add up if the project exceeds the expected finish date. A delayed completion will also cause the homeowner to make additional interest payments on the construction loan. If there is a Homeowner Association, you will be paying association dues without living in the association.

10. Structural engineers overspecifying. Because we live in a litigious society, structural engineers may specify more steel than necessary. Having your builder involved in the design process allows the builder to work with the architect in specifying what is necessary, without going overboard.

11. Homeowner Association fines. The Homeowner Association bylaws may have a set number of days to complete a new home construction project. Fines are imposed for each day exceeding that set number of days. The Homeowner Association may also impose fines for other bylaws broken by the construction crews.

12. Fees. Many fees must be paid in order to obtain a building permit. The homeowner had no idea and did not allocate enough money.

Builder Discussion Form

Architect issues _____

_____

Interior designer issues _____

_____

Consultant issues _____

_____

HOA issues _____

_____

Municipality issues _____

_____

Appliances _____

_____

Backing _____

_____

Built-ins _____

_____

Cabinets _____

_____

Carpentry _____

_____

Ceiling fans _____

_____

Ceilings _____

_____

Computer wiring _____

_____

Doors _____

_____

Driveway _____
_____

Electrical _____
_____

Electrical, exterior _____
_____

Excavation _____
_____

Exterior items _____
_____

Fireplaces _____
_____

Floors _____
_____

Foundation _____
_____

Framing _____
_____

Hardware _____
_____

HVAC _____
_____

Lighting _____
_____

Mirrors _____
_____

Paint _____
_____

Plumbing _____
_____

Porches, patios, decks, and balconies _____
_____

Protection issues _____
_____

Roofing _____
_____

Security alarm/integrated home automation _____
_____

Sidewalks _____
_____

Stereo speakers/equipment _____
_____

Stone/tile _____
_____

Telephones _____
_____

Televisions _____
_____

Walls _____
_____

Windows _____
_____

Appendix 1: Forms and the Binders They Go In

Form	Chapter	Page	Binder
Apartment Area Checklist	5	128	4
Appliance Shopping Form*	11	280	9
Architect Comparison Chart	2	42	2
Architect Contact Information	1	9	4
Architect Meeting Notes*	1	21	5
Architect Questionnaire*	2	38	2
Architect Site Visit Form*	2	48	8
Attic Checklist	5	129	4
Bar Checklist	5	130	4
Basement Checklist	5	133	4
Basic Bedroom Fact Sheet	4	71	4
Basic Design Fact Sheet	4	67	4
Bathroom Applications for Stone/Tile Checklist	8	251	4
Bathroom Checklist*	5	134	4
Bathroom Hardware Shopping Form*	11	285	9
Bathroom Storage Item Checklist*	5	140	4
Bedroom Checklist*	5	143	4
Bedroom Closet Checklist*	5	144	4
Bedroom Closet Hardware Checklist	8	243	9
Bedroom Closet Hardware Shopping Form*	11	289	9
Blank Comment Form*	1	18	various
Breakfast Room Checklist	5	152	4
Builder Comparison Chart	2	46	2
Builder Contact Information	1	11	4
Builder Discussion Form*	13	345	12
Builder Meeting Notes*	1	23	5
Builder Questionnaire*	2	40	2

*You will need multiple copies of these forms.

*You will need multiple copies of these forms.

*You will need multiple copies of these forms.

Form	Chapter	Page	Binder
Laundry Room Hardware Shopping Form	11	293	9
Library Checklist	5	186	4
Living Room/Great Room Checklist	5	188	4
Mechanical Room Checklist	5	189	4
Media Room Checklist	5	190	4
Miscellaneous Information Checklist	4	72	4
Miscellaneous Rooms with Cabinet Hardware Checklist	8	245	9
Miscellaneous Rooms with Cabinet Hardware Shopping Form*	11	295	9
Morning Kitchen/Counter Checklist	5	191	4
Mudroom Checklist	5	192	4
Municipality Information Fact Sheet	3	62	3
Nursery Checklist	5	193	4
Occupants of the Home Checklist	4	68	4
Office Checklist	5	194	4
Playroom/Game Room Checklist	5	196	4
Plumbing Checklist	7	229	4
Plumbing Plan Review Checklist	10	277	4
Pool House Checklist	5	197	4
Porch, Patio, Deck, and Balcony Checklist	5	198	4
Powder Room/Half Bath Checklist	5	200	4
Product Sample Fact Sheet*	1	20	10
Product Sample Manifest*	1	19	10
Real Estate Contact Information	1	16	3
Rooms in Your Home Checklist	4	69	4
Safe Room Checklist	5	201	4
Specialty Room Checklist	5	202	4
Stone/Tile Cuts Checklist	8	253	4
Subcontractor Meeting Notes*	1	24	5
Subcontractor Contact Information	1	12	4
Things That Make Noise Checklist	9	264	4
To Do List*	1	17	4
Utility Companies Contact Information	1	15	4
Wine Room Checklist	5	203	4

*You will need multiple copies of these forms.

Appendix 2: Standard Measurements and Dimensions

EQUIPMENT AND FURNISHINGS

AUDIO EQUIPMENT

Standard cable box, stereo receiver, CD player, VCR player, DVD player all are 17 inches wide. Depth and height vary.

DVD in a plastic case: $7\frac{1}{2}$ x $5\frac{1}{2}$ x $\frac{1}{2}$ inches

DVD or CD: $4\frac{3}{4}$ inches in diameter

CD in a plastic case: $5\frac{5}{8}$ x $4\frac{15}{16}$ x $2\frac{3}{8}$ inches

Video in a plastic case: 8 x $4\frac{13}{16}$ x $1\frac{3}{16}$ inches

Video without a plastic case: $7\frac{1}{2}$ x $8\frac{1}{8}$ x 1 inch

Cassette: $4\frac{1}{4}$ x $2\frac{3}{4}$ x $\frac{5}{8}$ inches

Album: $12\frac{3}{8}$ x $12\frac{3}{8}$ inches

BAR

Bar counter: 40 to 42 inches high

Bar stool: 30 inches high

Standard wine bottle: $11\frac{7}{8}$ to 12 inches high

Standard fifth of alcohol: $12\frac{1}{2}$ inches high

Half gallon bottle of alcohol: $11\frac{7}{8}$ to 12 inches high

Distance between bar and back bar counter: 36 to 42 inches

BED

King: 76 x 80 inches

California king: 78 x 84 inches

Queen: 60 x 80 inches

Queen extra long: 60 x 84 inches

Full or double: 54 x 75 inches

Full or double extra long: 54 x 84 inches

Single: 39 x 80 inches

Single extra long: 39 x 84 inches

Bunk beds: 30 x 75 inches

DINING TABLE STANDARD MEASUREMENTS

Round

40-inch diameter, seats 4 to 5

48-inch diameter, seats 5 to 6

60-inch diameter, seats 7 to 8

72-inch diameter, seats 8 to 9

84-inch diameter, seats 9 to 11

96-inch diameter, seats 10 to 12

108-inch diameter, seats 11 to 14

120-inch diameter, seats 12 to 15

Rectangular

2 feet 6 inches x 5 feet, seats 4 to 6

3 x 6 feet, seats 6 to 8

3 feet 6 inches x 8 feet, seats 8 to 10

4 x 10 feet, seats 10 to 12

4 x 12 feet, seats 12 to 14

4 feet 6 inches x 14 feet, seats 14 to 16

4 feet 6 inches x 16 feet seats 16 to 18

4 feet 6 inches x 18 feet, seats 18 to 20

Square

3 x 3 feet, seats 4

3 feet 6 inches x 3 feet 6 inches, seats 4

4 x 4 feet, seats 4 to 8

4 feet 6 inches x 4 feet 6 inches, seats 4 to 8

5 x 5 feet, seats 8 to 12

FURNITURE SPACING

Space between sofa and coffee table: 10 inches

Space between chair and dining table: 10 inches

Space between dining table and serving table or wall: 42 inches

Space per person at a dining room table: 24 inches, plus 2 inches for armchairs

Space between center of one bar/counter stool and center of adjacent stool: 24–30 inches

Height of counter stool: 24 inches

Height of bar stool: 30 inches

Space between foot of bed and furniture: 36 inches

Space between twin beds: 22 inches

GAME TABLES

Ping-Pong table: 9 x 5 feet

Pool table: 8-foot (44 x 88 inches) requires 13 feet 2 inches x 16 feet 10 inches if using full-sized cues

Pool table: 9-foot (50 x 100 inches) requires 13 feet 8 inches x 17 feet 10 inches for full-sized cues

Pool cue, standard: 57 inches

Pool cue, short: 48 or 52 inches

GARAGE VEHICLES

(The vehicles listed below represent a cross-section of vehicle sizes.)

These measurements do not include the side mirrors. If your vehicle has a brush guard on the front, you will need to add distance to the length.

Vehicle Sizes	Length (inches)	Width (inches)
Chevrolet Suburban	222.4	79.1
Ford Expedition	206.5	78.8
Hummer H3	186.7	85.5
Chevrolet Tahoe	202	79
Lexus LS	298	73.8
Chrysler 300	196.8	74.1
Honda Accord Sedan	191.1	71.6

KITCHEN AND PANTRY

CLEANING TOOLS

Allow 5 feet for height of brooms, mops, and other products such as Swiffers.

Upright vacuum cleaners such as Dyson, Bissell, and Eureka range 44 to 46 inches high.

KITCHEN CABINETS, COUNTERS, AND OVENS

Upper cabinet depth: 12 inches

Lower cabinet depth: 24 inches

Standard kitchen counter measurements: 24 inches deep, 36 inches high (depending on thickness of counter)

Distance between counter and bottom of upper cabinets: 18 inches

Distance between the sink counter and upper cabinets: 22 inches (if no window above the sink)

Distance above the top of a range to the hood: 30 inches

Distance between counter and island: 48 inches if there are appliances on both counter and island.

Standard cabinet shelves: 12 inches deep (measure your dinner plates; request oversized cabinets if they are larger)

Height of cutout for a single oven from finished floor: 32½ inches

Height of cutout for a double oven from finished
floor: 13¼ inches minimum

Most common length of slabs used for counters:
116 inches

KITCHEN PRODUCTS

12-pack of soft drinks: 5¼ inches x 4¾ x
15½ inches

2-liter bottles of soda: 12 inches tall, 4 inches
diameter

5-gallon water bottle: 19½ inches tall, 11 inches
diameter

Resealable sandwich bag box: 7¾ x 3 x 5 inches
(economy pack, 125 bags)

Resealable gallon bag box: 11¼ x 3 x 3½ inches

Plastic wrap or aluminum foil: standard length
12¼ inches

Extra length aluminum foil: 18¼ inches

Paper towels: 11¼ inches high

PIANO

Steinway Concert grand piano: 8 feet 11¾ inches
long, 61¼ inches wide, 990 pounds

Steinway Model B: 6 feet 10½ inches long,
58 inches wide, 760 pounds

MISCELLANEOUS ITEM MEASUREMENTS

Front-load washers and dryers on pedestals:
between 50½ and 51½ inches high; 27 inches
wide and 28 to 29 inches deep (Samsung
and Frigidaire models)

Ironing board: approximately 15 inches wide x
5 feet long

Outlets: 12 inches from finished floor

Shower curtains: 70 to 72 inches wide,
72 inches high

Shower curtains, extra long: 70 to 72 inches wide,
84 inches high

Towel bar: 48 inches from finished floor

Toilet paper holder: 2.6 feet from finished floor

Water dispenser with 5-gallon jug: 60 inches high

CLOTHING AND CLOSETS

CLOSET

Single hanging bar: 67 inches high

Double tier hanging bars: lower bar 38 inches
high, upper bar 78 inches high

Depth of hanging bar from wall: 11 inches

WOMAN'S CLOTHING

Length of dresses	50 inches
Length of evening dresses	68 inches
Length of blouses	34 inches
Length of knee-length skirts	34 inches
Length of shorts, cuff hung	28 inches
Length of coats	52 to 54 inches
Length of suits	40 inches
Length of robes	52 to 55 inches
Height of standard pair of cowboy boots	12 inches

MEN'S CLOTHING STANDARD MEASUREMENTS

Length of men's suits	30 to 40 inches
Length of men's slacks, cuff hung	44 to 53 inches
Length of men's slacks, double-hung	29 to 36 inches
Length of men's shirts	30 to 40 inches
Length of men's top coats	48 to 54 inches
Length of men's ties	60 to 62 inches
Height of standard pair of cowboy boots	13 inches

HANGING CLOTHING

Folded men's shirt: 9 to 9½ inches wide, 15 to 15½ inches top to bottom

Six pairs of pants folded over a hanger: 7 to 9 inches of hanging bar space

Six starched shirts on a hanger: 6 to 6½ inches of hanging bar space

Six suits on a hanger: 12 inches of hanging bar space

Six sweaters folded over a hanger: 12 inches of hanging bar space

Six pairs of jeans folded over a hanger: 11 inches of hanging bar space

For men, allow 2½ inches of hanging space per garment, 4 inches for heavy coats.

For women, allow 2 inches of hanging space per garment and 4 inches for heavy coats.

Allow 20 percent additional space for future purchases.

Appendix 3: Abbreviations Used in Architectural Plans

Below is a list of abbreviations commonly found on architectural plans and their meaning. This list will serve as a handy reference when you review your architectural plans.

" or **IN**: inch

AC: air conditioning
ACST: acoustic
AFF: above finished floor
AL or **ALUM**: aluminum
ARCH: architect or architectural
AVG: average

BD or **BRD**: board
BLDG: building
BLT-IN: built-in
BM: beam
BR: brass
BRZ: bronze
BSMT: basement

CAB: cabinet
CC and RS: conditions, covenants, and restrictions
CDR: cedar
CER: ceramic
CL: center line
CLG: ceiling
CLO or **CLOS**: closet
CLR: clear
CM: centimeter
CO: cased opening (doorway without a door)

CO: certificate of occupancy
COL: column
CONC: concrete
CONST: construction
CONT: continuous
CONTR: contractor
CT: countertop
CW: cold water

DEC: decorative
DEMO: demolition
DET: detail
DIA: diameter
DIM: dimension
DN: down
DR: door
DW: dishwasher
DWG: drawing
DWV: drain waste vent

ELEC: electric
EQL: equal
EQUIP: equipment
EST: estimate
EWC: electric water cooler
EXIST: existing
EXT: exterior

FAB: fabricate or fabricated

FAO: finished all over

FF: finished floor

FIN: finish

FL: floor

FLUOR: fluorescent

FP: fireproof

FS: floor supply and full size

FT: feet or foot

FTG: footing

FURN: furnish

GALV: galvanized

GEN'L: general

GFCI or GFI: ground fault circuit interrupter

GL: glass

GYP BD: gypsum board

HB: hose bib

HC: hollow core

HD: heavy duty

HDW: hardware

HDWD: hardwood

HH: head height

HOR or HORIZ: horizontal

HSWS: high side wall supply

HT or HGT: height

HTD: heated

HVAC: heating, ventilation, and air conditioning

HW: hot water

INSUL: insulation

INT: interior

J-BOX or JB: junction box

kW: kilowatt

LAV: lavatory

LIN: linear

LINO: linoleum

LOUV: louver

LT: light

LTG: lighting

M: meter

MAR: marble

MAS: masonry

MAT'L or MTRL: material

MAX: maximum

MECH: mechanical

MFD: manufactured

MFR: manufacture

MIN: minimum

MISC: miscellaneous

MO: masonry opening

MULL: mullion

NAT: natural

NEC: national electric codes

NIC: not in contract

NO: number

NOM: nominal

NTS: not to scale

OC: On center

OPG: Opening

OPP: Opposite

PH: telephone

PL: plaster

PLBG: plumbing

PL LAM: plastic laminate

PLY: plywood

PR: Pair

PROJ: projecting or projected

PRV: pressure relief valve

PT: partition

QT: quarry tile

QTY: quantity

R: radius
R: riser
RA: return air
RD: round or rod
REINF: reinforce
REQD: required
REV: revision
RF: reference
RGH OPNG: rough opening
RM: room
RMV: remove

SC: solid core
SCH: schedule
SD: smoke detector
SEC or SECT: section
SF or SQ FT: square foot
SH: shelf or sheet
SIM: similar
SPEC: specified
SPECS: specifications
SPLT: split
SQ IN: square inch
SQ: square
S ST: stainless steel
ST: steel
STD: standard
STRL: structural
SYS: system

T & G: tongue and groove (joint)
TEL: telephone
TEMP: temperature
THK: thick
TR: tread
TRM: trim
TYP: typical

UNF: unfinished
UR: urinal

VERT: vertical
VIF: verify in the field
V TILE: vinyl tile
VTR: vent through roof

W: width
W/: with
W/O: without
WC: water closet
WCT: wainscot
WD: wood
WH: water heater
WI: wrought iron
WIC: walk-in closet
WNDWS: windows
WP: waterproof
WT: weight

YD: yard

Appendix 4: Basic Architectural Symbols

ELECTRICAL SYMBOLS:

Ceiling light	
Wall light	
Wall light	
Pull switch	
Recessed light	
Fan outlet	
Fan with paddles and light	
Fan with paddles and no light	
Surface fluorescent	
Recessed fluorescent	
Spotlights	
Under-cabinet light switch	
Single pole switch	S
Three-way pole switch	S₃
Four-way pole switch	S₄
Weatherproof switch	S_WP
Automatic door switch	S_D
Switch with timer	S_T
Low voltage switch	S_L

Thermostat	T
Variable speed switch	V
Light, heater, fan switch	
Smoke detector	S.D.
Exhaust fan	
Door chime	CH
Electric door opener	D
Clock outlet	C
Single receptacle outlet	
Duplex receptacle outlet	
Split-wired receptacle outlet	
110 outlet	
220 outlet	220
Special purpose	
Garbage disposal	GD
Clothes dryer	D
Washer	
Range outlet	R
Floor single outlet	
Floor duplex outlet	

359

Floor special purpose outlet	△ (in square)	Washer	AW (in square)
Ceiling outlet	○	Dryer	D (in square)
Telephone outlet	◁	Toilet	⊡ ○
Telephone private system	◁P	Shower	⊠
Television cable	TV	Tub	▭
Whole-house vacuum	◁V	Water meter	—Ⓜ—
Weatherproof	⊖WP	Water heater	ⓌⒽ
Transformer	T	Hot water	—— — — ——
Push button	■●	Cold water	——— — · — · ——
Buzzer	◺	Vent	— — — — — — —
Bell	◻	Gas pipe	—— G —— G ——
Combination bell/buzzer	◻		

PLUMBING SYMBOLS

Built-in sink	⊙
Pedestal sink	⊙ PL
Kitchen sink	⊔
Dishwasher	DW
Range/oven	++ ++
Refrigerator	REF

Lighting panel	▬
Power panel	▨
Junction box	Ⓙ

OTHER SYMBOLS

Pocket door	
Bifold door	
Sliding door	
Hinged door	

Glossary

16 on center (16.o.c.): width between wall studs, in inches. Studs are installed 16 inches from the center of one stud to the center of another.

Aerator: the round screen screwed on the tip of a sink faucet that mixes air and water to create a smooth flow of water.

Anchor bolts: bolts used to secure a wooden sill plate to concrete, masonry floor, or wall; used in tornado, earthquake, and hurricane areas.

Backing: lumber installed between wall studs to give additional support for drywall or an interior trim-related item, such as handrail brackets, cabinets, and towel bars. This allows items to be screwed and mounted into solid wood rather than drywall, which may allow the item to break loose from the wall.

Back fill: dirt used to fill in around the foundation and footings, often the same dirt that was dug out.

Backset: the distance between the center of the hole for a door lock or cylinder to the edge of the door.

Backsplash: a wall covering, usually stone or tile, located on the wall area behind and above a countertop, a bathroom vanity, a bathtub, or any other area where water could splash onto the wall. Also protects walls from cooking splatters.

Ball catch: a type of hardware used to keep a door closed; a spring-loaded ball fits into a hole on the door or frame.

Balusters: the vertical posts in a railing; sometimes referred to as pickets or spindles.

Balustrade: the railing, posts, and balusters along the edge of a stairway or balcony.

Base or baseboard: a trim board placed along the wall where the wall and floor meet.

Base shoe: see *Shoe mold*.

Batch feed disposal: a type of disposal that uses a special stopper placed over the opening to the disposal, which you turn to activate the disposal motor.

Beadboard: a type of board that can be used as a wainscot, applied to an entire wall, applied to ceilings, and applied to cabinet doors. It has one or more half-round beads milled into the finished surface.

Bearing wall: a wall in a home that carries a substantial weight from the roof above or floor above. Not all walls in a home are load bearing. Also called a *load-bearing wall*.

Bifold door: doors that are hinged in the middle for opening in smaller areas, often an alternative to standard swing doors. Most common use is for closet doors.

Bi-pass doors: doors that slide by each other and are commonly used as closet doors. Also called sliding doors.

Blueprints: a type of copying most often used for architectural drawings. Blueprints are used by contractors and workers to guide them in the building process. The blueprints include floor plans, elevations, site plan, foundation and wall section plans, plumbing plans, electrical plans, HVAC plans, and construction details.

Bore: the diameter of the hole drilled in a door for a knob, lever, or dead bolt.

Breaker panel: the electrical box that distributes electric power entering the home to each outlet and switch. Sometimes called the fuse box or circuit breakers.

Building code: standards for the level of safety in buildings, used by builders, architects, engineers, and inspectors. In some municipalities, the building code is law.

Building permit: written authorization by a municipality such as a city or county, giving permission to the builder to construct or remodel a building or home.

Bull nose: a rounded edge or corner, as on a counter edge or drywall corner.

By-fold doors: see *Bifold doors*.

By-pass doors: see *Bi-pass doors*.

C.O.: see *Certificate of Occupancy*.

Can light: see *Recessed can light*.

Cantilever: where the area of the home extends beyond and over a foundation wall. Examples of items placed on a cantilevered area are a bathtub, fireplace, or bay window. The area does not normally extend over two feet.

Casement window: a window that swings open like a door, with hinges on one side.

Casing: wood or stone trim that is installed around the opening of a door or window.

Caulking: a flexible material used to seal a crack or gap between two surfaces to prevent moisture from entering, such as between pieces of siding on the exterior of a home or corners in a tub wall.

Certificate of Occupancy (C.O.): a certificate issued by a municipality granting approval for the home to be occupied. The home must pass final inspection by the code department before a Certificate of Occupancy can be issued. Also called Use and Occupancy Certificate.

Chair rail: interior trim usually installed 24 inches to 48 inches from the floor; provides accent to a room while protecting the walls from scuffs or dents from the back of chairs.

Chalk line: a line made by snapping a string or cord that is dusted with chalk, used for alignment during construction. Chalk can be blue, red, or black.

Change order document: spells out modifications to the plans, specifications, or the price of the construction contract.

Chase: a boxed-in vertical shaft in the framing that allows for mechanical equipment to run vertically. A *flue* would be located in a chase.

Chimney cap: the cover over the top of a chimney. These can be copper and very decorative, or be a plain and functional cap made of other metals, or even be faux stone made of concrete.

CMU foundations: stands for concrete masonry unit, often cinder block, which is used to build the *foundation* of a home.

Columns: vertical supports for the home made of steel, concrete blocks, brick, or treated wood. Some columns are decorative and offer no support.

Compressor: part of the air conditioning or heat pump systems; sits outside the home with a large fan as the main component.

Concrete test: a test done at the job site on the concrete that is ready to be poured. Concrete strength differs depending on the application which is spelled out by a structural engineer. The concrete test is done to ensure the correct strength of concrete that is specified is delivered.

Conductor head: an architectural accent that is part of a roof gutter system, located where the gutter meets the downspout. The conductor head is larger than the downspout; it catches the water and leads it into the downspout. It is not required for the gutters/downspouts to be operational. Also known as a *leader box.*

Construction fee: fee paid to builder, either as a percentage of job costs or a flat fee.

Construction manager: also known as the site supervisor; an individual who works for the builder to supervise day-to-day operations at the building site.

Construction protection: Plastic, paper, or other materials placed to prevent scratches, dents, nicks, and breakage to finished items during construction.

Construction soft costs: anything that is not tangible, such as a building permit, soil test, survey tests, structural engineer reports, and so on.

Contingencies: money built into the builder's quote to pay for mistakes that will appear on the *punch list.*

Covenants: restrictions and rules placed on homes and property uses, specifically found in homeowner associations.

Crown molding: used where the ceiling and wall meet; design and thickness can vary to suit the homeowner's taste.

Damper: a metal cover inside a fireplace chimney that is opened when a fire is burning to allow smoke to escape up the chimney. It is closed when the fireplace is not in use.

Dead bolt: a security lock usually installed on exterior entry doors that can be unlocked with a key on one side and a lever on the other, or a key on both sides. See also *Double cylinder dead bolt* and *Single cylinder dead bolt.*

Dedicated circuit: an electrical circuit that is dedicated to serve only one appliance or a series of smoke detectors.

Desuperheater: a mechanical device that uses the leftover heat from a geothermal system to heat a domestic hot water tank.

Distressed: a technique used on wood floors, wood beams, wood headers, and wood columns to give the wood an old, worn look. Can be done by beating heavy chains against the wood to create nicks, gouges, and other imperfections.

Doorjamb: the millwork or stone that surrounds the open area in which a door opens or closes. There are two upright pieces called side jambs and a horizontal piece called a *header.*

Doorstop: the wooden vertical *stile* that protrudes out from the door casing, which stops the door when it is in the closed position, or a piece of hardware that is installed in the wall, baseboard, door, or floor to stop the door from hitting a wall when fully opened.

Dormers: structural element extending out from a roof, usually with a window, giving head room to an attic area, giving light to an attic area, or creating a skylight in a room. The attic area may or may not be a finished room.

Double cylinder dead bolt: a dead bolt lock that is keyed on both sides. See also *Dead bolt.*

Double glass: window or door in which two panes of glass are used with a sealed air space between. Also called double pane or *insulating glass.*

Double-hung window: a window consisting of two sashes with an upper and lower half that can be slid up and down.

Downspout: attached to the roof gutter and empties water away from the home.

Dragging: A form of *faux paint,* in which a wide brush is dragged through a wet glaze on the wall with the brush bristles slightly bent.

Drawings: the original architecture plans or blueprints.

Dry in: to install black roofing felt on the roof so that the area below the roof will be kept dry when rain hits the roof.

Drywall: see *Sheetrock*.

Ducts: a pipe, usually made of metal, used to carry heated or cooled air to the vents throughout the house.

Due diligence: the research and analysis of a piece of property or condominium done by the prospective buyer and realtor before a final decision is made on whether to purchase the property.

Dummy door: a door, usually a closet door, that uses a ball catch at the top of the door to secure the door in the closed position. The doorknob does not turn or have any type of locking mechanism, and is used only as a grip to pull open the door.

Duplex outlet: the standard electrical outlet used in a home. (Two separate plugs can be plugged in, hence the term "duplex.")

Dutch door: a door that is split horizontally, giving the option of opening half of the door while the other half is closed or opening the entire door as one unit.

Eaves: the part of the roof that overhangs the outside wall of a home.

Egress: exit. Municipal codes require an egress window in every bedroom and basement. The minimum opening width is 20 inches and the minimum opening height is 24 inches, with the open area measuring a minimum of 5.7 square feet.

Electrical rough-in: work done by electrical contractor after the framing members are in place. The rough-in work includes running the electrical wires throughout the home and into mounted boxes to hold outlets and light switches and into mounted can light supports.

Electrical trim-out: installation of all outlets, light switches, face plates, light fixtures, smoke detectors, appliance "pigtails," bath ventilation fans, and other items by the electrical contractor.

Elevations (elevation drawings): straight-on views of either the exterior walls or selected interior walls. The drawings illustrate the locations of doors, windows, and built-ins, and the positions of electrical devices. They also give detailed information about wall finishes and decorative details.

Escutcheon: an ornamental plate that fits around the doorknob. Can also be used to hide extra holes in the door.

Espagnolette: a long vertically hung bolt, with a handle fixed at a convenient height for securing a door or casement at top and bottom.

Extras: see *Change order document*.

Face plates: the plate that covers light switches, outlets, cable connectors, and telephone jacks.

Faux paint: uses a variety of techniques to apply paint and glaze to a wall. See also *Dragging, Rag rolling, Sponging,* and *Stippling*.

Field changes: alterations made to a home on the construction site that differ from the blueprints. Also called a *change order document*.

Field measure: to take measurement (cabinets, countertops, stairs, shower doors, and so forth) in the home being built instead of using the blueprints.

Finial: an ornamental piece of hardware placed on a high point of a building.

Flashing: sheet metal strips installed around chimneys, where roof lines meet, and around skylights, vents, doors, and windows to prevent water infiltration.

Flatwork: concrete used on flat surfaces such as floors, basements, sidewalks, driveway, patios, and so forth.

Floor plan drawings: Drawings illustrating the size and location of all rooms and spaces in a home and designating the locations of built-ins, plumbing fixtures, closets, hallways, stairways, and fireplaces.

Floor register: a vent used to cover the heating, ventilation, and air-conditioning (HVAC) source coming out of the floor.

Flown topography: a photo used for topography taken above the land from a helicopter or an airplane. Not as reliable as *shot topography*.

Flue: a large pipe through which gas flows until emitted into the atmosphere. Normally double walled, galvanized sheet metal pipe, while fireplace flue pipes are normally triple walled.

Footings: the wide part of a foundation located beneath the foundation walls, designed to spread the weight of a house over a larger surface area of soil. Typically 18 inches to 24 inches wide, but can vary depending on the soil-bearing capacity.

Forced air heating: air that is heated in a furnace and distributed through ducts to various areas of the house. Common fuels for heating with forced air heat are natural gas, propane, oil, and electricity.

Foundation: the supporting portion of a home located below the first floor construction, or below grade.

Foundation forms: an area built with rebar and lumber to create a particular form for the foundation, into which concrete is poured.

Foundation plan drawings: drawings that establish the locations for the footings and the foundation, and basement if one exists.

Four-receptacle outlet: an outlet with four places to plug in a cord.

Four-way light switch: similar to a *three-way light switch* except with three separate switch locations instead of two. Refers to the four ways the switches can be operated: off from all switches, on from switch A, on from switch B, and on from switch C.

Framer: the subcontractor who installs the lumber and erects the frame, flooring system, interior walls, backing, door and window frames, trusses, rafters, and decking; and installs all beams, stairs, soffits and all work related to the wood structure of the home. The framer must adhere to local municipal building codes and regulations.

Framing: lumber or steel, such as studs, joists, beams, and rafters, used for erecting the structural members of a home.

Frost-proof hose bib: a *hose bib* that will not freeze.

Furdown: a ceiling or part of a ceiling that is lower than the primary ceiling, often made to enclose ducts or pipe that cannot be installed in the ceiling framing spaces and must be installed below the standard ceiling level. Also the rectangular finished structure above kitchen cabinets. Also called furred ceiling and drop ceiling.

Furniture plan: a floor plan showing the placement of furniture to scale.

Ganged switches: more than one light switch lined up next to each other.

Ground Fault Circuit Interrupter (GFCI): an ultrasensitive plug designed to shut off all electric current when it comes in contact with water. Used in bathrooms, kitchens, exterior waterproof outlets, garage outlets, and wet areas.

Grout: A wet mixture of cement, sand, and water that is applied in masonry or ceramic crevices to seal cracks between the different pieces. Commonly used with stone or tile pieces, and comes in different colors.

Halogen strips: a strip of lights that is sold by the foot and can be cut to any length. Halogen bulbs insert into the strip. Often used for under-cabinet lighting and above-cabinet lighting. If used for above-cabinet lighting, caution needs to be taken if objects are placed above the cabinet, as the lights become hot.

Hand-scraped: after floors are installed, a scraping tool is run over the floors either with the grain or against the grain (each creates a different look). Deep scraping gives a rougher look.

Hardware: accessories for the home such as doorknobs, towel bars, toilet paper holder, and cabinet and drawer knobs and pulls. Hardware is installed by the interior trim carpenter as the house nears completion.

Header: the horizontal structure member located over the opening of a doorway or window.

Hearth: the fireproof area directly in front of a fireplace. Usually made of fireproof materials such as brick, tile, or stone.

Heat pump: a mechanical device that moves heat from a cool space into a warm space during the heating season, and moves heat from your cool house into the warm outdoors in the cooling season.

Hollow-core door: a door whose interior is mostly hollow.

Honed: super fine finish on stone such as granite, but not as fine as a polished finish. A honed finish is dull.

Hose bib: a water faucet whose nozzle is threaded to connect to a hose.

House wrap: an energy-saving air barrier made from polyethylene fibers that is wrapped around a house during construction. House wrap is an insulator keeping air from penetrating the walls.

Humidifier: a mechanical device that increases the humidity within a room or house through the discharge of water vapor.

Hydronic heat: transfers heated water through tubing in floors, walls, and ceilings so that the heated water will radiate heat throughout a home.

Insulating glass: two panes of glass, with a sealed air space between them, used in windows or doors. Also known as *double glass*.

Joist: a horizontal framing member; a board that measures 2 by 8 inches, 2 by 10 inches, or 2 by 12 inches, and runs parallel to other joists and supports a floor or ceiling.

Keeper: the metal latch plate in the door frame that the plunger of a doorknob latches. Also called a *strike plate*.

Keyway: the actual key cylinder that is inserted into the doorknob.

Landing: see *Stair landing*.

Latch: the beveled metal tongue that is spring-loaded and sticks out of a doorknob or lever that allows you to close the door without engaging the locking mechanism or using a key.

Leader box: see *Conductor head*.

Level: A tool to measure true horizontal or vertical.

Lightweight concrete: a lighter strength concrete, such as concrete over the radiant heated water tubes used in the *radiant heat* floor.

Load-bearing wall: a wall in a home that carries a substantial weight from the roof above or floor above. Not all walls in a home are load bearing. Also called a *bearing wall*.

Louver: a vented opening on a door or window covered with sloping slats to prevent rain and other elements of weather from entering. A louver allows some daylight to enter through a door or window.

Millwork: all building materials made of finished wood that have been manufactured in millwork plants, including doors, windows and door frames, blinds, mantels, panel work, stairway, components, moldings, and interior trim. Does not include flooring, ceiling, or siding.

Miscellaneous concrete: random uses of concrete in a home building project, such as an area to stack wood and a dog pen.

Molding: a wood strip that may have an engraved, decorative surface used for a decorative finish around doors and windows, and for other applications.

Mullion: the vertical divider between windows or doors.

Muntin: a small piece that divides the glass on doors or windows to create window panes.

National Electric Code (NEC): a standard for the safe installation of electrical wiring and equipment. **NEC:** see *National Electric Code.*

Overhang: see *Eaves.*

Owner representative: an individual hired by the homeowners to represent them during the building process to ensure work is done properly and on time.

Painted design or landscape: landscape or other scene painted onto a wall.

Parquet floor: hardwood blocks glued individually to a subfloor. Designs include basket weave, diagonal basket weave, brick pattern, single herringbone, and double herringbone.

Passage door: a door in a home that does not lock. Usually a hallway door you would pass through, hence the name "passage."

Pavers: stone, brick, or slab used to pave an area such as a driveway, sidewalk, or patio.

Pinnacle: a vertical architectural ornament of a cone or pyramid shape; larger than a *finial* and smaller than a *spire.*

Plinth block: an optional block of wood or stone located at the corner of a doorway where the baseboard and door framing meet.

Plot plan: an overhead view plan that shows the location of the home on the parcel of land. Shows the setbacks and property lines and includes all easements and legal descriptions.

Plumb: exactly vertical and perpendicular, such as a wall. Placing a level on the area in the vertical plane will tell you if it is plumb.

Plumbing fixtures: plumbing equipment such as a sink, toilet, bidet, and shower/bath units.

Pocket door: an interior door that slides into a pocket in the wall.

Porte cochere: roofed structure extending from the entrance or side of a home or building over the adjacent driveway, protecting those getting in or out of vehicles from the weather.

Primer: a coating that is applied to prepare the surface for an even application of paint.

Privacy door: uses a lockset without a key so a door can be locked from inside the room, usually a bedroom, bathroom, or powder room.

P trap: a pipe shaped like a broken P used in drains. The pipe holds water to prevent sewer gases and fumes from entering the home through the drain.

Puck lights: approximately the size and shape of a hockey puck, these round light fixtures can be mounted under the upper cabinets. There should be one puck light per 8 to 12 inches of cabinet length.

Punch list: a list of items that are either missing, defective, poorly installed, and so forth, that need to be corrected by the contractor before the walk-through. During the *walk-through*, a new punch list is created with the homeowner.

Punch out: same as *Punch list.*

Quarter round: see *Shoe mold.*

Radiant heat: a method of heating using either water or electricity in pipes that are placed in the floors, walls, ceiling, or other surface.

Radon: a colorless gas formed from radioactive decay of radium in the earth, which can seep into a home and cause health problems. A radon detector can be installed to alert the homeowner if radon gas is present.

Rag rolling: A form of *faux paint* similar to *sponging*, using a bunched-up rag pressed against the wall.

Rail: the cross members of a door, cabinet door, or window.

Rebar: ribbed steel bars used to strengthen concrete

in foundations, walls, and other concrete structures. Rebar comes in various thicknesses and strength grades.

Recessed can light: ceiling lights that are flush with the ceiling.

Recirculation water pump: a pump on the water heater to keep hot water continuously flowing in the hot water line. It provides instant hot water when the faucet is turned on.

Redline: blueprints marked in red pencil that reflect changes to the plans.

Reflected ceiling plan drawings: drawings of a room shown as if you were looking down from the ceiling, showing light fixtures, ceiling patterns, or any item suspended from the ceiling.

Retaining wall: a wall-type structure built to hold back a slope and prevent erosion.

Ridge board: a board at the top of the roof that runs horizontally above the rafters.

Roof panel: usually copper, used to form the roof over a bay or bowed window.

Rope lights: a strip of lights that resembles a rope. Often used inside a cabinet with a glass cabinet door, underneath an upper cabinet, on top of an upper cabinet, on staircases, or to light the *toe kick*.

Rosette: a plain or decorative plate or trim piece placed behind the knob, pull, or handle of a drawer or cabinet pull. Usually round and may have scalloped edges.

Roughing-in: the initial stage of installing plumbing, electrical, heating, carpentry, or other materials. These materials are not hooked up to operate until the *trim* stage.

Sash: the framed area around a window pane.

Saw blade cut: a technique in which the surface of wood flooring shows the circular patterns of the saw used to cut the wood.

Schedules: the detailed specifications on the architectural plans listing finishes, materials, and products.

Setback: the distance a home must be located from the front, back, or side property lines, usually set by zoning laws or building codes and by homeowner associations.

Sheathing: a structural wood covering, such as plywood, that is the first layer of outer wall covering used on studs, floor joists, and rafters/trusses.

Sheetrock: a manufactured panel made out of gypsum plaster and nailed or screwed to studs to create walls and ceilings. Sheetrock comes in sheets that are usually $\frac{1}{2}$ inch thick and 4 by 8 feet or 4 by 12 feet. Also called drywall, plasterboard, or gypsum.

Shingles: Roof covering to prevent water seepage. Materials are made of asphalt, asbestos, wood, tile, slate, or other material.

Shoe mold: molding used where the floor and baseboard meet. A carpet strip or quarter round may also be used here.

Shot topography: topography shot by a surveyor on the ground using survey equipment. More accurate than *flown topography*.

Sight line: what one sees when standing in any location of a home.

Single cylinder dead bolt: a lock where a key is needed on the exterior of a door and a turn lever on the inside.

Site plan drawings: plans that show the locations of a home on a lot. Also identifies property lines and the location of utilities, and shows the driveway and other paved areas plus instructions for grading the land.

Skip trowel: a technique using a watered-down mixture of joint compound that is applied to a wall or ceiling. The trowel is gently dragged across the mixture that has been applied to the wall, leaving some of the mixture on the wall.

Slab: flat, sometimes ribbed, reinforced concrete building element that provides a base for the floor or roofing materials.

Sleeves: pipes installed under a driveway, sidewalk, or other type of surface before concrete is poured or *pavers* are laid, so that in the future, sprinkler system pipes or low voltage wiring can be run through the pipe. Usually PVC pipes are used.

Sliding door: see *Bi-pass door*.

Soffit: the underside of the roof overhang on the outside of the home, usually with vents to allow air into the attic.

Soundboard: a special board applied to studs under drywall, used to reduce sound transmission through the wall.

Spire: tapering conical or pyramidal structure on the top of a building, usually larger than a *finial*.

Sponging: A form of *faux paint* that involves dipping a sponge and pressing it against the wall.

Stair landing: a platform between flights of stairs, usually no less than 3 feet by 3 feet square.
It can serve as a resting place, a place to change the direction of the staircase, or the end or beginning of the staircase.

Stair rise: the vertical distance between each step, not to exceed 7 1/2 inches.

Stair riser: the vertical area at the back of each step on a staircase.

Stenciled floors: various designs or borders copied directly onto an installed wood floor, using different applications of stain colors or sometimes paint.

Stile: a vertical framing member in a panel door or cabinet door.

Stippling: A form of *faux paint,* in which a brush dipped into paint is dabbed against the wall, with the bristles of the brush slightly bending.

Stone cap: a fabricated piece of stone glued onto the flat edge of stone. Can be a decorative cap on the top of the pieces such as a stone backsplash, the top of a stone chair rail, or the top of a stone baseboard.

Stop order: a formal, written notification to a builder to discontinue some or all work on a project. The reasons to issue a stop order could be safety violations, defective materials, poor workmanship, or cancellation of the contract.

Strike plate: the plate on a door frame where the latch or dead bolt strikes.

Stucco: a durable material made mostly of Portland cement, sand, and lime, which is applied in several layers to an exterior wall while wet.

Tap fee: fees charged for hooking up utilities to be used on the construction site.

Three-way light switch: allows you to turn a light on or off, or turn the power to an outlet on or off, from a light switch located in two locations. Three-way refers to the three ways the switches can be operated: off from both switches, on from one switch, and on from the other switch.

Threshold: the bottom metal or wood plate located across the floor of an exterior door frame. Generally, they are adjustable to keep a tight fit with the door slab so air, moisture, or bugs cannot enter the home.

Toe kick: the area between the bottom of a cabinet and the floor. The toe kick usually extends 2 to 3 inches out from the cabinet and 3 to 4 inches up from the floor. It allows your toes to fit slightly under the cabinet so that you can be closer to the counter when working on the countertop.

Touch pads or **touch monitor:** a security system control pad used to activate or deactivate the system by touching buttons on the pad or monitor.

Transom: a window above a door. These can be used on interior doors or exterior doors.

Tread: the flat surface or stair step on a stairway on which the foot is placed.

Trim (plumbing, heating, electrical): the final work done by mechanical contractors to finish their areas of work. This would include installing the plumbing fixtures and HVAC vents and putting on face plates.

Truss: a framing member that is engineered to support the roof. The truss does the same job as a pair of rafters but is designed to have a longer span.

Tub deck: the surface around a tub that is built into a platform.

Tub skirt: if a tub is built into a platform, the tub skirt is the vertical side of the deck. If you have a jetted tub, you will need to be able to remove the skirt in order to reach the motor for servicing.

Vapor barrier: first layer of an outer material used to prevent or retard the movement of water vapor, the absorption of moisture, and to prevent condensation in your home.

Veranda: a roofed porch with open walls attached to a residential structure usually surrounded by railing.

Wainscot: material applied to the lower portion of a wall, usually made of wood panels, beadboard, stone, or tile.

Walk-through: a final inspection of a home, usually with the homeowner, builder, and realtor, done before the "closing" to identify and document problems that need to be corrected. A *punch list* is created during the walk-through.

Warranty: guarantee for any manufactured product such as a roof or an appliance, or for labor on a job.

Warranty reserve: funds designated for completing the one-year warranty list.

Water board: water-resistant *sheetrock* used in a shower, tub area, dog wash area, or any other area whose walls will be sprayed or splashed with water. Usually green or blue colored.

Water closet: a closet-sized area with a door in a bathroom or powder room where a toilet is located.

Water tap: the point where the water line coming from your home connects to the main municipal water system.

Weatherproof receptacle cover: a cover placed over any exterior electrical receptacle to prevent water from reaching the receptacle. These are required by the municipal codes.

Window treatment: covering used on windows to protect the occupant's privacy, such as curtains, shades, and shutters. Can also be used to protect possessions in the home from sunlight.

Zone: for construction, an area served by one heating or cooling loop. For landscaping, the area of the lawn that will be watered from a sprinkler system.

Zoning: a governmental directive that limits the use of a property, such as single family use, high rise, residential use, industrial use, and so on. May limit the size of your structure, and the location of the structure on the property. Also see *Building codes*.

Bibliography

AARP. "Bathroom Checklist."http://www.aarp.org/families/home_design/bath/a2004-03-02-b-checklist.html.

AARP. "Checklist for Doors, Floors and Hallways." http://www.aarp.org/families/home_design/doors_floors/a2004-03-02-d-hallwaychecklist.html.

AARP. "Checklist for Safety, Lighting and Storage." http://www.aarp.org/families/home_design/safety_lighting/a2004-03-02-s-checklist.html.

AARP. "Kitchen Checklist." http://www.aarp.org/families/home_design/kitchen/a2004-03-02-k-checklist.html.

Dechiaral, Joseph, Julius Panero, and Martin Zelnik. *Time-Saver Standards for Interior Design and Space Planning*, Second Edition. New York: McGraw-Hill, 2001.

Energy Match. "Geothermal Heating Systems." http://www.energymatch.com/features/article.asp?articleid=46.

Energy Right. "Geothermal Heat Pumps." http://www.energyright.com/heatpump/geothermal.htm.

Eubank, Karen. "Aging in Your Home." Park Cities People Newspaper. December 22, 2005: 1D and 6D.

FEMA. "Preparing a Safe Room." http://www.fema.gov/hazard/tornado/to_saferoom.shtm.

Ferguson, Myron E. *Build It Right,* Revised Sixth Printing. Salem, Oregon: Home User Press, 2000.

Greene, Fayal. *The Anatomy of a House.* Illustrated by Bonita Bavetta. New York: Doubleday, March 1991.

Mullin, Ray C. *Electrical Wiring Residential,* 12th Edition. Based on the 1996 Electrical Codes®. Albany, New York: 1996.

PPFA. "Cross-Linked Polyethylene." http://www.ppfahome.org/pex/index.html.

Salant, Katherine. *The Brand-New House Book.* New York: Three Rivers Press, 2001.

Smith, Mark A. and Elaine M. Smith. *The Owner-Builder Book,* 3rd Edition. Provo, Utah: The Consensus Group, Inc., 2003.

Ultimate Guide to Wiring. Upper Saddle River, New Jersey: Creative Homeowner®, 2004.

U.S. Green Building Council. "LEED® for Homes Pilot Rating System." Version 1.1a, January 2007. http://www.usgbc.org/ShowFile.aspx?DocumentID=2267.

Suggested Readings

Fields, Alan and Denise Fields. *Your New House,* Fourth Edition. Boulder, Colo.: Windsor Peak Press, 2002.

Irwin, Robert. *Tips and Traps When Building Your Home.* New York: McGraw-Hill, 2001.

Locke, Jim. *The Well-Built House,* Revised Edition. New York: Houghton Mifflin Company, 1992.

About the Author

Susan Lang was born on the Mississippi Gulf Coast, and grew up in the town of Pass Christian. As a child, she admired the beautiful beachfront houses in her hometown, and often drew rough floor plans of her dream home. Susan has been a consultant for the design, construction, and decorating of many homes and condominiums, and has served as a general contractor on remodeling projects. She lived in Dallas and Fort Worth, Texas, for 23 years before moving to Nashville, Tennessee, in 2005.

Susan encourages you to e-mail her your own "thank goodness I read this book" moments, and to share suggestions based on your own home design experiences. You can e-mail Susan at info@designwithsusan.com or visit her website at www.designwithsusan.com.